Worshiping Power

An Anarchist View of Early State Formation

PETER GELDERLOOS

Worshiping Power

An Anarchist View of Early State Formation

PETER GELDERLOOS

Advance praise for *Worshiping Power*:

"*Worshiping Power* succeeds in making sense of one of the most baffling anthropological problems: that of origins of state and state-like institutions. This book is testament to Gelderloos's innovation and engagement with anarchism, state-centered social science and anthropology—a work of ethnographic theory thats suggests stimulating new avenues of empirical research and theoretical inquiry. The book is also an excellent read!"
   —Andrej Grubačić, author of *Living at the Edges of Capitalism: Adventures in Exile and Mutual Aid*

"By questioning the myths we have collectively inherited around the formation of the state, Gelderloos dares to do what most contemporary thinkers blindly refuse. For far too long we've been gripped by an unshakable faith in statist politics, where anything beyond this stifled and masochist imagination is dismissed as wishful thinking at best, or savagery at worst. Gelderloos cuts through the rhetoric that has us bend and bow to the predation, elitism, and parasiticism of the state, not as a politics of exploring terra incognita, but as a recognition of how alien these ideas were to the world we once knew. *Worshiping Power* is not just a reclamation of our history, it offers a glimpse into the reconvening of our humanity."
   —Simon Springer, author of *The Anarchist Roots of Geography: Toward Spatial Emancipation*

"*Worshiping Power* is an insightful, sweeping analysis of how and why states have arisen (or haven't), delivered in sparklingly clear prose. It is everything that an anarchist history should be: heretical, tentative, and provocative, as well as deeply researched, persuasive, and above all, relevant."

—Kenyon Zimmer, author of *Immigrants against the State: Yiddish and Italian Anarchism in America*

"Contemporary radical state theory owes much to an anarchistic ethos. Gelderloos important little book surveys and reinterprets this literature, and then gives it a coherent anarchist politics."

—Alex Prichard, Department of Politics, University of Exeter

This edition © 2016 AK Press (Chico, Oakland, Edinburgh,
Baltimore)
ISBN: 978-1-84935-264-2
E-ISBN: 978-1-84935-265-9
Library of Congress Control Number: 2016941988

AK Press   AK Press
370 Ryan Ave. #100   33 Tower St.
Chico, CA 95973   Edinburgh EH6 7BN
USA   Scotland
www.akpress.org   www.akuk.com
akpress@akpress.org   ak@akedin.demon.co.uk

The above addresses would be delighted to provide you with
the latest AK Press distribution catalog, which features books,
pamphlets, zines, and stylish apparel published and/or distributed by
AK Press. Alternatively, visit our websites for the complete catalog,
latest news, and secure ordering.

Cover design by Margaret Killjoy | birdsbeforethestorm.net

Printed in the USA.

"And perhaps solving the mystery of the birth of the State might also permit us to clarify the conditions of the possibility […] of its death."
—**Pierre Clastres**

"Acudid los anarquistas
empuñando la pistola hasta el morir
con petróleo y dinamita
toda clase de gobierno
a combatir
¡y destruir!"
—**"Arroja la Bomba"**
Spanish anarchist song composed in prison in 1932,
popularized in the revolution of 1936

Dedicated to Harold H. Thompson and Kuwasi Balagoon, who died in the dungeons of the State after decades of confinement, to Matías Catrileo, shot down in the struggle to regain his people's land, and to all those who continue fighting, inside and out.

Special thanks to Elizabeth Cobb, for vigorous proofreading; to Tariq Khan, for suggestions and pointers; and to Jennifer Coffman, for the hearty criticism and research pointers that aided my first forays into scholarly writing more than ten years ago.

CONTENTS

Introduction

FOR OVER A HUNDRED years, anarchists have been accused of both romanticism and of radical cynicism; the former, for insisting that humanity's original condition is total freedom and that even now we can create societies free of coercive institutions and live on the basis of mutual aid, solidarity, and voluntary association; and the latter for maintaining that all forms of government, from the most dictatorial to the most democratic, are fundamentally oppressive, and that capitalism is incapable of producing anything but misery. Now, mainstream scholarship is finally lending credibility to the anti-authoritarian intuition of revolutionaries like Mikhail Bakunin and Emma Goldman, and to the subversive theories of scientists like Pyotr Kropotkin and Élisée Reclus.

The question of how and why states were formed is the keystone of Western civilization's creation mythology. Most readers will share my experience of having been brought up in a society where history begins with the appearance of the State. Anything outside its domain is a Dark Age, *terra incognita*, a savage and barbarian land. We are taught that communities created the hierarchical structures of territorial governance that would eventually solidify as states out of a need to organize more efficiently, to respond to natural disasters or population growth, to administer large-scale infrastructure, to defend against hostile outsiders, to protect individual rights through a social contract, or to regulate economic production and surplus value. All of these hypotheses are demonstrably false, yet we are continually indoctrinated to accept them, to keep us from grasping the predatory, parasitic, elitist, and completely unnecessary nature of the State. Official versions of the story of state formation can be triumphant, portraying the State as an escape from barbarism, or they can be cynical, acknowledging the State to be a continuation of human savagery, but at all costs we must believe that state formation was necessary to human progress and that states are an indispensable part of global society today.

Thanks to social movements and anti-authoritarian struggles in the streets, and a growing recognition—starting with the near nuclear disasters of the Cold War and accelerating with climate change and mass extinction—that the State may well be the death of us all, room has finally been created for the scholarship that backs up what has been obvious for centuries: that the State is the enemy of freedom, human well-being, and the health of the planet. The available data demonstrate the universality of resistance to state formation, the predominance of failed states over successful states, the parasitical and coercive nature of states, and the existence of stateless societies with high population densities, a capacity for defensive warfare, complex infrastructure, and other presumed instigators or products of state formation.[1] Both Hobbesian and

---

1   Representing the conservative end of the academic spectrum, with narratives that are frequently Eurocentric and state-privileging, we have the collection edited by Grinin, Bonda-renko, et al. They acknowledge that "nowadays postulates about the state as the only possible form of political and sociocultural organization of the post-primitive society, about *a priori* higher level of development of a state society in comparison with any non-state one do not seem so undeniable as a few years ago. It has become evident that the non-state societies are not nec-essarily less complex and less efficient" (Bondarenko, Grinin, and Korotayev, "Alternatives of Social Evolution" in *The Early State, its Alternatives and Analogues,* edited by Leonid E. Gri-nin, Robert L. Carneiro, Dmitri M. Bondarenko, Nikolay N. Kradin, and Andrey V. Korotayev [Volgograd, Russia: Uchitel Publishing House, 2004], 5). Note that while questioning the unilineal statist mythology, the idea that history comes down on a single track, called progress—thus the present social forms are the best yet—they still cleave to Eurocentric and ultimately statist concepts like "primitive," linear complexity (as in, more or less complex, utilizing culturally specific criteria that favor Western civilization). They also frequently impose Western meanings that privilege a certain, cynical vision of

social contract doctrine about the State, which pop historians and social scientists perpetuated for ages through a selective culling of evidence, have been irreparably discredited. The State was not a survival measure to help people aggressively elevate themselves from a "nasty and brutish" struggle for survival in a dog-eat-dog world; nor was the State, at any point, the result of a consensual process designed to protect people's liberties and well-being.

What's more, the State is losing its place as the default protagonist of history. Most academics and writers are forced to acknowledge the antipathy the State has had to overcome throughout its development, though they continue to sympathize with this coercive institution. No longer able to glorify it, they try to rescue it as a necessary evil. Today, only pop historians can get away with writing the unqualified tale of great men and the empires they commanded. More serious thinkers, studying social networks, the diffusion of power, or the universality of resistance, are increasingly recognizing the ways that history has been shaped by the conflict between rulers and the ruled.[2] Others, like anthropologist James C. Scott, are picking up the torch carried forward by Pierre Clastres to conduct research from the perspective of populations directly in resistance to state authority.

An increasingly convincing picture of the origins of the State is emerging. However, participants in anti-state movements have

---

power in human relations, on social structures, customs, and interactions in societies operating under a completely different paradigm, without showing the slightest courtesy of acknowledging the meanings and values as they are understood in those societies. On the parasitical nature of states, see James C. Scott, *The Art of Not Being Governed: An Anarchist History of Upland Southeast Asia* (New Haven: Yale University Press, 2009). For examples of stateless societies organizing complex infrastructure and technologies, see Peter Gelderloos, *Anarchy Works* (Berkeley: Ardent Press, 2010).

2   See, for example, the history of resistance under the British Empire, Antoinette Burton, *The Trouble with Empire: Challenges to Modern British Imperialism* (Oxford: Oxford University Press, 2015).

not necessarily been paying attention, perhaps due to a residual mistrust in the very academic institutions that have systematically played the role of state apologists. I would argue that we should not hold back in modifying and updating our theories in light of new research, especially since our struggles have been the force that has revealed the failings of the dominant world structures and made such research conceivable and necessary. Only by constantly renewing our theoretical frameworks can we show how the manner in which states emerged thousands of years ago is in fact immediately relevant to our daily struggles and tribulations. Unfortunately, many people who oppose the State, or who at least reject the dominant models of governance, fall back on one of several stock theories that are almost as dogmatic and inaccurate as the statist doctrine. For anarchist theory to advance in the question of state formation, the answers provided by the approaches of dialectical materialism, environmental determinism, and primitivism need to be discarded or heavily revised.[3]

In order to critique these three approaches, it would help to clarify the concept of the State. I think it is useful to refer both to the ethical, idealist, and oppositional definition proposed by anarchists, for example the framework Bakunin lays out in "Rousseau's Theory of the State" and *Statism and Anarchy*: "If there is a State, there must be domination of one class by another

---

3   Though primitivism is usually the only one of these approaches accused of ideological cherry-picking, they all bring to their historical analysis the very vision they seek to prove; to primitivism, history is a lie covering the primary evil of civilization; to dialectical materialism it is an objective tension of productive forces; and to environmental determinism a mechanistic and humanistic belief that everyone, everywhere, is the same, moved only by the primacy of that physical environment which can be claimed to predate and thus determine human activity. See Frederich Engels, *The Origin of the Family, Private Property, and the State* (1884) for the materialist view; Jared Diamond, *Guns, Germs, and Steel* (New York: W.W. Norton, 1997) for environmental determinism; and on primitivism John Zerzan, *Future Primitive and Other Essays* (New York: Autonomedia, 1994).

and, as a result, slavery; the State without slavery is unthink-
able—and this is why we are the enemies of the State"; as well as
the structural, evolutionary definition of anthropologists, which
gives quantitative and analytical criteria to differentiate the State
from other forms of social organization. The latter, in its simplest
form, identifies a bureaucratic, territorial, coercive organization
with multiple levels of administration, in which power is institutional rather than personal, and power-holders monopolize
(at least ideally) the legitimate use of force and the codification
of morality.[4] Both of these definitions will be further developed
throughout the text. I think it is useful to combine them in an
unresolved tension in order to achieve both strategic clarity and
analytical clarity, the latter to allow us to distinguish historical
changes and the former in order to root our new understanding
within a struggle for freedom. There is no learning without taking sides, and there is no theory that does not also project a vision
of the future.

According to dialectical materialism, the State is a product
of class divisions in society: government is an organizing tool of
the owning class, and different forms of governance are determined by a society's economic mode of production. The problem
with this theory is that state formation cannot be the product
of class divisions in society because it precedes such divisions,
as argued by Pierre Clastres. A mechanism of political power is
required to permit class divisions to grow, and a mechanism of
spiritual power to allow concepts like surplus and duty to appear.
On the whole, what early Marxists analyzed as material conditions and superstructure tend to evolve simultaneously, but if one

---

4   Bakunin "Rousseau's Theory of the State" (1873) and *Statism
     and Anarchy* (1873), Leonid E. Grinin, "The Early State and
     Its Analogues: A Comparative Analysis," in *The Early State, Its
     Alternatives and Analogues*, edited by Grinin, Carneiro, Bond-
     arenko, et al., 88–136; and Dmitri M. Bondarenko, "Kinship,
     Territoriality and the Early State Lower Limit," in *Social Evo-
     lution and History* 7, No. 1, edited by Henri J.M. Claessen,
     Renée Hagesteijn, and Pieter van de Velde (Moscow: Uchitel
     Publishing House, 2008), 19–53.

had to simplify, numerous timelines of state evolution show that what materialists assume to be a cause is more often an effect. Turning material and other forms of determinism on their heads, Christopher Boehm, in an extensive survey of stateless societies, demonstrated that the key factor allowing a society to be stateless was not its mode of production or geographic conditions, but an ethical and political determination to prevent the emergence of hierarchy: what he referred to as "reverse dominance hierarchy," in which special functions were compartmentalized rather than centralized and potential leaders were closely watched, and were abandoned, exiled, or assassinated if they exceeded their powers or acted in a greedy or authoritarian manner. In contrast to a mechanistic trend in academia that would dismiss freedom as a subjective illusion or meaningless concept, we anarchists assert that will, both individual and collective (at which level it is often read as culture), is an indispensable force for shaping our society, our mode of production, and our relationship to the earth.[5]

Capitalism can easily be read as the motor of the modern state, and at a certain moment in European history, the needs of an emerging class of investors, merchants, and workshop owners exceeded the political capacities of the absolute monarchies, with their cumbersome, unresponsive bureaucracies oriented towards the needs of a landowning aristocracy. The bourgeois class forced the creation of rationalized, democratic governments capable of proactive social reengineering, a sort of top-down terrorism that would leave the parasitism of earlier states behind and transform the whole of social life into an accessory of economic production and state power. Never mind that this process can be more accurately read as the imposition of social control than as the accumulation of capital, though the latter has also been an essential force. A longer-term analysis shows that such power struggles have transformed models of state organization many times

---

5   Pierre Clastres, *Society Against the State: Essays in Political Anthropology*, trans. Robert Hurley, Abe Stein (1974; repr., New York: Zone Books, 1989). Christopher Boehm, "Egalitarian Behavior and Reverse Dominance Hierarchy," *Current Anthropology* 34, No. 3 (June 1993).

in the past, and that with great frequency states have taken the initiative to transform society and implement new productive models. Sometimes capitalists have modernized government in order to increase their power, and sometimes governments have imposed proactive measures to rescue capitalists from their own shortsightedness. However, capitalists and their predecessors—slaveowners, moneylenders, merchant-investors—owe their very existence to the State. In early states, concentration of political and spiritual power precedes economic stratification in society. Many societies at the cusp of state formation lacked significant forms of economic exploitation. As a general rule, reciprocity is the basis of society and culture.[6] It was the political power that early states accumulated that allowed them to rework the basic foundations of society in order to make exploitation feasible.

Hundreds or even thousands of years of social evolution, along authoritarian or "homoarchic" lines, were required for the emergence of haves and have-nots, individual property, quantification of value, toilers and parasites. And parallel to these proto-state societies, we have examples of alternative forms of social evolution with an equal technological complexity and similar productive techniques, that chose decentralized forms of organization, and non- or even anti-authoritarian cultural values. As regards societies with little or no economic stratification, there are hundreds of examples of human societies practicing a variety of modes of production and different forms of political organization, from hunter-gatherers in California to agriculturalists in southwest Asia, with no clear pattern, no deterministic link between one and the other. Even among primates of the same species, practicing the exact same "mode of production," one can find significant differences in the level of hierarchy between different groups.[7]

Looking at the native populations of the Americas, Pierre Clastres cites examples of societies that switched from sedentary agriculture to nomadic hunting without any significant change

---

6   Clastres, *Society Against the State*, 49.

7   Bondarenko, Grinin, and Korotayev, "Alternatives of Social Evolution," 6.

to their kinship and other social structures; hunter-gatherer societies that developed sedentary agriculture again without significant changes to what Marxists would term "superstructure"; and multiple cases of neighboring societies with completely different modes of production but almost identical forms of social and political organization.[8]

I would also be remiss if I did not mention early Marxism's intrinsic racism as a reason for contesting its explanations of state formation. Such racism, implicit in a pro-imperialist framework that lauds Alexander, Caesar, and Napoleon, and portrays the colonization of less developed (read: non-Western) countries as progress, becomes explicit when Marx and Engels speak of "barbarian nations," "lazy Mexicans," "energetic yankees," "the interests of civilization," and so forth. Either we abandon the project of forcing non-European societies to pass through a Eurocentric dialectic, or we must erect absurd figures like an "Asiatic" or "African mode of production" to shore up a theory that simply does not square with the historical record.[9]

---

8   Clastres, *Society Against the State*, 194–95.

9   Quotes and criticisms of Marxism from Tariq Khan's "'Come O Lions! Let Us Cause a Mutiny:' Anarchism and the Subaltern," *Institute for Anarchist Studies*, anarchiststudies.org, April 2, 2015, which summarizes the opposing takes of anarchism and Marxism on imperialism, peasant and indigenous populations, and anti-colonial movements. On the African mode of production, see Catherine Coquery-Vidrovitch Catherine, "Research on an African Mode of Production" in *Perspectives on the African Past*, edited by M.A. Klein and G.W. Johnson (New York: Little, Brown and Company, 1972). For a typical Marxist view of a non-Western society practicing "primitive communism," see L. Baudin, *Une théocratie socialiste: l'État jésuite du Paraguay* (Paris: Génin, 1962). Regarding the Guarani tribe, the author asserts that, "their mentality is that of a child" (14). And as we anarchists prefer to base our evaluations on actions rather than words, it is worth noting that every single Marxist-inspired regime to date has carried out genocidal policies against any indigenous or non-Western group within its borders, as it

Environmental determinism fares better under scrutiny than materialism, since there is a solid correlation between environmental factors and social evolution. However, we can easily fail to notice that environmental determinists are far better gamblers than theoreticians. Albeit with great acuity, they perform what is in the end a simple, if not simplistic, operation: the selection of geographical factors that advantage state formation, like river valleys, distance from the equator, fertile plains where major irrigation works are feasible, etc. The problem is, they set these factors to masquerade as an explanation when in fact they tell us absolutely nothing about causation. This is where gambling comes in. Geography clearly aids or impedes state formation. If you can correctly identify just one of a hundred factors that make state formation more feasible, given a broad enough sample (like, say, all of human history) you will statistically come out on top. That doesn't mean that the one factor you have been able to identify is the only factor, nor that it is a trigger or cause. What it comes down to is that environmental determinists are unable to take any single river valley or fertile plain and predict that in a certain moment in history, there will or will not be a state there.

Hindsight also plays a big role. An alien observer, knowing only the geography of Earth and using the determinist method, would probably select China as the likeliest spot for a world-dominating state to emerge. We can explain why this wasn't the case, as Jared Diamond does: China had *too many* factors working for it, allowing political unification to occur too early, so that

---

sought to impose its particular vision of the Western trajectory of economic development. This is nothing but a socialist alternative to the practices of the World Bank and IMF. We would do well to heed the insistence of a radical group of Mapuche at the forefront of their struggle for land reclamation: to identify themselves as proletarian would be to willingly complete the process of genocide that, in their case, has not yet fully erased their traditional, communal way of living. I think it is fair to assert that neither Marx nor the vast majority of Marxists who have had access to state power ever intended to allow "primitive communists" a place in their future world.

the evolving state did not benefit from the positive pressure of a dozen disunified, competing states, as did Europe. But it's always easier to tailor an explanation when we know the outcome. And I doubt that the environmental determinists would have been able to predict the alternating patterns of statism and statelessness in the European subcontinent, in the Rif, or in North America, or that they would have wagered on the Andean plateau as the locus of state formation in South America, as opposed to the Plata or Bío-Bío river valleys.

Although Jared Diamond, nearly alone among neo-environmental determinists, has gone a long way to distance the theory from its white supremacist and colonialist origins (see Friederich Ratzel and Ellsworth Huntington), he still relies on an excessively monistic explanation for human social evolution that entirely cuts out the political will of societies to exercise coercive power or practice reciprocity and cooperation. Within his optic, every society, given the proper geographic opportunity, will develop a state and commit the same atrocities of slavery, genocide, imperialism, and exploitation as the West. This starry-eyed humanism, in the end, is an alibi that naturalizes and universalizes certain oppressive values promoted by Western elites. Anti-Western nationalism is not the answer, since elites of other cultures have also organized atrocities, as Diamond correctly points out. Casting the problem as universal, and thus inevitable, is nothing but complicity with the atrocities our rulers systematically carry out, which we can choose to support or resist. The answer to the quandary lies in the theoretical realization that elites around the world must be atrocious in order to wield power, and the recognition that today, the predominant power structure, and thus the one that it is most relevant to criticize, is the one imposed by Western civilization. The gravest consequence of Diamond's humanism, insisting that everyone everywhere has always been the same (thus, carriers of the dominant social values) is to invisibilize the very real and often effective struggles for horizontal, cooperative societies. Freedom and well-being become the mere consequences of external factors. Moral qualms solved: get back to work.

Finally, primitivism can make a legitimate ethical argument against sedentary civilization and animal husbandry, but on a theoretical level it cannot account for hierarchical cultures in some hunter-gatherer groups, nor for agricultural societies with high population densities that were resolutely anti-authoritarian and ecocentric before colonization. Primitivism enjoys an absolute legitimacy insofar as it constitutes a revindication of what is probably the healthiest way that people can relate to their environment, and a way of life that tens of thousands of people around the world still practice, despite the efforts of states to forcibly colonize and settle them. No society is free that does not permit nomadism and ecocentric forms of living; democratic rights, seen from the perspective of hunter-gatherers, are just another recipe for genocide. Primitivism, therefore, is commendable for championing what Marxism callously assigns to the dustbin of history and environmental determinism writes off as a non-competitive economic mode. But on the theoretical level, primitivism is demonstrably mistaken as regards the origins of oppression and hierarchy, and such a mistake is relevant to our attempts, here and now, to win back our freedom. Also, paradoxically, certain expressions of primitivism fall into an ironically rationalist absolutism—for example, in their consideration of language, tools, and social planning—that is by no means a faithful expression of an ecocentric or "primitive" worldview. And certain expressions of primitivism fall into the positive racism of romanticizing an exotified Other; the term itself, in fact, preserves the exotification implicit in the statist dichotomy between the civilized and the primitive.

All three of these approaches, in addressing the question of state formation, tend to focus on explaining the creation of the very first states rather than the spread and survival of different state models that have been created and adapted throughout history. At most, they identify a mechanism that limits or impels a unilineal growth in the power of the State, whether that be geographical conditions, economic development, or the inner principles of civilization itself. This focus assumes the State to be a superior model, a Pandora's box that spreads its evil throughout the world from the moment it is opened. While state organization can produce certain advantages in the conquest of other societies, the supposed superiority of state organization, even from a strictly administrative-military standpoint, must be problematized.

Complementary to the simplistic view of state formation is a simplistic view of statelessness, almost entirely restricted to one anthropological type, the hunter-gatherer. This anthropological view is either fettered by the romanticism of the primitivists, or the conservatism of a Harold Barclay or Ted Kaczynski, both of whom can be commended for appreciating their subject without imposing a rosy, idyllic lens to make the subject more palatable, but not for their failure to question and reinterpret the patriarchal and Eurocentric ethnologies that have corrupted their data sets.[10] They deal, in other words, with an anthropological view of statelessness that internalizes at least a part of the characterization, inserted by European observers, of stateless peoples as static, backwards, and brutish, ignoring the historicity of stateless peoples and their ability to champion and implement ideals of liberty, however imperfect the practice. Lacking this vital human element, they nonetheless cut the crap and advance a hard-to-dispute claim that the misery of statelessness is far better than the misery of the State.

Far and away the best anarchist description of state formation is Fredy Perlman's *Against His-story, Against Leviathan!*[11] Perlman is writing myth, this is the strength and limitation of his essay, but in many ways he hits the nature of state formation on the head, providing a convincing historical, structural, and psychological explanation for the development of states. On both a factual and mythical level, the greatest weakness of his argument is its unitary intent. He tries to portray a single event of original

---

10   See, for example, Harold Barclay, *People Without Government: An Anthropology of Anarchy* (London: Kahn and Averill, 1996); and Ted Kaczynski, "Letter to a Turkish Anarchist," *theanarchistlibrary.org*, 2003.

11   Perlman, when he declares he is not an anarchist, does so in direct contrast to contemporaries of his who declare themselves anarchists but do not live up, in Perlman's eyes, to the anarchist ideal. Perlman, meanwhile, consistently champions anarchy and anarchism.

state formation, explaining all other states as consequences of the Mesopotamian experience. Here more than anywhere else he contradicts the factual record and gives us a myth that is profoundly unhelpful, the Pandora's box of state formation, an evil that once unleashed cannot be contained.

Because politogenesis[12]—state formation—has tended to be such a fragile, fragmented, halting, and often unsuccessful process, I will focus first on the far more common phenomena of secondary state formation and state re-formation before working back to the rare occurrence of original states forming without any guiding model. This should also situate the conversation where it belongs: how to understand and prevent the resurgence of state power wherever it has been toppled, rather than mystifying the first states in order to plot the exact alchemical combination that allowed their appearance. After all, human societies are capable of organizing anything, including states. Is it such a mystery that societies without the experience to know it was a very bad idea would do such a thing?

When we talk about states, we should keep in mind that we are discussing a social arrangement that evolved following a wide variety of evolutionary pathways, in very different conditions, on different continents. As previously mentioned, there are also different reasons for studying and thus defining the State.

As Howard Zinn said, "You can't be neutral on a moving train." Anarchists study the State in order to attack it, and to create something that will be more conducive to total freedom and

---

12   Though the word *politogenesis* was originally coined as a synonym for state formation, more recently, some scholars talk about non-state alternatives of politogenesis (e.g. Bondarenko, Grinin, Korotayev, "Altenatives of Social Evolution"). However, given their lack of interest in exploring the reality of anti-authoritarian societies (or more accurately, their interest in preventing the emergence of any such category), and given the anarchist critique of a fundamental social alienation resulting in the division of political and economic spheres, an alienation that is not present in all societies, I opt to use the term in its original sense.

a healthy relationship with the planet. We lay at the State's feet a great many atrocities. It is the primary culprit for slavery and genocide on every continent, for the worst wars in human history, for mass incarceration, and for the destruction of the planet. Anarchists define the State as a centralized, hierarchical system of political organization based on coercion and alienation, the primordial alienation being the theft of each person's ability to decide over their own lives, the suppression of self-organization so that power could be centralized, delegated, and institutionalized.

Anarchist definitions of the State, like the one offered by Bakunin, tend to be imprecise precisely so they can be inclusive. Anarchists have not dedicated their lives to the Idea, the dream of total freedom, or died on the barricades and on the scaffolds to replace one form of hierarchy with another, softer hierarchy. A broad, inclusive definition allows anarchists to confront domination in whatever form it might take, including within our own movements, and to be ever ready to adapt to an unfolding understanding of how power operates. Anarchism, therefore, has been able to grow beyond the European workers' movement in which it first achieved a named existence, to recognize parallel roots in anti-authoritarian struggles on other continents, to become a part of early anti-colonial struggles, and to play a leading role in the fight against patriarchy. This latter is an important example; patriarchy, it turns out, is a system of oppression that precedes and can exist independently of the State. Anarchism, as the formulation of a desire to combat all domination, is best served by a broad definition based on opposition to any impediment to freedom rather than to a specific historical structure.

Social scientists offer us more precise definitions, though these are devoid of any commitment to take a stand against elitism or defend free communities. In fact, their more mechanical, detached analysis allows them to be useful to states. There are certainly more career opportunities in advising international agencies how to prop up failed states than there are in advising rebellious movements how to destroy their oppressors. Nonetheless, the extensive resources they command have allowed them to make precise distinctions and to shed light on evolutionary processes that were lost to popular memory. Some of the key factors of current definitions that may be useful to contemplate are:

- a minimum of three levels of hierarchical organization (e.g. the capital, provincial capitals, and towns or local administrations) which allow for delegation and chains of command;[13]
- unitary decision-making and an explicit chain of command, which ideally do not permit contradictions, even if contradictions are regularly produced in practice (i.e. the whole apparatus strives to avoid contradiction, and when different governing bodies arrive at different decisions, the conflict must be arbitrated to decide which body has jurisdiction or constitutes a superior authority);
- the administration of a redistribution of resources, from the toilers to government functionaries, which can include symbolic rulers, bureaucrats, soldiers, priests, and others, or to government projects, such as the construction of infrastructure or monuments;
- authority that can be delegated (i.e. it is institutional rather than pertaining exclusively to a charismatic individual) and that flows from a centralized point of legitimation, often abstract (the gods, the law, the people);

---

13 Others propose a four-level site-size hierarchy in the archaeological record to qualify as a state. This criterion requires four types of settlements, from the smallest—the household or hamlet—to the village, to the regional capital, to the largest—the supreme capital (H.T. Wright, "Recent Research on the Origin of the State," *Annual Review of Anthropology* 6 (1977): 379–97). However, four levels of settlements could be incorporated in a three-tier political organization, as the smallest settlements would be too small to host agents of the central authority and would be politically dependent on the nearest village, the smallest unit to be organized by the central authority.

- this centralized point of legitimation, though it may be operated upon by a variety of institutions and social groups, is collectively held to be singular, and in its ideal form harbors no inner contradictions, despite incessant struggles by elite factions to control it;

- identity and authority are territorial rather than kinship-based (although new states are rarely powerful enough to fully suppress the kinship paradigm, and have to gradually undermine it while also making use of it, allowing territorial and kinship paradigms to coexist);

- the execution of war-making, punishment, conflict resolution, and normative authorities, and the intent to monopolize these authorities.

The astute reader will notice a substantial gap between these two classes of definition. In fact there have been a great many societies that were not anarchic, that had hereditary or religious elites and did not place a high value on the rejection of authority, but had little or no coercive powers and no bureaucratic organization; perhaps the elites were not even able to parasitically exploit the labor of their subordinates and neighbors. The academic definition, focused on exact typologies, cannot include such polities as states. This reflects scientists' colonial past and present; the implicit purpose of their definition is to spread the model and oversee the evolution of primitive societies into the club of statehood. Because the anarchists' definition is ethical, and their goal is just the opposite—to destroy state organization and help societies free themselves from coercive authority—they cannot give a free pass to hierarchical societies that lack the degree of stratification and institutionalization that the anthropologists are looking for. The ambiguity created by relying on two different definitions with a vast grey space between them does not, however, present any real methodological problems for my investigation. On the contrary, the intermediate group that inhabits this grey space is of great theoretical importance. Sometimes, "grey" polities resisted transitioning to statehood, while in other cases they developed states at the first opportunity.

Different case studies can help illustrate the role that economics, social structure, and culture played in this open-ended evolution.

Now we know what we are looking for when we investigate politogenesis, and we know the sorts of explanations that are inadequate or discredited. In broad strokes, then, how can we explain state formation? It is now undeniable that there are multiple pathways in the evolution of states. I will not offer a single cause nor a single evolutionary model. There are several models we could consider, building off the work of a great many specialists. However, within each model, I find more particularities than similarities. As such, throughout the following chapters, which are divided thematically, I highlight the basic models when they appear, but place the weight of the narrative on the particularities of each case. This may not be the best format for rapid summarizing, but its advantage is in avoiding potentially dogmatic simplifications.

I.
Take Me to Your Leader:
The Politics of Alien Invasion

It is now a commonplace that colonizing states appoint leaders to horizontal societies they are trying to absorb through trade or warfare. This is not particular to one stage or type of state formation, but state formation as a constant activity. British colonizers bestowed titles on local intermediaries from Africa to Central Asia. US and Canadian occupiers set up tribal governments. Bourgeois states used repression and subsidies to encourage hierarchical organization in the labor unions of the workers' movement. The media appoint spokespeople to heterogeneous rebellions.

Writing about Southeast Asia, James C. Scott explains the process:

> Every state with ambitions to control parts of Zomia—
> Han administrators in Yunnan and Guizhou, the Thai
> court in Ayutthaya, the Burmese court in Ava, Shan chiefs
> (Shabwa), the British colonial state, and independent
> national governments—has sought to discover, or, failing
> that, to create chiefdoms with which they could deal. The
> British in Burma, Leach noted, everywhere preferred auto-
> cratic "tribal" regimes in compact geographical concentra-
> tions with which they could negotiate; conversely, they had
> a distaste for anarchic, egalitarian peoples who had no dis-
> cernible spokesman.[1]

Nor was this a British phenomenon.

---

1   Scott, *The Art of Not Being Governed*, 211–12.

Armed with ethnographers and deterministic theories of social evolution, the French in Vietnam not only drew boundaries around the tribes they dimly discerned and appointed chiefs through whom they intended to rule but placed the peoples so designated on a scale of social evolution. The Dutch accomplished much the same administrative alchemy in Indonesia by identifying separate indigenous customary law (adat) traditions which they proceeded to codify and use as a basis for indirect rule through appointed chiefs.[2]

Why would they appoint chiefs to peoples that had none?

Peoples whose vernacular order was egalitarian lacked the institutional handles by which they could be governed. Those institutions would have to be provided, if necessary, by force.[3]

The reasoning is simple. Hierarchical societies are easier to control, and hierarchies cannot defend themselves from more powerful hierarchies. Officials from a state cannot easily communicate with members of a society in which decisions are made in open assemblies, or societies with chaotic rather than unitary decision-making.

As an important aside, I would challenge the reader to accept chaotic organization as a superior form, even though we are usually only presented with a pejorative vision of chaos. In unitary decision-making, an entire polity must abide by a single decision, or there must be a clear hierarchy to govern and rank the decisions made at different levels, whether in a bureaucratic or federalistic system. All governments, from fascist dictatorships to direct formal democracies, share the principle of unitary decision-making and disseminate the assumptions on which such decision-making is based. Chaotic decision-making fosters the recognition that society can function spontaneously as a decentralized network,

---

2   Ibid., 258.
3   Ibid.

permits conflict as a healthy force in our lives, encourages a multiplicity of decision-making spaces pervading all moments of life, well beyond the formal, masculine sphere of the congress or the dictat, and allows different, even conflicting, decisions to be made at different points in the human network, while encouraging a collective consciousness so all decision-makers can maximize their intelligence and accordingly harmonize. Humans have an evolutionarily tested ability to utilize chaotic decision-making at a macro scale, and the only people who dispute this are those who wish to permanently infantilize their compatriots so as to control them by monopolizing decision-making in unitary structures.[4]

In fact, these two logics of communication, chaotic and unitary, are mutually exclusive. When a state communicates with another society, it is interested in transmitting orders or legislating agreements, not in contributing its perspective to the multitude. Furthermore, the population of a hierarchical society is already organized, in some form or another, in order to be ruled, whereas an egalitarian society is in fact organized, to varying extents, specifically so as not to be ruled. The forms of organization are not at all—contrary to conventional anthropology—orders of complexity on an evolutionary scale; rather they are qualitatively different and mutually exclusive. They represent either the strategies of the rulers, or the strategies of those who refuse to be ruled.

There is, however, a scale of intensity as regards the ability of a state to foist hierarchies on a traditionally stateless people. When an encroaching state has less direct power in a region it wishes to conquer, or the society it wishes to conquer has fewer institutional, authoritarian "handles" to make use of, the process

---

4   For a further elaboration of this view as it pertains to differing strategies in a social movement (direct democracy vs. anarchy), see Anonymous, "Fire Extinguishers and Fire Starters: Anarchist Interventions in the #SpanishRevolution," *CrimethInc.*, June 2011, http://www.crimethinc.com/texts/recentfeatures/barc.php. As it pertains to social theory, see Marianne Maeckelbergh, *The Will of the Many: How the Alterglobalisation Movement is Changing the Face of Democracy* (London: Pluto Press, 2009).

is distinct, as is the resistance to this process. The British tried to appoint chiefs among the horizontal Chin of Southeast Asia, and to increase their prestige and authority, the chiefs, subsidized by their powerful allies, threw lavish feasts, in accordance with the feasting culture prevalent in their society. In response, a new cult arose among the Chin that "repudiated community feasts while continuing the tradition of individual feasts that served to increase personal, not chiefly, status."[5]

In the end it is a matter of common sense. A society needs to be accustomed to having leaders for a foreign power to effectively be able to appoint puppet rulers. Those societies that already have traditional forms of hierarchy, though these might not be enough to qualify them for statehood, are more easily forced into a statist logic. If a stateless people has no local, traditional forms of hierarchy that can be exploited by a colonizing state, or if the local leadership—the potential chiefs—cleave to the popular values of anti-authoritarianism and autonomy, a colonizing state has very few possibilities to expand its control. It can either attempt a policy of genocide through extermination or resettlement, or accept the autonomy of the stateless society, at most demanding tribute, a sort of blackmail by which the stateless people produces trade goods to buy reprieve from punitive military actions.

The Roman Empire contented itself with tribute from the Germanic tribes it could not conquer. French colonization in North America largely failed to induce the decidedly anti-authoritarian Algonquian tribes to develop state structures. Instead they sought tribute in the form of the fur trade, and opted for slower, less dramatic forms of genocide—like kidnapping native youth and forcing them into abusive Jesuit schools where they would have to adopt the language and culture of the colonizer. The modern Botswana state uses forced resettlement against the horizontal San hunter-gatherers. Examples of colonizing states using total extermination against resolutely anti-authoritarian peoples abound, such as the Dutch extermination of the natives of the Banda islands, the British genocide in Tasmania, or the repeated massacres of California natives by US settlers.

---

5   Scott, *The Art of Not Being Governed*, 212.

Portuguese and Dutch colonization of Ceylon (Sri Lanka) provides a good example. In the sixteenth century, the island was inhabited by a patchwork of chiefdoms and kingdoms—stateless areas and weak state powers—that were generally not unified in a single polity. The kingdoms of Kotte, Jaffna, Raigama, Sitawaka, and Kandy contested for dominance or at least tribute in the well-known cycle of empire building and collapse, with the shifting centers of power and autonomy that characterize early state-building processes. The stateless, feudal areas of the Vanni chiefdoms in the north of the island paid tribute to now one, now another of the neighboring states in the south. Occasionally a monarch would conquer multiple kingdoms or even unite the whole island, but in general power was not institutionalized and was not easily passed on from one ruler to the next, so that the empire rarely outlived the emperor.

Neither the Portuguese Crown nor the Vereenigde Oostindische Compagnie (VOC)—the Dutch East India Company— could project the military force needed to conquer the island. In fact, guerrilla resistance on the island decimated more than one European army. Faced with this situation, the Portuguese and then the Dutch tried to play different native kingdoms off against one another, appointing client rulers whenever they could. With their naval power and their ability to control trade, the Portuguese were quickly able to gain control over the Kotte kingdom with the use of client and puppet rulers. But state-building is rarely a straightforward process. Kotte dependency caused a backlash, allowing the Sitawaka kingdom to take over its territories and control most of the island. This political centralization caused another backlash, and the newly conquered territories rebelled, allowing the Portuguese to step in and reassert their control. The turning of the tables gave an advantage to the Kandy kingdom, strategically located in the interior of the country, where it enjoyed military superiority. Subsequently, the Dutch allied with Kandy to sweep out the Portuguese, but no sooner had they won than they turned on their erstwhile partners.

Readers can imagine the impact this process of continual warfare and trade had. Local elites, unless they were willing to give up their privileges to take part in the total leveling of society that an effective guerrilla resistance would require, had to develop more effective war-making hierarchies, invent more effective mechanisms of diplomacy and legitimation, and engage in more intensive forms of trade and production in order to acquire the bargaining power and the imported military hardware that would allow them to stay in power. Even though the Portuguese and the Dutch failed to occupy the island and impose direct control, their commercial empires profited and their state-building mission succeeded. As political and economic organization along the coast developed on Western lines, in 1815 the British were able to capture Ceylon's previously indomitable guerrilla interior without a fight. The Kandyan aristocrats signed a treaty and consented to a British protectorate.

In the East Indies, the VOC established "factories" (representatives of English trading companies were known as "factors") throughout the areas where they tried to monopolize trade. These factories were fortified port settlements with warehouses, barracks, administrative centers, courthouses, prisons, and other buildings that fulfilled the joint functions of commerce and state-building. At times, the colonial factories also served as points of production for the assembly or refinement of trade goods.

> Starting from these factories the VOC obtained spheres of influence or even occupied territories. In this way the VOC, which was in the Netherlands only a trade company, had real sovereignty rights in these territories of the "East." So, the VOC had the right of declaring war and concluding a peace treaty.
>
> All this is dominated by trade, namely to obtain spices for the lowest possible price. For this aim, contracts were signed with native princes. In such a contract was fixed that spices only should be delivered to the VOC. In exchange, the native rulers were military [sic] supported by the VOC.
>
> By mutual rivalry between two princes the VOC offered aid to one of them, mostly the weakest. Only with the help of the VOC this prince could go on fighting. The VOC didn't give so much support that he really could win

his war. So he was dependent. His opponent also started negotiations with the VOC to get rid of the problems. But every kind of VOC support had his [sic] price; exclusive delivery of spices for a low price.[6]

If a prince didn't fulfill his "obligations" (not fulfilling production quotas or allowing spices to be smuggled out to other buyers) then a punitive expedition was organized.

As colonizers on different continents and in different centuries have learned, state-building is indispensable for effective economic exploitation. The agents of colonization use diplomacy and commerce, with a symbolic battle or massacre thrown in to demonstrate their superiority. They make alliances, give gifts, play local enemies off one another, win trading partners, favor compliant leaders or representatives, kill or marginalize defiant ones, and gradually try to bring their new allies into a client relationship, seeking their dependence.

As an encroaching state's influence grows, the influence of its appointed spokesperson within the stateless society also grows. Even when the state does not occupy the stateless society and lacks the ability to restructure it on hierarchical lines, as more decisions, more resources, and more forms of power flow through the appointed chief or spokesperson, the symbolic force of their relationship with the external state begins to outweigh the symbolic force of the horizontal forms of self-organization that are being eclipsed. To clarify, leaders in non-state societies had little or no coercive power, and played a function within a largely horizontal relationship with the rest of society. Sponsorship by an outside state invested them with a new symbolic power and subverted the idea of reciprocity that had previously been both the basis and the limit of their authority.

This is not a case of one state simply expanding itself into new territory and subjugating new captives to a hierarchy of its

---

6   Henk Rijkeboer, "History of the Dutch East India Company—The Asian Part," European Heritage, 2011, http://european-heritage.org/netherlands/alkmaar/history-dutch-east-india-company-asian-part.

own creation. It is in fact the formation of a new state that often flows out of a strategy of resistance of the stateless society. We can call it the **reluctant client state**. When a stateless society comes into contact with a state that is interested in establishing an exploitative relationship, it is not uncommon for members of the stateless society to enter into a limited relationship, hoping to acquire some material gains (rare trade goods or better weapons, for example) while keeping the foreign state at arm's length. Rather than inviting foreign state agents to participate in the horizontal social life, they accept the appointment of an intermediary who would seek to arrange favorable deals while limiting contact. But as the foreign state's presence increases, and their ability to leverage demands or different forms of blackmail grows, the intermediary increasingly has to work on behalf of the state's interests, and they exercise a growing amount of power in their own society. They become the cathode that galvanizes a new state, employing helpers to organize the intensifying exploitation demanded by the foreign state, and eventually organizing a coercive apparatus under their own control so they do not have to rely on the often-obtuse military force of the foreign state.

In the US colonization of the Great Plains, trade posts played a vital role. Often accepted by autonomous nations as a way to minimize the influence of the encroaching state while availing themselves of the benefits of trade, the trade posts became the nuclei around which a "reservation" (concentration camp) would be constituted. Trader envoys (often of mixed descent) and native police forces played a key role in this process, which invariably led to the appointment—by the bureaucracies in Washington—of a tribal government.

With a little bit of pressure, the logic of the state infiltrates the stateless society, whether that society is a social movement or an entire country. What appeared to be the easier path of state avoidance becomes the path of state formation.

A similar process characterizes at least a part of the state formation that was triggered by the European slave trade in West Africa. For the period of the Triangular Trade, European states had neither the military resources nor the political will to engage in a wholesale occupation of the African continent. Most of the states that formed in sub-Saharan Africa before the Berlin Conference of 1884 were not the direct creation of European colonizers. Rather, European traders, with or without the direct involvement of their states, carried out punitive raids against West African communities and then entire nations that would not help them capture people to be exported as slaves. They also engaged in military action to keep coastal communities from centralizing or becoming too strong, ensuring that they could impose favorable trade terms. African intermediaries tried to get the best bargain for guns and other tools, while trying to minimize the impact on their local society. The cost of the deal was passed off onto neighboring societies, from whom slaves were taken with the aid of European weaponry.

The competition between different nations to avoid the worst of a raw economic deal imposed by foreign states led to an explosion of state formation in West and Central Africa. Intermediaries often became the poles around which new states formed. Because such intermediaries came from privileged strata in pre-existing non-coercive hierarchies, they were able to adapt such hierarchies to the new coercive, statist logic. Old power relations were eroded, but old forms were preserved in appearance.

Many stateless societies in Africa had weak hierarchies uniting entire nations at the time European merchants started arriving. Those whom the Portuguese, and later Dutch, French, and English, classified as kings were often religious or military figures who played a ritual or defensive role for the whole nation, but who had no power over simple village chiefs and councils, and no authority in the daily life of people outside the "royal" court. Such leaders might have prerogatives in trade and negotiation with neighboring societies, and so they became intermediaries and organizers in the growing trade of ivory, gold, and slaves.

In the case of the Ashanti state, power derived from trade with the Europeans allowed the royal court to establish a bureaucracy and rule the villages in a hierarchical chain of command, with appointed officials whose authority came to supersede that of the chiefs. Ashanti acquisition of firearms through trade with the Dutch, and the royal organization of a disciplined, professional army, allowed the Ashanti to conquer neighboring societies and expand their territory dramatically. Offensive warfare, in turn, allowed them to kidnap more people and sell them into slavery.

In the Dahomey kingdom, access to firearms also allowed a royal army controlled by a supreme leader to achieve a major territorial expansion. The king's prerogative of control over trade allowed him to sharply increase his power over the rest of society. Traditional forms of warfare were transformed as war captives were now sold into slavery, exchanged for guns. It was the king and his retainers who monopolized the new firearms and allowed them to subordinate the councils and other power-sharing mechanisms that were typical in West African societies prior to the effects of the Atlantic slave trade. The Dahomey also excelled in another important tactic of state-building: the suppression of local customs and social structures in conquered territories.[7]

The Oyo empire was one of the most important West African states of the period. Before the slave trade had begun to wreak its worst effects, the Oyo were already a hierarchical society with a supreme leader aided by sub-chiefs, though whether they could be defined as a state is debatable; for example, the sub-chiefs could exercise a considerable amount of power over the paramount ruler. Around 1535, the Nupe invaded, sacking the capital and forcing the royal family to flee into exile. The Nupe were a stateless people organized in a confederation of decentralized villages, but recently united by a single military leader, Tsoede, who had been living with the royal family of a neighboring society, and who returned bearing symbols of leadership. The Nupe enjoyed a military advantage owing to their decentralized structure and their use of cavalry. The Oyo royals spent eighty years in exile, presumably dreaming and scheming of returning to power. When they finally recovered their prior territory and constructed a new capital, they organized a more centralized government and adopted the military use of cavalry. This act of state formation came just in time for the Oyo state

---

7   R.A. Guisepi, ed., "Africa and the Africans in the Age of the Atlantic Slave Trade," *History World International*, history -world.org (accessed January 7, 2016).

to benefit from the slave trade, which it did immensely, enjoying near continuous success as an expansive, militarist state. This was also a survival strategy. West African societies that did not turn to aggressive slave-raiding were depopulated to the point of extinction by the voracious European slavers and their proxies.

Intensive, bloody trade and constant warfare in West Africa were the ingredients that fueled state formation on the continent, the plantation economy in the Americas, and industrialization in Europe. Capitalism had gone global.

But not all hierarchical West African societies seized on the slave trade as a motor for state-formation. The Benin kingdom or megacommunity, which some anthropologists argue did not constitute a state (see Chapter VII), tried to discourage slaving. They limited trade with the Europeans to pepper, ivory, and textiles. "Eventually European pressure and the goals of the Benin nobility combined to generate a significant slave trade in the eighteenth century, but Benin never made the slave trade its primary source of revenue or state policy."[8]

The influence of the slave trade was not uniform across Africa. In the Congo basin, far from the European slave forts, local populations were not as pressured by nascent capitalism's growing appetite for labor as were the societies farther west, and the slave trade was not so intense as to present a threat of liquidation. In fact the locals did not enter into direct contact with European or Arab-Swahili slave traders and explorers until the nineteenth century. States in the basin did not face an urgent need to grow in military power *vis-à-vis* their neighbors, nor was there a pronounced influx in weaponry. State elites in the Congo basin could comfortably finance themselves by selling war captives to European or Arab-Swahili traders, therefore decreasing their need to exploit their subject population.[9] In fact, the more involved a Congo basin state was in the slave trade, the less developed its internal hierarchies and systems of exploitation.

---

8   Ibid.

9   Eleonora L'vova, "The Formation and Development of States in the Congo Basin," in *The Early State, Its Alternatives and Analogues*, 291.

Understanding local complicity with the international slave trade also requires us to distinguish between different paradigms of slavery. Even in the eighteenth and nineteenth centuries, white proponents of the slave trade justified their systematic profiting off of genocide and torture with the argument that slavery was already practiced in Africa, or that even before European contact, one-third or 50 percent of the population in such-and-such society were slaves. This is a confusion going back at least to Roman times, when Tacitus—used to the brutal chattel slavery of his own empire—wrote that the Germanic tribes also practiced slavery. In societies with a warrior class, there frequently also existed a class of dependents. These might be war captives, oath breakers, or people who did not participate in warfare. In some societies such dependents could be bought and sold, but in general they had rights that might include prohibitions on beatings and severe punishments, on the breaking up of families, and guarantees to food, housing, religious freedom, and dignity. Masters also had an obligation to protect their dependents. In many African societies, masters and so-called slaves worked side by side in the fields and enjoyed roughly equal living conditions. Using the same word to refer to this kind of servitude and to the murderous, totalitarian chattel slavery of the Europeans is completely misleading and inappropriate. Let's use another example. Wage labor can accurately be described as a kind of slavery: a universal slavery in which autonomy, self-sufficiency, or running away are impossible, and the conditions of slavery are only mitigated by the fact that the slaves have the right to hire themselves out to other masters. In our society, then, some 95 percent of the population are slaves. The prior existence of dependents in African societies in no way changes the fact that the Atlantic slave trade constituted a genocidal interruption to their ways of life, just as our practice of wage slavery would not make it any less brutal for an alien civilization to cart away half our population for forced labor on an asteroid colony.

In response to threats of extermination first from English slavers and colonizers and then from US settlers, the Cherokee made a number of initial steps towards state formation before integrating themselves as subjects of the US government. It is interesting to note that before colonization, the Cherokee had already experienced an anti-authoritarian revolution. Oral histories and scholarship both suggest a popular rebellion against the *Ani-kutani*, a hereditary priestly class that, though not constituting a state, held a number of privileges. Before the nineteenth century, Cherokee priests had taken on a different function as medicine men, acceding to the office not through inheritance but by having their personal abilities recognized by the community.[10]

After the British decimated the indigenous opposition to the Virginia colony, they implemented an extensive campaign to sign alliances with indigenous groups, whom they used as agents of economic production and as proxy forces to fight the French for dominance of North America. The Cherokee accepted an alliance with the British, selling them deerskins and slaves and fighting against French proxies like the Shawnee. By the mid-eighteenth century, population pressures and land encroachments by the settlers caused the alliance to break down, and the Cherokee fought a series of wars, first against the British and later against the new American state. Before these wars, English traders and government officials had frequently tried to appoint leaders or even "emperors" to the Cherokee people, but the Cherokee resisted and retained their decentralized structure, with communal land holdings, autonomous villages, and elected leaders with strictly limited powers. After being conclusively defeated by the English and Americans, and with dispossession and forcible resettlement on the rise (but still before the Trail of Tears), the Cherokee opted for a strategy of acculturation. This was not, however, a consensus position: a band led by Dragging Canoe established eleven towns on the Chickamauga Creek and fought a guerrilla war against the settlers from 1776 to 1794.

George Washington, the greatest landlord and slaveowner of the Virginia colony and first president of the new American state, encouraged the assimilationist Cherokee to give up communal land tenure. They adopted European methods of agriculture and industry, modified their traditional gender divisions,

---

10   L. Irwin, "Cherokee Healing: Myth, Dreams, and Medicine," *American Indian Quarterly* 16, No. 2 (1992).

invited Christian missionaries to convert them, and established a government in 1788. Their first three leaders, up until 1827, were all resistance figures who had fought alongside the famous Dragging Canoe. In 1821, the recently statist Cherokee were instrumental in defeating the indigenous resistance in the Creek War, handing a victory at Horseshoe Bend to General Andrew Jackson, the very man who as president would force them onto the Trail of Tears a few years later. The statist Cherokee practiced slavery, operated businesses, and engaged in commerce. In 1827, they adopted a constitution modeled on the US document, with two-tiered legislature and three branches of government. It is worth pointing out, however, that these cultural changes were most pronounced among the ascendant Cherokee elite. The majority fought for and preserved traditional ways of life, until and after the Indian Removal Act of 1830 forcibly evicted them.[11]

It is curious to note that in the first two centuries of contact between the Cherokee and the English, most of the Europeans who integrated themselves in Cherokee society were Scots, and secondarily Irish and Germans, whereas the settlers most notorious for encroaching on Cherokee lands were Scots-Irish from Ulster. The Scots-Irish were originally Scottish settlers whom the English Crown resettled as part of a strategy of state-formation in historically anarchic Ireland. The Scots and the Irish were people who had historically resisted state formation; meanwhile in Germany there were a great many peasants suffering from primitive accumulation and the late imposition of a modern state. Processes of state formation or state resistance create cultural differences that can last over centuries and affect whether or not people facilitate or resist state power.

The Muskogee Nation of southeastern North America faced a similar process of colonization. A part of the Muskogee clung to peaceful resistance and negotiations while others took to guerrilla resistance to try to end encroachment on their lands. Settlers practiced genocidal tactics, like slaughtering all the deer to starve out the Muskogee hunters. Eventually, the Muskogee were partially

---

11   Roxanne Dunbar-Ortiz, *An Indigenous Peoples' History of the United States* (Boston: Beacon Press, 2014), 87–90, 110.

acculturated. Relations with the expanding state had created a "privileged class [that] was dependent on their colonial masters for their personal wealth." Roxanne Dunbar-Ortiz writes:

> This small elite in the Southeast embraced the enslavement of Africans, and a few even became affluent planters in the style of southern planters, mainly through intermarriage with Anglos. The trading posts established by US merchants further divided Muskogee society, pulling many deeply into the US economy through dependency and debt. [...]This method of colonization by co-optation and debt proved effective wherever employed by colonial powers in the world, but only when it was accompanied by extreme violence at any sign of indigenous insurgency. The United States moved across North America in this manner. While most Muskogees continued to follow their traditional democratic ways in their villages, the elite Muskogees were making decisions and compromises on their behalf that would bear tragic consequences for them all.[12]

The Rickahoken of central Virginia provide an even more tragic example. Defeated in an early war against the Virginia colony along with other members of the Powhatan confederacy, they resorted to an alliance with the British. In exchange for weapons and permission from the Crown to continue existing, they had to provide the British with tobacco and slaves. It is believed that the Rickahoken decimated the Shanantoah (who lived in the valley named after them, the Shenandoah) some time after the 1660s, when a German-Czech explorer found the valley to be heavily populated. Perhaps the Rickahoken themselves resettled the area, because in 1705 another white invader reported the valley to be so densely populated by "Tobacco Indians" that there were no remaining sites for settlement. Curiously, just twelve years later, Lt. Governor Alexander Spotswood led a party of patricians— land speculators and surveyors—over the Blue Ridge Mountains and into an empty Shenandoah Valley, which they divided up as

---

12   Ibid., 91–92.

planned. How did he know they would find the area depopulated? It is believed that in the preceding years, the Rickahoken,
distrusting their greedy allies in the Virginia colony and fleeing
warfare in the increasingly volatile Appalachian corridor, took
refuge with the Huron in the far north. The history textbooks (of
the settler state that grew out of Virginia and the other colonies)
tend not to mention this complex set of conflicts, instead assur-
ing their readers that European settlers found the Shenandoah
Valley uninhabited.

All of these processes of genocide, each with different
results, are standard effects of the extension of state power. The
extreme disparity in military technologies allowed Europeans
to create settler states, enslaving, depopulating, and repopulating the territories they conquered. However, the earlier stages
of this process show how an aggressive state can cause its stateless neighbors to either form their own states in the hopes of
securing an alliance, or to engage in rebellion, flight, and defensive warfare, potentially undergoing an anti-authoritarian social
evolution. Even the most peaceful, trade- or conversion-oriented
states, seeking to maintain relations with other populations,
have sometimes ended up disrupting their new neighbors to the
point of destroying them. All states view stateless populations
as potential property, and deny their fundamental right to exist.
"We had to destroy the village in order to save it," that phrase of
bureaucratic insanity from the Vietnam War, expresses the statist
mentality in the most lucid, logical way possible.

Negotiation with a state tends to result in domination,
whether the form that takes is inclusion in exploitative trade networks, imperial annexation, or total annihilation. True independence from states can only come through warfare.

In Suriname, Jamaica, and Haiti, Africans running away
from enslavement by the Dutch, British, Spanish, or French, and
banding together to form communities of resistance in the mountains and forests formed a number of stateless societies. Many of
these groups were firmly anti-authoritarian. After failing to subdue Suriname's Boni maroons in a guerrilla war that lasted 150
years, the Dutch tried civilizing them by signing treaties promising peace if the maroon communities would help hunt down and

recapture slaves who escaped thenceforth. The maneuver failed, and today seventy thousand descendants of the "bush maroons" still live in relative autonomy in Suriname.

The English had a little more success on Jamaica, but they also ended up fighting guerrilla wars for a hundred years against the maroon communities that began to form there in the 1650s. The most noted resistance figure of the Windward Maroons, who were organized in a decentralized, anti-authoritarian fashion, was Granny Nanny. The Leeward Maroons, on the west side of the island, were organized hierarchically. Their leaders were men, the most famous of whom was named Kodjo. It was the Windward Maroons who resisted signing peace treaties with the English the longest. After signing the treaties, the maroons on Jamaica were obliged to help the British return newly escaped slaves and suppress slave rebellions, in return for peace and partial autonomy. The British thus forced the maroons to accept a kind of border, a differentiation between the maroon citizens, who were entitled to the right of freedom, and the colonial subjects, governed by British slave laws. The border was a first step towards creating distinct nationalities, ending the subversive hospitality with which the maroons had previously welcomed all runaways into their community. In the end, what was most important for the British was not to reassert control over specific people or a specific territory, but to close an open space in which their divisions of race, nationality, and class lost all meaning.

The most dramatic example of maroon resistance comes from Haiti. In the 1750s, Mackandal led a group of enslaved African plantation workers in a rebellion against the French colony. The movement was hierarchically organized, and when its leader was executed, it quickly died out. In 1791, the rebellion that would eventually defeat the French Crown, the English, the Spanish, and then the French republican troops under Napoleon broke out and spread in a horizontal, decentralized fashion, not developing hierarchical forms for several years. The most influential people in sparking the uprising were two Voudun priests, a man and a woman. It is noteworthy that among all the maroon resistance movements, the decentralized ones were the only ones in which women also held leadership positions, and leadership was more often shared, whereas the centralized movements, which were also more likely to imitate European cultural and political forms, were exclusively led by men.

Eventually, Toussaint L'Ouverture claimed the title of general and organized a European-style army, centralizing the resistance movement. On the cusp of victory, he submitted to Napoleon's demands, helping the French to restore a certain kind of order to the island. This betrayal sparked a new decentralized rebellion, which forced the French out. A number of Toussaint's officers, however, inserted themselves into leadership positions, establishing a European-style state with French assistance. One after another, first Dessalines and then Henry Christophe, ruled like tyrants and were eventually assassinated by their own people.[13]

Haiti provides an example of the **rebel state**. This model arises from the militaristic pressures of a resistance war, from the possibilities a rebellion offers for charismatic figures to ascend and come into control of a proto-state structure (the rebel military), and from the cultural dominance of the occupying state (which implants statist forms of legitimacy, a statist cultural pedigree, and statist methods of military organization in the collective consciousness of the occupied people). Though it seems paradoxical, in the end it is a common occurrence for a colonized people to imitate the colonizer even as they rebel against him, such that a movement for freedom from a specifically statist oppression becomes a reproduction of state authority.[14]

---

13   Information on the maroon rebellions in Suriname, Jamaica, and Haiti can be found in Wade Davis, *The Serpent and the Rainbow* (New York: Simon & Schuster, 1985); C.L.R. James, *The Black Jacobins* (New York: Random House, 1963); and Wim S.M. Hoogbergen, *The Boni Maroon Wars in Suriname* (Leiden: E.J. Brill, 1990). Readers whose interest is in overthrowing states, not jut studying them, will also find the following source interesting: Russell "Maroon" Shoatz, "The Dragon and the Hydra," 2010, https://russellmaroonshoats .wordpress.com/2012/08/10/the-dragon-and/.

14   Frantz Fanon, *The Wretched of the Earth* (New York: Grove Press, 1961).

II.
Ze Germans:
A State-Making Technology

IN THE YEAR 983, the Slavic inhabitants of that forested plain south of the Baltic sea, where the river Spree winds past a series of placid lakes, the spot where a city known as Berlin now stands, rose up against their masters. The Slavs, known as Wends, were ruled by a Germanic elite who imposed on their subjects Christianity, military discipline, feudal obligations such as forced labor and the tithe, and a culture of reverence for divine and secular authority. The Wendish rebellion was successful, as were many rebellions against early states. The population killed off or drove out all the German nobles and priests, and for the next century and a half, lived as pagans, stateless and free.

It required a much larger apparatus of state formation than the elite German warrior brotherhoods to subdue them. No less than the Catholic Church, the most potent agent of state formation in the entire European subcontinent[1] (and subsequently in the South American continent as well), declared a Holy Crusade against the Wends in 1147, organizing the various states, state fragments, and *politogens*[2] of Central Europe to conquer and colonize them.

---

1   I don't know of any geographical society or academic institution that advocates the redesignation of Europe as a subcontinent; nonetheless only the obstinate self-importance of the white supremacists who founded such institutions can explain the continental classification. Not tectonically, not geographically, not historically, not even culturally can Europe qualify as a continent. On all grounds India has a far better claim to continent-hood.

2   Inventing new terms can be an obnoxious habit; nonetheless in the literature on state formation I found no term for a body

Other Slavic peoples who lived farther to the east, some of them inhabiting lands vacated by Germanic tribes moving into the collapsing Roman Empire, did not develop states until significantly later. In what is now Ukraine, the Rus—forebears of the Russians—settled on the Dniepr River and began what would eventually become a powerful state. But the Rus were a brotherhood of Norse warriors who colonized the Slavic locals, just as happened with the Wends.

At Wielkopolska, over the course of the ninth and tenth centuries, the Polanie tribe formed the first endogenous state in Central Europe. Unlike the colony states on the Spree and the Dniepr formed by invading politogens, Wielkopolska provides a clear example of another model of state formation: **the imitative state**. Local elites within the preexisting autochthonous hierarchies were impressed by the greater power amassed by elites in neighboring societies, and sought to copy them. Having a model close at hand conferred two great advantages for state formation.

Firstly, it decreased the risk entailed by seizing the power necessary for state formation. Unlike original states, imitative states had an example they could follow, and proof that increasing their level of stratification and hierarchy was possible. As in early states, power was by no means stable in non-state societies. Tribes and chiefdoms also faced rebellion and fracturing that toppled the leadership, and unlike their homologues in state societies, the leadership of non-state societies was largely subordinate to the population and did not enjoy coercive capacities. They had to protect themselves with status and charisma alone. Being seen as power-hungry and tyrannical was a proven way to undermine those qualities and end up deposed, exiled, or assassinated.[3]

---

that acts intentionally and aggressively as a vessel and vector for state-making technologies and as a direct agent for state formation, but does not in itself constitute a state, lacking the requisite host population.

3   Boehm ("Egalitarian Behavior and Reverse Dominance Hierarchy") details the frequency with which leaders of stateless societies were deposed or even killed by others with less status. Among the two most frequent motives for such topplings are

Secondly, having states as neighbors changed the political situation faced by a society and made the option of militarization more attractive. States are highly dangerous to their citizens and to the externalized barbarians alike. They obligate neighboring societies to consider the question of self-defense. This question does not have an inevitable answer in state formation, as some historians have wished to assert. Many societies, from the Mapuche and the Lakota of the Americas to the Wa of Zomia, were able to organize for effective defensive warfare against far more powerful state neighbors without an increase in social hierarchy (in fact their collective self-defense sometimes even led to an accentuation of their anti-authoritarian characteristics, as a way to mobilize enthusiasm for defensive warfare and differentiate themselves from the statist neighbors).

More precisely, the need to organize for warfare offers up a trajectory of state formation for those societies where an elite already exists and is prepared to seize the situation and sell a solution to their lower-ranking kin. This is especially the case when self-defense can be sold, by the local elite to their subordinate kin, as a kind of national independence rather than the rebuffing of any kind of domination, whether endogenous or exogenous. This same tension was evident in the state-formation processes of post-colonial countries, where national liberation movements tended towards nationalism (liberation as cultural and political independence attained through inter-class unity).

In the case of what is now Poland, increasing populations and belligerent pressure from neighboring states did not make state formation inevitable. The rest of the region faced the same conditions, and also experienced a growth in the construction of fortified settlements, but only at Wielkopolska did a state emerge in the ninth and tenth centuries. It seems that their pathway was to use the increase in construction and military measures (both of which can be accomplished with relatively egalitarian means) as an opportunity for political unification, first perhaps in the form of a strong confederation of tribal leaders enacting an ambitious

---

the perceived greediness and the authoritarianism of the leader.

plan to administer the closely related concerns of trade and war-fare, and then to support a monarchy.

Poland's unique position as an endogenous state surrounded by states of Germanic origin indicates the first strands of an interesting pattern. Elsewhere, the Visigoths, another Germanic tribe, poured into the Iberian Peninsula and founded a rudimen-tary kingdom in the vacuum left by the Roman collapse, over three hundred years creating an increasingly effective, central-ized authority when Tariq ibn-Ziyad swept across from northern Africa and established an emirate at Córdoba. The Muslim state spread quickly, soon reaching as far as the Pyrenees. Formation of a Muslim state in the Iberian Peninsula was aided by the apathy of the local population who scarcely raised their hands to defend their burdensome Visigoth lords,[4] preferring the lenient Moorish rulers. This is another mechanism for stable state-formation: **the progressive state**, a lesser of two evils that takes advantage of the popular rejection of a more onerous form of state. This category could include those democratic states that restored governing institutions after popular revolt made it impossible for dictator-ships to rule with any kind of stability (the early French Republic, democratic Spain, democratic Greece, Albania…). Ironically, the Iberian inhabitants of the Peninsula's northern coast, who had long resisted full inclusion into the Roman and then the Visigothic states, finally formed a state—the Kingdom of Asturias—when the remnants of the Visigothic nobility allied and intermarried with local tribal leaders in order to organize a defense against the incursions of the more effective Umayyad state.

In the Italic peninsula, Germanic tribes invaded Rome itself, not exclusively to destroy its power, as Hannibal's army from New Carthage (Cartagena, in modern day Spain) had attempted centuries earlier. On the contrary, the ostensible goal of the Ger-manic barbarians, from Odoacer to Theodoric the Great, was

---

4   Tacitus singles out the Goths as the most "autocratic" of the
     Germanic tribes, "but not to such a degree that freedom is
     destroyed." Tacitus, in *The Agricola and the Germania*, trans-
     lated by H. Mattingly (98; repr., Baltimore: Penguin Books,
     1948), 138.

to rule Rome, generally in concert with Roman authorities and political institutions.

The British Isles present another case. The tribes of the Angles and Saxons came over from modern-day Denmark and Friesland to conquer the Gaelic inhabitants (rallied unsuccessfully under the legendary Arthur)[5] and establish a kingdom that, depending on the criteria, potentially qualified as an early state. Five hundred years later, other Germanic politogens came over with a more perfected state model. In the same year, 1066, Vikings under King Harald Hardrada and Normans under William the Duke of Normandy invaded Eng-land (the land of the Angles). The latter were successful. And though the politico-military force from Normandy was French-speaking, Normandy's state model was another Germanic import, arriving a century earlier in the form of a successful Viking invasion—the eponymous "North-men" of Nor-mandy, who quickly integrated themselves with another Germanic early state, that of the Franks, founded by Clovis at the end of the fifth century, when a confederation of Frankish tribes under Clovis's leadership conquered northern and then southern Gaul, subordinating other Germanic tribes as well as the Gallo-Roman inhabitants, "eliminating the tribal chiefs (kings) and taking over their rights" (although the tribes retained semi-autonomous existence for a few more centuries.[6] Also in the eleventh century, the Normans were instrumental in state-building efforts in fractiously diverse southern Italy, where Byzantines, Catholics, Jews, and Muslims had competed for control. The Frankish crusader states in Syria and Jerusalem, where Arabic and Turkish state-building efforts were largely decomposing, also deserve mention.

Since we have mentioned the Norse, we shouldn't forget the three Scandinavian states of Germanic origin. And of course

---

5   Arthur, though he is presented to us as a king, is a good exam-
     ple of a non-state leader: it is not institutional legitimation but
     charisma and magic attaining specifically to his person that he
     needs in order to rally his warriors, who sit together in a circle.

6   Michal Tymowski, "State and Tribe in the History of Medie-
     val Europe and Black Africa—A Comparative Approach," in
     Social Evolution and History, 177.

there are those territories that we have naturalized as "Germany," as well as Austria and Switzerland. Within those territories, for a while unified as the Holy Roman Empire, are dozens of duchies, counties, principalities, and kingdoms formed by various Germanic tribes.

> The last tribal [stateless] areas in Europe were taken over by state organizations in the 13th century. These were the territories settled by the Baltic peoples; the Prussians, the Yadzvingians, the Lithuanians and the Latvians [...] Most of their tribal organizations were destroyed by the expansion of the Order of the Teutonic Knights, which created the Teutonic Order state in the conquered areas. Only the Lithuanians managed to beat back the invasion and to create their own state.[7]

If you were to take a map of Europe and color in all the areas where state authority was introduced or reintroduced by Germanic tribes, you might surpass the area tamed by their predecessor, the Western Roman Empire.

With such a track record, it would be easy to fall back on the ready stock of cheap stereotypes regarding *ze Germans*. But still, looking at state origins in the graveyard of the Roman Empire during the first millennia of the Common Era, one must ask, what gives? One is almost reminded of the franchising Phoenicians, a Semitic people originating in what is today Lebanon, who crossed the Mediterranean world and made their home in settlements far and wide, founding, for example, the cities of Málaga, Cádiz, Tarragona, Tangier, Carthage, and Genoa. But instead of establishing trading posts, the Germanic tribes were establishing states. Incidentally, the linguist John McWhorter hypothesizes a Phoenician influence on ancient German, by way of a possible Phoenician settlement in Jutland, modern-day Denmark, all the way on the other side of the European coast.

James C. Scott talks about certain ethnicities as state-making technologies. Such ethnicities are a complex of religion,

---

7   Ibid., 174.

historical narrative, customs, administrative tools, kinship and lineage systems, agricultural techniques and productive modes that all converge to enable state formation. What might be the specific characteristics of this "technology"? The religion probably won't involve an adoration of Mother Earth, of specifically local-based deities, and a worship of animals, rivers, and trees as the brothers and sisters of human beings. On the contrary, the religion will probably be patriarchal, and if it is not monotheistic, the pantheon will be hierarchical. Worshiping authority will be key. The historical narrative will focus on warrior-kings and father figures. Organizational forms will be centralized rather than decentralized, and even if the culture still contains acceptance of things like general assemblies, there will also be a tradition of officials with well defined ceremonial and administrative duties. The kinship system might allow for nuclear families or large extended clans, but elder males will have authority and the inheritance of property should be a relatively unambiguous affair (and they will, of course, have the concept of private property, even if the elite have not yet managed to destroy the parallel custom of communal property). Agriculture will focus on the production of field crops that can easily be controlled and taxed (with irrigation and milling constituting choke points).

Because the cultural technologies of a specifically statist ethnicity are evangelist and colonizing, a politogen can be a small group of warriors and administrators who conquer a larger population and eventually absorb it into a common identity. This is the **conquest** or **colony state**. A politogen is a cultural group that constitutes a state-making technology and often takes the form of an ethnicity or proto-ethnicity. It is like a virus that will form a state once it acquires a host population. The conquest state is a process of secondary state formation, a politogenesis that is the result of or at least influenced by other, previous processes of state formation. In the nineteenth century, Humplowitz and Oppenheimer published the "Conquest Theory" of state origin, suggesting that the first states arose when warlike nomadic societies, such as the Magyar or groups like the Vikings, conquered sedentary agricultural societies. And, while there are numerous examples of such occurrences, I cannot find any examples of primary state formation that follow this model. In other words, all such militaristic nomads already had examples of preexisting states to learn from. The politogen capable of forming a conquest state must have passed through a process of direct or indirect tutelage under a preexisting state, as the German tribes did with the Romans, whereas the colony state is formed when a patron state orders or permits a group of its subjects to undertake the conquest, subordination, and administration of a stateless territory.

In the conquest state, the economic mode and agricultural techniques are almost always imposed by the colonizing group, even where they might gain a greater profit margin and competitive advantage by adapting more fully to local conditions; their own way of life is adhered to religiously as a sign of identification with the governing authority. Meanwhile, the religion of the conquerors tends to syncretize with that of the conquered, co-opting local deities and festivals within its framework, giving the locals an incentive to adopt the new religion, and adapting old practices to a new moral universe. As for the language of the conquered group, it tends to affect the conquerors' language in unpredictable ways, changing the grammar but not the vocabulary, as Welsh did to Old English, shedding grammatical complexity and taking in a duplicate set of vocabulary, as Old English did during the Norman and Viking invasions, or replacing the conquerors' language entirely, as the local Slavs did with their Rus colonizers.

How exactly does a state-making technology come about? One early account of the Germanic tribes comes from the pen of Tacitus, a highly placed Roman historian. The description he gives is easy to synthesize into one unified picture, as he often conflates one tribe with another, or projects his ethnography from one group to the others. Looking past Tacitus's exotification, we can argue that the Germans are the creation of the Roman Empire. Given the name of "German" and assigned a singular identity by their imperial neighbors, they were actually a multiplicity of peoples only loosely linked by linguistic and other cultural similarities.

No doubt the Suebi (or Schwaben) themselves saw some affinity with the Cherusci, the Goths, or the Vandals, as they could communicate with one another, speaking related dialects, worshiping the same or similar gods, and practicing similar forms of social organization. But they were not a unified group. They fought wars against one another, there is no record of a majority of them ever coming together in one political formation, and they generally maintained their autonomy, although there is record of members of one tribe referring to other tribes as kinsmen, especially in the face of Roman hostility.

The process of an empire constructing the barbarians is by no means unique to the Germans. Empires habitually manufacture ethnicities at their frontiers. Ethnicity begins where sovereignty ends, to cite James C. Scott.[8] In order to control an uncontrollable, it must first be named. All domination flows from an original categorical enclosure. The very category of "tribe," so influential in classical anthropology and pregnant with a sense of the primitive and pristine, is in fact an imperial creation. In the Roman Empire, tribes were administrative units for populations that defied direct rule but could be intimidated into paying protection money (or "tribute"), participating in "tribunes," and taking part in other aspects of imperial business. Over time, they were increasingly integrated into the Roman state, holding on to a semi-autonomous status. Clearly, the tribes were never intended to remain autonomous forever. Identification and constitution as a tribe were early rungs on the ladder of colonization.

Germany as an entity existed in the Roman imagination, whence it was transposed to a German imagination (nor is this a unique process: Benedict Anderson and Alfred Kroeber describe how colonial state administration was able to create separate ethnic "tribes" that eventually became self-identifying, in the case of a separate Chinese ethnicity in Dutch Batavia or distinct ethnic tribes as understood in the Western sense in North America).[9] Germany as a political reality was not born until 1871, created by Chancellor Bismarck on the grave of the Paris Commune. But its imaginary existence up until that point was by no means insubstantial. It reflects greatly on the worldview of

8   Scott, *The Art of Not Being Governed*, xi.
9   Cited in ibid., 259, 264–65.

the Germanic tribes in the era of the Roman collapse that they
named the greatest state they eventually built the Holy Roman
Empire. This would be the first Reich referred to by the Third
Reich, whose ideologues also found great validation in the fact
that Tacitus casually referred to the tribes across the Rheine as
having "pure blood."

What else did Tacitus find among the Germanic tribes?
At the time he published *Germania*, in 98 CE, there was little
to suggest the German ethnicity as a state-making technology.
The different German peoples were stateless. Many of them had
chiefs or kings, though it was often the Romans who appointed
these among the conquered tribes or allied tribes living along
the border. The chief, however, was not a coercive figure. Tribes
made decisions in open assemblies, generally held after drunken
debates during feasting. Tacitus, with both pleasure and irony,
records the almost constant feasting and the unlimited hospitality of the Germans. Both of these are common features of stateless societies.

Tacitus refers to the Germans as a "free people," in contrast
to the "autocratic" or "despotic" nations Rome was at war with
in the east. He himself notes that the self-organized, decentralized Germans presented a much greater military threat to
the Roman Empire, and over a period of two hundred years
at that, than the despotic empires on their eastern border ever
had. The three hundred years of history after his account bear
out the assertion a hundredfold. Again, the evidence shows that
stateless societies have an even greater capacity for self-defense
than statist ones.

While Tacitus's classification of the Germans as a "free"
people sometimes uses the same criteria as anarchists might—
general participation in decision-making, the lack of coercive
authorities—we have to be aware that the Roman historian
entertains a patrician's notion of freedom. Consider the following passage:

> Bordering on the Suiones [the predecessors of the Swedes]
> we have the nations of the Sitones. They resemble them in
> all respects except one—woman is the ruling sex. That is

the measure of their decline, I will not say below freedom, but even below decent slavery.[10]

In comparison to the Roman patriarchy, we know that Germanic societies were relatively egalitarian in their gender relations. In a clearly androcentric way (for we cannot doubt which gender the Roman talked to, whose activities he granted legitimacy, and on whom he focused his attention), Tacitus gives some indication of this: "they [the German men] believe that there resides in women an element of holiness and a gift of prophecy; and so they do not scorn to ask their advice, or lightly disregard their replies." Tacitus moderates what he sees as a contemptible respect for women by amending that the German men do not shower any women with "servile flattery or any pretence of turning women into goddesses" as some contemporaneous Roman cults did the wives of emperors. However, according to his own account they did not shower anyone with servile flattery, and they did worship goddesses and consider some earthly women divine.[11]

Although Tacitus talks of "noble families" and "slaves," there is little evident class differentiation. "In every home the children go naked and dirty, and develop that strength of limb and tall stature which excite our admiration [...] The young master is not distinguished by the slave by any pampering in his upbringing. They live together among the same flocks and on the same earthen floor."[12]

The class of people among the Germanic tribes whom Tacitus calls "slaves," referring back to a well defined class in Roman society, are probably better understood as dependents, in that they had their own homes, land, and families, they were rarely flogged or otherwise punished, they were not given specific duties but instead were expected to pay a sort of rent or tithe, contributing to the household economy of their master or patron, who in turn had the responsibility to protect them. In large part, the

---

10   Tacitus, *The Agricola and the Germania*, 98.
11   Ibid., 108.
12   Ibid., 118.

determining factor separating slaves from free men was the obligation to go to war. By honoring warriors, Germanic tribes were
able to create a soft hierarchy, largely non-coercive, that provided
additional sustenance for a specialized warrior class. However,
these warriors were not entirely freed from the obligation to
toil, as were Roman patricians, and they could not subject their
dependents to conditions of misery or hyper-exploitation. We
could even imagine this history from a different perspective, in
which the so-called slaves preferred to spend more time farming
in order to liberate themselves from dangerous military duties.
Tacitus recorded a value hierarchy among the warriors that honored bravery, but perhaps the toilers, whose voices were never
recorded, reproduced another set of values that honored sharing
and fertility. We have no way to know if this is true; the hypothesis simply illustrates how statist ethnographers can distort their
subjects and record reflections of their own cultural prejudices.

Tacitus claims that the Germans were lacking in gold
and silver, though discoveries that postdate his account would
demonstrate this was due to the local disinterest in these sub-
stances, and not to their absence beneath the soil. He also notes
that "the employment of capital in order to increase it by usury
is unknown in Germany." In a number of passages that contrast
with modern stereotypes (and that contradict the anthropomor-
phism of climate, in which geographical conditions determine
social character, literally hot weather leading to metaphorically
hot blood), the Roman chastises the Germans for their laziness,
their lack of discipline, their preference for gambling and feasting over labor and husbandry, and—most hilariously from a
present-day standpoint—their utter unpunctuality.[13]

To put it bluntly, how did this lazy, hospitable, sharing,
egalitarian, decentralized, uncapitalistic smattering of tribes
turn into one of the principal producers of states across an entire
subcontinent?

The answer I propose lies in the one characteristic of these
tribes that interested Tacitus the most. His curiosity, after all,
was motivated by state interests, as tends to be the case with

---

13   Ibid., 122–23.

ethnographers. This interesting characteristic was their militarism. Though the armies of Germanic tribes were voluntary, mobilized by collective notions of honor rather than the coercive powers of a military apparatus, these tribes proved a major threat to Roman power. A large part of Roman affairs in the north of their empire centered on allying with particular tribes and playing them against one another to prevent their turning against Rome.

Tacitus talks almost exclusively about the warrior brotherhoods of the tribes, though this was only one segment of their society. Agriculture and nearly all productive activity among the tribes, except for hunting, was carried out by women, dependents, old men, and the non-warriors whom Tacitus terms the "weaklings of the family."[14] Though he places a nearly exclusive emphasis on the warriors, we cannot assume this to be a value generalized in the tribal society itself. The warriors thought it beneath them to dirty their hands in the fields or win wealth by the sweat of their brows rather than by bloodshed, but we do not know what those who did work in the fields thought about such labor or about warfare. We do know, however, that women played an important role in mobilizing the tribe for warfare, urging the warriors on through a mixture of encouragement and shaming. We can also assume that as these tribes fractured and spread into the vacuum left by the collapsing Roman Empire, when bands of warriors colonized populations previously subject to the empire, they generalized their value hierarchy that placed warfare—and by extension affairs of state and ownership—at the top, and labor—what in their societies of origin had been the work of women and war captives—on the bottom. In effect, what was potentially an egalitarian, complementary division of labor between the masculine and the feminine became a hierarchical and patriarchal division of labor when the masculine half of Germanic society was able to spread and conquer other populations. As warfare became the more important activity in the reproduction of Germanic societies, the warrior half was able to impose its own value system, regardless of whether it had truly been the dominant half previously.

14   Ibid., 114.

(As a useful contrast, we can consider an inverse situation; centuries later, when it was trade and artisanal production rather than warfare that became more important for the spread of the dominant social model, it was the descendants of the servants and dependents—commoners—who began to take power away from the descendants of the warriors—the nobility—though it was also necessary that changes take place in the techniques of warfare favoring the military units of urban citizens over the mounted nobility before this democratization process could reach fruition.)

Roman colonization and contact had a great impact on the Germanic tribes. Highly developed Roman patriarchy encouraged and empowered nascent forms of Germanic patriarchy (ever present as a possibility in a gender-divided society, even an egalitarian one). This in turn is related to a motor of state formation that I will refer to as **militarization**. The contest of arms made inevitable by Roman expansion found a certain resonance in the warlike German society. For the Germanic tribes, already accustomed to competitive warfare, battle with the Romans was not only a question of winning their freedom, but also of winning. Some warlike societies are fiercely libertarian, but those that exhibit democratic characteristics—such as the Germanic tribes with their warriors' assemblies presided over by war leaders who introduced proposals for common voting—can operate as a centralized polity and are much more likely to be induced into the competitive aspect of war. David Graeber makes a similar argument with respect to the ancient Greeks, asserting that democratic organization was typical to state-forming warrior societies whereas consensus-based organization was typical to stateless societies.[15]

It is noteworthy that the Germanic armies that not only defended against but also invaded Rome tended not to be pristine barbarians fighting for their freedom. On the contrary, they were usually led by warriors who had served in the Roman legions and were now trying their own hand at the Roman project of conquest.

15   David Graeber, *Fragments of an Anarchist Anthropology* (Cambridge: Prickly Paradigm Press, 2004).

Warrior brotherhoods such as those that existed in Germanic society are egalitarian on the surface, especially as judged by democratic criteria of freedom. But they have proven themselves inclined and able to constitute politogens. Rome itself, which evolved inexorably from Kingdom to Republic to Empire—and was at every point in that process authoritarian and hierarchical, a fact obscured by the democratic criteria of freedom—started out as a warrior brotherhood similar in many ways to those of the Germanic tribes.

When the Romans founded their city in the eighth century BCE, they had a patriarchal social organization dominated by a king, thirty *curiae*, and *gentes* or clans. It was a democratic organization in the true militaristic, authoritarian, patriarchal sense of the word. (I understand that this assertion will rankle many readers. The arguments that back it up—and there are many— are material for an entire book. That is exactly, however, the topic of a future book that is already in preparation.)

The king was a symbolic leader who could also institute organizational reforms and push the whole society to accept ambitious new strategies or projects, provided he had the support of the other two groups.

The *curiae* were egalitarian groups of free men, probably composed of one hundred infantry warriors each. Etymologically, *curia* derived from *co-viria*, co-manhood. Each *curia* had a leader, the *curio*, and each elected two priests. "Curial hierurgies were often accompanied by joint dining [...] which confirms the parallel with Spartan *syssitiae* [...], egalitarian (brotherhoods) of messmate warriors."[16] All the men could vote, and they divided land won by conquest on an egalitarian basis. Related to the *curiae* was the *populus*, the people-host, which had an assembly in which free men could vote. Incidentally, extended kinship bonds were weak and communities of commoners were united by neighbor bonds, with each household led by a man. This may not

---

16   Dmitri V. Dozhdev, "Rome," in *Civilizational Models of Polito-genesis*, edited by Dmitri M. Bondarenko and Andrey V. Koro-tavey (Moscow: Institute for African Studies of the Russian Academy of Sciences, 2000), 261.

seem rare to Western readers but in a broad historical perspective
was quite uncommon and bears important ramifications for state
formation that will be discussed in a later chapter. To summarize,
though, such conditions of alienation and relative individualism
were likely the result of displacement, slaving, and turmoil—
basically, refugee crises—caused by expansive states and their
continuous warfare throughout the Mediterranean in prior centuries. In other words, we are dealing with state effects. One of
the most significant of these effects for subsequent developments
was land alienation: given the atomized family structure, land
was doled out as individual property.

Finally there were the *gentes*, the clans, whose leaders were
patriarchal, noble families with legendary ancestors, private
hierurgies (rituals led by a priest), and private places of worship.
In the militarized schema of Roman social organization, these
were the equestrians, the mounted warriors, who commanded
retainers and enough economic resources to be able to maintain
horses and the corresponding arms and armor. A clan might be
able to field a thousand warriors, nobles and commoners bound
by a common loyalty oath to the military chief of the *gens*. They
also had clients who swore allegiance in exchange for protection.
The clients had to perform some duties for the clan, needed the
chief's permission to marry, and were expected to support the
clan chief in public office, but the chief also had responsibilities
to them, for example having to support them and acquire them
legal defense if they were put on trial. Legally and symbolically,
they had the status of dependent children to the clan. Politically,
the clan chiefs had the *patres*, their council. The assembly and the
council existed in relative political equality; for example both had
to legitimate a new king.[17]

The perceptive reader will have noticed here the prototype
for the oldest existing democratic governments, those of the
United Kingdom and the United States, along with that of
numerous other states. Bicameral legislation, a House of Lords
and a House of Commons, or Senate and House of Representatives; this is a structure that finds its root in the caste system

---

17   Ibid., 265.

of ancient Rome, in which a noble elite enjoyed many economic and symbolic privileges, and enjoyed a potent hegemony in the economic mode that was naturalized, based in individual, alienable property rather than communal or collective holdings (which constituted an obstacle to state formation in many other societies but which the Romans never had to deal with). The equality of this system, which is formal and meaningless in terms of quality of life, stems from a militaristic and patriarchal idea of organization, in which male commoners were motivated to fight by being promised a piece of the pie, and given symbolic status recognition (in lay terms, ego boosts). The huge, despotic empires of the Fertile Crescent had proven time and time again that armies composed largely of slaves could not stand up to smaller, democratic armies. We can't know if the Romans were conscious of this lesson, but we can't help but think that it filtered through to them at least indirectly, given that the Italic Peninsula had been a part of the Mediterranean world system for more than a millennium.

With a city, the Romans established their state. First they conquered and absorbed the other members of the Latin League, before expanding across the Italic Peninsula and then developing continental ambitions. In time, the office of king was deposed and the plebeians won more rights, establishing the patriarchal, militaristic, imperialistic, and slavery-based Republic that Western thinkers admire so much.

Militarization, in sum, is a culturally driven, non-inevitable process by which the exigencies of warfare—either socially manufactured or imposed by bellicose neighbors—are exploited by an endogenous proto-elite to create a pathway for increasing social discipline and hierarchy. Frequently, militarization functions as a process of communication, even of mutuality, between two adversaries, in which the more decentralized society adopts characteristics of the more centralized one, or both societies at war increase their relative centralization and hierarchy, to win a competitive advantage. This advantage may be illusory, or it may allow one polity to avoid subjugation, but in any case, the winner in any militaristic contest is the principle and model of militarism itself.

I have already argued that decentralized societies enjoy a military advantage in terms of self-defense, but one thing they are incapable of is effectively planning and administering the conquest of a neighboring society. This trend even pertains to anarchist militias in the twentieth century. The Makhnovists in the Russian Civil War and the volunteer anarchist columns in the Spanish Civil War were easily the most effective fighting units in each of those wars, relative to their size and resources, but every time they had to go on the offensive beyond their base territory, they fell into stalemates. The ability for conquest is one "competitive advantage" a militaristic centralization provides. Additionally, chronic warfare can allow a war-making proto-elite to erode or diminish the other social structures and centers of power that hold them in check.

It should be emphasized that militarization is not synonymous with a warlike disposition nor is it antonymous with pacifism. Nor are its military advantages uniformly real, as many societies that have availed themselves of a greater mobility have demonstrated tremendous effectiveness in fighting invading states while increasing, rather than limiting, their decentralization and egalitarianism. It should also be noted that it is not a principle restricted to processes of early state formation. The impact of the Popular Front strategy during the Spanish Civil War was to militarize both the anarchist movement and the social revolution, spelling disaster for both. Militarization in the Spanish Civil War reinstated state power where it had been overthrown. It is in fact from this episode that I draw the name for the phenomenon: *militarization* was the term batted back and forth in anarchist debates, regarding the demands from the republicans and Stalinists who controlled the government that the volunteer militias be disbanded and incorporated into the regular military.

The Spartans of ancient Greece are depicted as extremely warlike. This vision has come down to us, however, through a notably pro-Athenian historiography. Arthur Evans argues that this picture is the twofold result of the homophobia of modern-day historians (who wish to portray the Spartans as uncultured), and the contemporary Athenians' fear of a relatively egalitarian Sparta in which women enjoyed higher status and the whole population was armed.

It is true that the early Dorians [whose capital was Sparta] were militaristic, but they were actually less militaristic than the previous Mycenaeans. For example, the Dorians were not dominated by a militaristic aristocracy, and they had no government bureaucracy devoted especially to war, as did the Mycenaeans.[18]

Homosexuality "was more highly regarded [in Sparta] than it was at Athens during the later classical period," and women enjoyed a relatively elevated status and could hold property and censure men.[19] In an ambitious history, *Witchcraft and the Gay Counterculture*, Arthur Evans traces a direct relationship between militarism, state formation, the emergence of class society, and the intensification of patriarchy, the latter resulting both in a decline of the status of women and in the suppression of homosexuality and transgender identities. From the modern standpoint, Classical Greece and Republican Rome seem to be broadly accepting of homosexuality and even libertine in their sexual practices, but compared with the societies they supplanted, they were in fact conservative. Moreover, as these societies became more militaristic, homosexuality was gradually suppressed, and important political, philosophical, and military leaders played a proactive role in this process.

On many occasions throughout history, it was the very act of conquest that allowed an aggressive society to develop the exploitative and administrative forms necessary to become a state. So far, we have looked at the model of the conquest state using a specific optic: militarization, whereby a relatively egalitarian society cleaves, and masculine organizations, the military brotherhoods of the Romans or the Germans, become a politogen, conquering other populations and forming states. **Imitation** was another motor in this process, certainly with the Germanic tribes, who had been under the tutelage of the Roman Empire, and probably with

---

18   Arthur Evans, *Witchcraft and the Gay Counterculture: A Radical View of Western Civilization and Some of the People It Has Tried to Destroy* (Boston: Fag Rag Books, 1978), 45.

19   Ibid., 46.

the Romans as well, who had plenty of contact with neighboring states or militaristic chiefdoms as they were founding their city.

The Congo basin states, the Lunda, Bakuba, and Baluba, provide a different example. Until the nineteenth century, they had no direct contact with other states. At that point, they adapted their endogenous forms of statist organization, shifting from exacting tribute to seizing captives or condemning criminals, whom they sold to European and Arab-Swahili slave traders. But they already had a state organization prior to Western contact.

These states were constituted by militarily aggressive ethnic groups that conquered other peoples. The Balunda conquered several peoples, such as the Chokwe and Aushi, to form the Lunda state; the Bushongo (*shongo* was the name of the double-edged blades they used) conquered the Bteng, Pyang, Bangongo, and another fourteen tribes to form the Bakuba state (*Bakuba* means "men of lightning," another reference to their weaponry); and the Baluba (whose name means "conquerors" or "destroyers") conquered the inhabitants of what is now Northern Zambia.[20]

Initially, the eventual conquerors practiced forms of external exploitation, robbing their neighbors through raiding. Over time, they ritualized and pacified this process; instead of raiding and plundering, they took to exacting tribute. At the time, the Balunda, Bushongo, and Baluba barely practiced internal forms of exploitation, though they had kinship hierarchies based on lineage: families who enjoyed a higher status and so constituted a form of nobility, although there were scant economic structures to differentiate them on a material level.

Eventually, the tribute-paying populations who were nearest and most vulnerable to the political power of the conquerors became fully integrated into a state society, and divided into provinces. War raiding and the exacting of tribute continued against external populations, whereas in the provinces, the tribute took on the form of a civic obligation.

So, while a fisher caught ten baskets of fish, he reserved for himself only four baskets. The rest of it was distributed

---

20   L'vova, "The Formation and Development of States," 288–89.

[...] as follows: one basket was for the old men of his village, three baskets were for the village chief and his clan,
and two baskets were a tribute in favor of [the] supreme
power.[21]

Land was inalienable, but peasants had to pay a tribute in
agricultural goods, as in the feudal system, and to turn over a
portion of their catch from hunting and fishing, as described
above. They also had obligatory labor duties, corvée labor, but
these were irregular, in contrast to many other early states. Any
status goods, such as ivory, leopard skins, and eagle feathers, had
to be given to the chiefs, who could then redistribute them as
status and political needs dictated.

The hierarchies of the conquered peoples were integrated
into the new states (showing the wisdom of having horizontal internal relations as a means for avoiding conquest and co-
optation by a state).

The chiefs of conquered ethnic groups were also included
into the top governmental strata of Kuba, Luba, and
Lunda states. But they were forced to recognize the rulers [...] as supreme chiefs. Sometimes, these new relations
were registered through real [or] symbolic matrimonial
rituals between the supreme chief and chiefs of conquered
peoples.[22]

Interestingly, this symbolic matrimonial ritual shows a parallel with the *immixtio manuum* ritual in the vassalage ceremonies of Western Europe, as pointed out by Jacques Le Goff.[23]

These states also had armies, law courts, secret fraternities,
councils of nobles, and the institutions of servility and client-
age. The armies were not regularized, but functioned as a "home

---

21   Ibid., 290.
22   Ibid.
23   Jacques Le Goff, *Time, Work, and Culture in the Middle Ages*,
      trans. Arthur Goldhammer (Chicago: University of Chicago
      Press, 1980).

guard," with all the adult males of a certain age group liable to be called into service. In the Kuba state, unlike the other two, "a number of war leaders [...] conserved their posts in peacetime." In all three cases, however, the armies were at the service of the government, being "used for territorial usurpation, war robbery expeditions, suppressions of revolted vassals, and so on."[24]

The law courts were most extensive in the Kuba state, with a multi-stepped structure spanning village, province, and capital. The highest judges were the paramount ruler and the head of the council. There were also "different judges for making decisions on definite crimes and cases: on sorcery, on killings, on fights and mutilations, on stealing, on heritage, on trade and so on."[25] The secret fraternities, for their part, executed the sentences. In early states on multiple continents, such fraternities played an important role in backing up what was otherwise a weak state power, both symbolically and physically. A famous example is the cult of Ares in the Athenian city-state, which carried out executions on the hill of Areopagus.

Sometimes the secret fraternities comprised young men recruited to support the old men who occupied the positions of judges and rulers. Recruits were given the privilege of being sanctioned to commit what would otherwise be blood crimes, a great power both symbolically and psychologically (and also quite revealing in terms of the psychology of state supporters: the "anti-social elements" that apologists for the State always warn us against have from the very beginning been the agents of the State itself). Other times they were power-holders in their own right. Their anonymity played multiple functions: ritualizing the mystical execution of justice and encouraging the view that justice was the dispensation of a divine principle and not the politically motivated action of specific people with names and faces; excusing the families of the executed from the obligation for vengeance, in cases where they supported the justice process; and protecting the executioners from vengeance, in cases where the families of the executed were defiant. This last element is perhaps

---

24   L'vova, "The Formation and Development of States," 295.
25   Ibid., 295, 294–95.

the only one that has remained unchanged today, when state executioners are still faceless, and police in anti-terrorism or other high-profile operations of a political nature cover their faces and badge numbers.

In all three Congo basin states, the authority of the paramount ruler was complemented by that of a council of nobles. In the Kuba state, this council had a leader.

> The relations between the council and the [paramount ruler] were ambiguous. Members of the council outwardly showed obedience but they were very powerful in reality [...]. Having meetings not less than once a week the council decided practically all the important questions. The nyimi [paramount ruler in the Kuba state] was allowed only to submit proposals for consideration. He was not allowed even to be present at the sittings of the council. A kikaam [head of the council in the Kuba state] could make a decision opposed to the will of a nyimi.[26]

The paramount rulers were also surrounded by a large number of noble courtiers, some of whom played a "crucial part in the state apparatus" while others were only the bearers of honorary titles. It is important to note that while the paramount rulers may seem like figureheads from a modern standpoint, they played a vital role as "priest-king," which will be discussed in Chapter XI. The ascendance of the council and other institutional forms of leadership in the Kuba state reflect a push by the elite to extend their power beyond what is attainable through the symbolic and religious forms of domination that are prevalent in early states.

The three Congo basin states practiced servitude, whereby war captives, condemned criminals, or their relatives had to toil in fields, act as domestic workers, porters, personal servants, or bodyguards. The labor they provided was minor, far from constituting the primary form of economic exploitation, and the conditions and labor demands they faced were significantly lighter than those of the slaves under the Roman Empire or the later

---

26   Ibid., 294.

European nation-states. Clients (most typical in the Baluba state) enjoyed a much higher status than servants. Attaching themselves to a noble family, they played the role of bodyguards or assistants. Over time, the mutual obligations of clients and patrons took on a hereditary form. The societies that preceded these states were all non-patriarchal or only lightly patriarchal, whereas all three states pushed to institute more patriarchal relations.

These internal processes, perhaps more important in the formation of the Congo basin states than their practices of warfare and conquest, correspond to patterns that will be discussed in a subsequent chapter.

III.
Save Me from Yourself:
The Statist Spread of Salvation Religions

"ADOPTION OF THE [STATE] model was tantamount to adoption of Christianity, which legitimized the political order of the state."[1]

The parastatal Catholic Church had attached itself to the Roman Empire, using that structure's last centuries to spread the religion considerably, converting the elites and then the peasants of barbarian societies. When the empire fell, the Church held on to the dream. Even where it was too weak to constitute an imperial state, it spread a common cultural language that favored state formation and preached obedience to authority. Over centuries, it served as a centralized network to mobilize resources for state formation, until the power of those states increased to a point where they either monopolized the resources of the Church or rebelled against it, creating their own autonomous churches with a doctrine modified to legitimize the transformed basis of their power.

What is often missed in the progressive telling of history is that the Romans came closer to the creation of capitalism than subsequent societies, up until the end of the Middle Ages and the beginning of colonization beyond Europe. In the meantime, the Eastern Roman Empire, the Byzantines, and the Arab states kept capitalist structures alive in the Mediterranean world system. A major cause of the peasant rebellions that began to occur in Western Europe in the Late Middle Ages was the restoration of Roman law by local elites, which allowed land to be bought and sold as a commodity. As a direct result and parallel, the condition

---

1   Tymowski, "State and Tribe in the History of Medieval Europe and Black Africa," 174.

of peasants—who were much better off in the Middle Ages or under the earlier German tribes than their Roman homologue, the slave—began to deteriorate gravely, as the worker was created, on the one hand, and on the other the institution of slavery was brought back—not from nonexistence, but from decline—and intensified and expanded immeasurably.

The epidemics, poverty, starvation, servitude, intolerance, witch hunts—basically all the features assigned to the stereotypical image of the Dark Ages—were in fact characteristic of the end of the Middle Ages, the Renaissance, and the beginning of the Enlightenment. The Dark Ages were only dark for states, because their power, relative to their subjects, was greatly diminished compared to the centuries before and after. Many areas under Roman rule slipped from state control for a number of centuries, and as Kropotkin documented, many medieval towns freed themselves from lordly authority in the tenth and eleventh centuries.[2]

When state power was restored, it was accompanied by another Roman practice that might have slipped into obsolescence were it not for the diligence of the Catholic Church: usury. Contrary to its own doctrine, the Church encouraged finance—lending with interest—in order to fund its own power pursuits. In the fourteenth and fifteenth centuries, the most powerful financiers of Europe did business with, and were located close to the Vatican. Significantly, the promotion of usury was one major corruption of the Catholic Church that the Protestants did not consistently criticize. Only the Anabaptists, slaughtered by their erstwhile Protestant allies, harped on the sin of finance. (It is also curious how, nowadays, the frequent demonization of Islamic shari'ah law almost never mentions shari'ah's prohibition of lending with interest, a detail that certainly worries the owners of Western media outlets more than questions of women's rights.)

As both the Protestant Reformation and early Christianity demonstrate, salvation religions can subvert state authority and subsequently create new, more powerful authorities.

---

2   Pyotr Kropotkin, *Mutual Aid: A Factor of Evolution* (London: Heinemann, 1902).

The extension of new state structures through the southern reaches of the defunct Roman Empire and beyond, riding the wave of Islam, was even more dramatic than the German explosion in the north. In many parts of the Arabian peninsula prior to Islam, the emergence of a state was impeded by the strong tribal organization of society. Tribal leaders would brook no other leaders standing over them, nor a bureaucratic organization diffusing their power; whereas tribal members typically considered submission to anyone but the proven leader of their own tribe an indignity (and the leader, in practice, won respect more than he enjoyed the *a priori* submission of his fellows). The exception to this dynamic had to be found in an exceptional and extrapolitical space: religion.

> The solution to this impasse was worked out even prior to Islam by the evolution of the organization centred upon the sacred enclave, managed by an hereditary religious aristocracy respected and protected by the tribes.[3]

Islam, by being thoroughly monotheistic, could achieve the centralization of these enclaves; and by preaching the holiness of submission to God they could convince the tribal leaders to bow to a higher, apolitical authority in a way that preserved and even amplified their dignity, and left their own political authority symbolically intact. Religion broke the intense localism that often prevented state formation, and masked the emergence of a professional class. In the Yemeni highlands, the *sayyids*, who traced their decent to Muhammad, constituted the new hereditary religious aristocracy, and they were aided by a second-tier, the *qadis*, learned families who could not claim descent from the Prophet. Islamic shari'ah law also influenced the transformation of a collective property regime "towards the individual possession of the arable lands by all the adult members of the tribes."[4]

---

3   R.B. Serjeant, quoted in Andrey V. Korotayev, "The Chiefdom: Precursor of the Tribe? (Some Trends of Political Evolution in North-East Yemeni Highlands)," in *The Early State, Its Alternatives and Analogues*, 301.

4   Korotayev, "The Chiefdom," 305 (earlier data from 300–301).

In Yemen, which was to provide vital military power for
the Arab expansion, a central state was integrated, in a common
system, with surrounding non-state tribes through a number of
economic, religious, and political links. Islam intensified this
sense of unity, not only in the highlands but across the Arabian
peninsula; influenced by Islam's insistence on genealogies, the
Yemeni quickly elaborated their own, thus joining the Arab
ethnos, which previously had not included them. The militarily
potent tribes each included 20,000–30,000 members, as well as
tens of thousands of non-member dependents with varying levels of status, from the *sayyids* and *qadis*, to the unarmed "weak"
population under tribal protection,[5] butchers, barbers, heralds,
merchants, horticulturalists, craftspeople, Jews, and lowest of
all, servants.[6] (Interestingly, the tribal organization of the region
has proven much more durable than the state organization, and
persisted intact well into the twentieth century. It still remains
partially intact today.)

Islam and the state model it linked to spread on the back of
an Arabic population expansion, and also through the intercontinental trade expansion that was occurring in those centuries. The
Islamic state already had some experience with incorporating
into their social system non-Muslims and people who fell outside their Arab genealogies. When the non-Muslim population
in their administrative purview began to increase exponentially
with the first conquests, so too did the state apparatus. The social
presence of non-Muslims, as well as non-Arabic converts to
Islam, provided a solid social hierarchy as well as ready-made jus-
tifications and metrics for taxation and tribute (Arabic Muslims
were the most privileged stratum, and then non-Arabic Muslims,
and then non-Muslims). The well-known historical tolerance of

---

5   This relationship was probably not as cynically threatening as
     it might seem, given that the tribes owed the "weak" castes a
     real responsibility. If unarmed dependents were harmed, it was
     a great dishonor for the tribe, and reparations or fines for any
     injury to such a person was much higher than if the injury were
     committed to a member of the tribe itself.

6   Korotayev, "The Chiefdom," 300–301.

Islam may be related to the fact that, by tolerating internal differences, they also provided a stable basis for the hierarchies on
which their states relied.

Soon, Islamic states were at the scientific and commercial
center of a nascent world system that spanned Europe, Africa,
and Asia. However, the Arabic countries in the cradle of the
Muslim world experienced chronic problems with state formation. Amin Maalouf speculates as to why the Arab states were
so fragmented and ineffective just a couple centuries after the
golden age of the Umayyad Caliphate, which had dominated an
area extending from Persia to Spain. The Abbasid Caliphate that
succeeded it lost most of its domain within half a century, and
the caliph of Baghdad was soon little more than a religious figure
bestowing symbolic authority on—and sometimes held hostage
by—Turkish sultans or other warlords. The Turks, who themselves had recently been a stateless, nomadic people, also failed
to achieve any lasting political unification (excepting a small
portion of the empire, the Anatolian peninsula that would later
come to bear their name, and not for another four hundred years).
Charismatic war leaders like Imad al-Din Zangi or Salah al-Din
would unify a large territory, but their deaths almost always led
to civil war (or were in fact the first blow in a civil war, in the case
of frequent poisonings and assassinations). A regular succession
and institutionalized transference of power was a rare occurrence. In effect, the vast former empire was a disunified collection of city-states. Islam had, however, succeeded in destroying
a stateless imaginary. With few exceptions, such as non-Arabic
mountain populations in the Caucusus or the Rif, Islam had
succeeded in centralizing symbolic power and creating a statist
imaginary, such that state-building was henceforth the goal of
nearly all political activity, ineffective as it might be.

Specifically, Malouf asks why the Frankish crusaders were so
much more successful at building stable states in Syria and Palestine than the Arabs. After all, the Arabs perceived *franj* practices of hygiene, medicine, and justice as insanely ignorant and
monstrous, and modern Western criteria would have to corrob-
orate such a view. Beyond the typical culturalist explanations of
Western innovation—the Arabs rested on their sense of cultural

superiority whereas the Europeans actively sought to appropriate new knowledge—Malouf points out that Muslim political culture placed no limits on the authority of rulers, whereas a democratic spirit among the Franks limited the arbitrary power of rulers, encouraging peasant industriousness and the free development of commerce, as the undertakers of such labor could expect to enjoy a larger part of the fruit of their efforts. It should be noted, though, to prevent any excessive orientalizing, that the often celebrated "democratic spirit" was a militaristic fraternity and a shared identification with power that always relied on the enslavement or extermination of an Other. Likewise, Arabic absolutism was not much different from Roman absolutism at the height of that empire's power.

Malouf continues: the "nomadic origins" of the Arabs and Turks might also explain "their inability to build stable institutions," such that "every transmission of power provoked civil war."[7] Malouf hints that the frequency of "successive invasions" in the Middle East made stable states an unrealistic objective for the political class. The elite culture of frenetic conquest may have been a rational adaptation to such uncertain circumstances. The Middle East was a hub of culture, trade, and other sources of power, and as a result, it was demographically unstable, to put it lightly. If you are unlikely to be able to establish a dynasty due to frequent invasions (which also put an end to the more stable Frankish states after little more than a century), then it makes more sense to live high on the hog, to pillage and despoil and generally create heaven on earth, rather than thinking of legacies and the stability of your political structures. In this respect, state builders on the European subcontinent may have benefited from inhabiting a backwater that no one in their right mind would want to invade.

Islam was an important force for state formation for more than a millennium. In recent times, Muslim fundamentalism has been an effective state-building movement in places like Afghanistan or Iraq/Syria, where Western, post-colonial states have

---

7   Amin Maalouf, *The Crusades Through Arab Eyes,* tran. John Rothschild (New York: Schocken Books, 1984), 262.

failed. But for most of its history, a more tolerant form of Islam linked to global trade expansion was the active motor of polito-genesis. When Musa I of Mali went on a pilgrimage to Mecca, the sheer abundance of lavish gifts he brought with him notice-ably reduced gold prices throughout the entire world system. It was Muslim traders who truly kicked off the cycle of accumu-lation linking Africa, Europe, India, Central Asia, China, and the East Indies, which Portuguese and Dutch merchants would later take over. With Islam and intensified trade came a number of new states in South Asia and North Africa that tended to be more robust than their Hindu or animist predecessors.

Trade expansions often go hand in hand with state expan-sions, as trade creates networks that states can exploit, and states create infrastructures and impose conditions of alienation that make the accumulation of wealth possible. While trade occurs anarchically and can be organized without states, a state may decrease its costs and risks, allowing it to be pursued purely in the interest of profit, and also create dependent populations vul-nerable to exploitation. Traders, therefore, come together as a class to favor states and state formation, but this same process eventually allows them to become powerful enough to threaten certain forms of state organization and impel others. States, as they become more powerful, can be the greatest threat to trade, thus powerful states will enter into conflict with the merchants on whom they become increasingly reliant. If this conflict is resolved in a way that mutually increases the power of rulers and merchants, it is through the greater inclusion of merchants in state decision-making, and through the modification of produc-tion and commerce in order to favor state power, for example through war industries.

Because trade supersedes state borders, merchant classes will often come into conflict with the zeal and dogmatism of state reli-gion; frequently collaborating with foreigners who perform other religions, and having the experience of operating in foreign coun-tries, they develop a peculiar internationalism. Salvation religions, because they are universalizing, can flatten out the cultural differ-ences that localized religion only enhances, and help merchants create a common culture in their transnational networks.

On the other hand, by expounding universal truths antagonistic to other truth claims, salvation religions may initially pose a problem to power-holders. The Roman Empire was hostile to Judaism and initially to Christianity, and the Mecca elite expelled Mohammed for his teachings. The chauvinism of power-holders would prevent them from taking full advantage of the transnational opportunities presented by the merchant class. Yet a ruling class can never adopt a true internationalism. They need a provincial chauvinism to mobilize and militarize their society when trade wars turn into hot wars, as the Arab expansion and the Crusades both demonstrated.

Salvation religions can spare elites this dilemma by fragmenting society into secular and ecclesiastical spaces, as Christianity did, or by practicing tolerance, as Islam did during the peak centuries of overland intercontinental trade, or as Buddhism did in its expansion through stateless parts of Asia. In the former model, certain religious rules are suspended for a specific class of people, which may eventually give rise to a power struggle between the Church and the semi-autonomous class (as happened in Western Europe); in the latter model, the claim to a superior truth is maintained, but the consequences are reserved for the afterlife (or reincarnation), with the authorities benevolently protecting infidels from punishment in this life. The former gives a competitive advantage to autochthonous merchants but sacrifices the primacy of the priests, whereas the latter model allows the national religion to maintain its dominance but also allows foreign merchants to gain dominance within the national territory. This is more or less what happened in the neighborly system constituted by Christendom and Islam.

Given that there are multiple solutions to the conflict between the chauvinism and universalism of salvation religions, such religions can complement trade and state expansions better than localized pagan spiritualities. Unlike pagan religions, salvation religions are mutually exclusive; therefore states can use them as a tool for war mobilization. But salvation religions bring advantages to state formation in other ways as well.

As salvation religions spread, they can prove subversive to preexisting states as commoners seize on them to rally popular rage and differentiate themselves spiritually from their rulers. However, salvation religions are easily recuperated and hijacked by forward-thinking states. The spread of such religions, therefore, serves to shake up the conservatism that often plagues states and to allow more potent, proactive governments to clear away defunct regimes and open a new path for state advancement. Just as the Roman Empire seized on Christianity to supersede the zero-sum imperial competition that was bleeding the Mediterranean world dry, a rekindled Islamic fundamentalism is reinvigorating the process of state formation in the stagnating, post-colonial states of Saharan Africa.

Fortuitously for them, a shared religion does not end competition between states, which would cause them to atrophy, but it does create a unified cultural field that establishes certain protections, shared norms, and informational networks that are invaluable to merchants in the absence of a unified state structure governing diverse territories. Merchants become key agents of the new religion, also increasing their connectivity to whatever progressive states have succeeded in recuperating that religion. The materially intense channels and networks created by merchants can then be used as paths for state expansion, as was the case with European colonialism in Africa and Asia. Incidentally, missionaries of salvation religions can also play this role, acting as advance troops to establish beachheads, collect information on the natives, and prepare them for occupation.

Because nearly all the states in Southeast Asia before the modern period adhered to Buddhism and one of their major struggles was the constant civilization and recapturing of subjects, who were prone to run to the hills, the universalization of Buddhism to all regional states deprived hill peoples and barbarians of the chance to use one competing salvation religion subversively against another. Buddhism and civilization were symbolically united, increasing the former's allure and cultural sway. And even though the states of east and southeast Asia were in competition with one another, by creating, almost federalistically, a unified substrate of religion they increased their collective civilizing power, and all of them gained. After all, once subjects were brought down from the hills and put to work, they could be fought over, captured and recaptured by the competing states. It was easier to change their nationality than to civilize them in the first place.

> Given the influence of the clergy (*sangha*) in Theravada countries like Burma and Siam and a cosmology that potentially made the ruler into a Hindu-Buddhist god-king, it was at least as vital for the crown to control the abbots of the realm as it was to control its princes—and at least as difficult [...]

> Despite their syncretism and incorporation of animist practice, Theravada monarchs, when they could, proscribed heterodox monks and monasteries, outlawed many Hindu-animist rites (many of them dominated by females and transvestites), and propagated what they took to be "pure," uncorrupted texts. The flattening of religious practice was, then, a project of the padi state to ensure that the only other kingdom-wide institution of elites besides the crown's own establishment was firmly under its control. A certain uniformity was also achieved because the larger abbeys were, after all, run by a surplus-appropriating elite that, like the crown itself, thrived best on the rich production and concentrated manpower available at the state core.[8]

Clearly, salvation religions advantage states because they provide a psychological weapon against the disorderly byproducts of exploitation and suffering, and they focus a people's symbolic and spiritual attention on a domain that is both within state control (the publicly subsidized temples) and conveniently away from the ugly terrain of state effects (in Nirvana or Heaven), away from the fields, the prisons, the gutters, the battlefields. Unlike animist and pagan religions, which may also be used to awe and pacify subjects, salvation religions do not have a potentially subversive, anti-authoritarian attachment to the local; their god is omnipresent and their teachings are designed to be transported. Thus they alienate access to the divine while maintaining a mobility befitting an army.

---

8   Scott, *The Art of Not Being Governed*, 155–56.

However, all religions can be subverted by mystical cults or heretical movements. Heterodox believers claim the state religion, usually (but not always) protecting themselves from the full zeal of a holy war waged against them, and also benefiting from trade and other peaceful relations with their co-religionists. By propagating heterodox beliefs, they can subvert state authority and carve out a sphere of independence while claiming the privileges that attain to believers.

The trend is transcontinental. Peasant rebellions in Europe that challenged feudal authority frequently adopted Anabaptism, or one of many Marian or Manichean heresies. Heretical forms of Buddhism have long been popular among the highland communities in resistance to state encroachments in Southeast Asia. A similar pattern can be observed among the Berbers of Northern Africa.

> When the Romans who controlled the province of Ifriqi-yah [Africa] became Christianized, the highland Berbers (whom they never fully subjugated) also became Christians—but Donatist and Arian heretics, so as to remain distinct from the church of Rome. When Islam swept the area the Berbers became Muslims, but soon expressed their dissent from the inequalities of Arab Muslim rule by becoming Kharijite heretics.[9]

Heterodox and heretical sects were manifold in Christian Europe, being attached both to dissident movements among elites promoting alternative strategies for the organization of power, and also to popular, anti-authoritarian movements that contested the exploitative practices of power-holders. However, in the twelfth and thirteenth centuries, secular power-holders, particularly in certain French territories where processes of state formation were most advanced, began pressuring the Catholic Church to justify the purging of competitors. Under the guise of a war on heresy, whoever could secure the approval of the Church could humiliate or even eliminate their rivals, sometimes

---

9   Ibid., 158.

even when these had the favor of the king. In effect, this constituted the gradual abolition of the Peace and Truce of God, the
result of a tenth- and eleventh-century popular movement that
had pressured the Church to severely limit feuding by nobles,
thus protecting commoners from the ravages of warfare and from
the elevated tax burden that went with it. By demonizing their
rivals as heretics, secular rulers could get around the prohibitions
enacted by the Peace and Truce of God. But as feudal warfare
gained steam, the war on heresy developed mechanisms of its
own, under control of the Church. The earliest targets were elites,
but Rome's bloodhounds quickly turned their attention against
the commoners. These two movements, the secular and the ecclesiastic, and their targeting of the upper and lower strata of society,
found their maximum point of harmony in the crusade against
the Cathars of the French Pyrenees. Subsequently, the renewal
of secular warfare diverged to foment processes of empire building that ended in the modernization of the State, whereas the
ecclesiastic purges later took on gender and class overtones and
transformed into the witch hunts, a tool that municipal authorities quickly appropriated, together with the early enclosures and
debt policies laying the groundwork for capitalist social relations.

Religious **purification** was an important motor for state formation among the Israelite tribes after they settled in the territories
that would become their homeland. The tribes were organized in
a loose confederation, but hostile incursions by bellicose neighbors
encouraged them to band together under a common war leader or
king (a common occurrence in stateless tribal confederations). Up
to that time, Israeli monotheism (which in practice was still quite
open to polytheism, *Yahweh* perhaps being viewed as a special god
of the tribes rather than the only true God) proscribed the establishment of a single human ruler, since such a ruler was ostensibly
usurping a power position that belonged only to God. Such a view
shows how religious practices that later became important motors
of state-formation were originally tactics of state-resistance (similar to how Christianity was initially a state-resistant practice). The
implications of early Israelite anti-statist monotheism should have
obvious subversive implications, given that its practitioners had
been slaves of the Egyptian god-king, the pharaoh.

Contrary to the exaggerations in the Bible, the United Kingdom of Israel was not a state, and the level of unification it achieved was minimal, limited to the battlefield and a few acts of temple construction, the most famous being in Jerusalem, a city that at the time only had a few hundred inhabitants.[10] Perhaps only the last of the three supposed kings—Saul, David, and Solomon—actually exercised a leadership role over the whole of the confederation. Significantly, the conquest story of the origins of Israel was made up a couple centuries later by state historians who wanted to invent a militarist pedigree in which the country was founded on the slaughter of heathens. Archaeological evidence shows that in reality, the Israelites and the Canaanites peacefully coexisted.

The northern tribal confederation of Israel, which contained the majority of the Israelite tribes, rejected Solomon's attempt to found a dynasty, so that his son only had authority in the smaller, southern Kingdom of Judah. Politogenesis actually occurred over the following century, as the Kingdom of Judah and the Kingdom of Israel fought each other and also waged wars against the Moabites, the Assyrians, the Egyptians, and the neo-Babylonians. The Old Testament reflects the Kingdom of Judah's disdain for Israel's tolerance of polytheism, and documents Judah's use of monotheism to legitimate the role of a supreme monarch supported by a priestly class. The Kingdom of Israel promoted polytheism—particularly the worship of the Phoenician god Baal—partly as a way to prevent their religious-cultural domination by Jerusalem (the capital of Judah) and partly as a reflection of their greater tolerance (or weaker control by a priestly class). Though the northern kingdom was more populous and architecturally more advanced, it can be argued that they did not develop into a state until later, under the Omrides dynasty.

Polytheistic states largely described the fickle, shifting fortunes of nature or geopolitics (e.g. invasions, declines in trade) as the result of wars or conflicts between the gods; in

---

10   Israel Finkelstein and Neil Asher Silberman, *The Bible Unearthed: Archaeology's New Vision of Ancient Israel and the Origin of Its Sacred Texts* (New York: Simon & Schuster, 2001), 133.

other words, society and the state were peripheral to extremely important changes in the world around them. Such a view, in which human society is at the mercy of fortune, created a crucial barrier to the expansion of state power. The monotheistic state of Judah, on the contrary, could develop a *cratocentric* worldview in which divine will and state interests were completely fused. Any misfortune, whether a plague or the supposed division of the United Kingdom, was a result of the wrath of an extremely demanding God. Any good fortune was the result of obedience to God's will. The will of God and the will of the State, incidentally, were synonymous.

This new moral universe enshrined total obedience and also made sure that the priests always had a useful culprit every time things went wrong, given that total obedience is impossible in practice. Millennia before the prison-industrial complex would come to manufacture the crime and incarceration it profits off of, monotheists had learned to produce the sins that could create a demand for more monotheism.

Purification, in the Israelite case, went hand in hand with militarization, though it was the function of the priestly class in legitimizing and expanding state authority that was most highly privileged.

Sleeper States and Imperial Imaginaries:
Authority's Afterlife and Reincarnation

THE ANTHROPOLOGICAL AND EVOLUTIONARY typology of *band, tribe, chiefdom, state* does not accurately describe the historical existence of states and stateless societies. Many bands have been post-state groupings whose organizational structure helps them resist capture and inclusion by neighboring states. "Tribes" as classically defined tended to be the projections and inventions of states (or as Korotayev documents in the Yemeni highlands, evolutions of chiefdoms), whereas societies defined as "chiefdoms" could be stable, mildly hierarchical megacommunities that actively constituted state alternatives rather than stepping stones to state-formation. Rather than existing as discrete ethnic units, societies tend to be differentiated articulations of cultural, socio-economic organization that only function as part of an interconnected regional or global system.

From an anarchist standpoint, there is something else lacking in the evolutionary typology. Namely, there have been some societies that, although in organizational terms may be defined as chiefdoms, already contain within them more than just the first steps of state formation, and therefore act as vehicles for state-formation rather than independent and resistant hierarchies.

Quite apart from their organizational reality, states include a projectual dimension (as we have seen in Chapter II) and an imaginary dimension (Chapter III), that are wholly real, even though they must be relegated to the immaterial sphere according to an erroneous dichotomy (and sometimes dialectic) once in vogue. A more nuanced, realistic version of this dialectic, such as the Foucault- and ethnology-influenced method of history espoused by Jacques Le Goff, would describe these two dimensions as aspects of a society's mentality, "'that which changes least' in historical evolution."[1] However, within this framework, a mentality without the institutions, economies, and social structures to support it can only be understood as archaic, vestigial. Such a mentality is nothing but a residue of the hard structures that have presumably evolved and left it behind. Even though an unsupported mentality indisputably constitutes part of the social reality, it lacks a claim to reality because within a progressive framework it belongs to the past, it constitutes a dead-end, whereas the supposedly more evolved structures represent the only way forward. Even if this view is not the aim of historical ethnology, it is still the likely outcome of the evolutionary worldview built into and only partially excised from ethnology, history, and all other Western scholastic disciplines. In 1974, Pierre Clastres wrote how "behind the modern formulations, the old evolutionism remains, in fact, intact."[2] The same observation could be made today. I don't think the intellectual culture of scientists can be completely purged of this pervasive mythology as long as the interconnected economies, institutions, structures, and parallel mentalities (of both popular and elite culture) are infused with an implicitly supremacist and accumulative progressivism.

(Many academics from the Early State Project, for example, though they recognize the basic precepts of multilinear evolution, the historical commonplace of state failure, and the possibility of a stateless complex social organization, still frequently use a temporal language that implicitly identifies the state as the most advanced form of organization. And how could they entirely purge this component of their ideology, even once they have the capacity to recognize it as erroneous and mythological, when the only economic opportunities for Early State scientists, aside from teaching at universities, is to advise dominant states on effective methods for propping up failed states, from Somalia to Iraq. And as for the teaching posts or museum jobs, these are hardly refuges of pure research, as the number and quality of such posts is directly related to the profitability with which the discipline can be applied outside of academia.)

---

1   Le Goff, *Time, Work, and Culture in the Middle Ages*, 229.
2   Clastres, *Society Against the State*, 184.

To shed a little light on the importance of the projectual and imaginary dimensions, let us turn to early medieval Europe. Because of the strong pretensions of post-Roman European elites to be commanders of states, it took a long time for modern scientists and historians to recognize that by their schema, they were actually looking at chiefdoms and not states.[3] In other words, the European term had connotations of sophistication, and thus statehood, whereas non-Western terms communicate primitivism, and thus chiefdoms.

According to an evolutionary analysis based on organizational complexity and territoriality, many European kings of the early Middle Ages were "in fact" chiefs. While accurate within its own terms of analysis, this view is erroneous for not giving importance to the imaginary organization of these societies.

Before identifying a few significant aspects of the collapse and reemergence of the State in Western Europe, it would do well to problematize a crucial element of social scientists' definition of the state: its territoriality. Control of a territory rather than the unification of specific kinship groups seems to be a universal and essential feature of the state. Yet many social scientists have uncritically taken state pretensions of their own territoriality at face value, perhaps because they share the state's ideology and believe in the projection of its legitimacy. As Scott conveys in his discussion of "Mandala states," a state's territoriality is often fictive, imaginary, and projectual.[4] In other words, states

---

3   And it may be equally if not more true that academic Eurocentrism abetted the confusion. *King, rex, roi,* et cetera, originally denominated chiefs whose authority more often than not was temporary, charismatic, and/or primarily military. Centuries later, European monarchs, and the heads of true states, chose these same titles, perhaps to anoint themselves with an aura of historical continuity or eternal supremacy. In the modern era, early researchers did not know to distinguish kingdom-chiefdoms and statist monarchies, a problem they would not have had if the symbolic, mythologized term at play had been *longko* or *nyimi* rather than *koning* or *rei.*

4   Scott, *The Art of Not Being Governed,* 60.

throughout history, up until today, do not exert control over
the entirety of the space (and here we can consider both social
and geographical space) they claim to dominate. The functional
aspect, then, are elite claims. A state's territoriality resides most
perfectly in its rulers' imaginary. What other aspects of state formation are produced by the imagination? Let us return to the
example at hand.

The Western Roman Empire collapsed in 476, and the
politogens with some direct connection to it (for example, Germanic war leaders who had served in the Roman military) were
only able to subject a portion of the old empire to new state
authority. Before 600, there were few polities, besides that of the
Franks, the Saxons, and the Longobards, that could boast both
a significant territory and a political structure worthy of classification as a state. The economic and organizational basis of
statehood dissolved throughout most of Europe. Cities declined,
private ownership of land disappeared, horticulture became the
predominant economic activity and, as Western Europe refor-
ested even hunting became important again. Elite hierarchies
were often redundant, overlapping, and ambiguous, lacking
multiple levels of administration, a uniform legality, or a defined
chain of command. The Church and the courts of warrior-kings
worked fundamentally in alliance but also in competition, their
hierarchies overlapping and often conflicting, a sort of inefficient
double-measure to tie the population down in the absence of any
unified measure. The land was divided into a patchwork of territories promising their obedience to multiple masters who competed
endlessly, working out a pecking order that remained ambiguous
for centuries. On an organizational and economic level, the system was similar to that of the Waha in central Africa,[5] although
the latter developed in completely different ways, preventing
state formation for centuries whereas Western European societies continuously climbed that hill no matter how many times
they fell down. In contrast, what has been described as Chinese
or Japanese feudalism differs strongly from European feudalism
in terms of organization and property relations, as hierarchies

5   Le Goff, *Time, Work, and Culture in the Middle Ages*, 279–82.

were unitary and well defined, with a relatively unambiguous chain of command and source of sovereignty and legality. The point of commonality was a partially self-sufficient peasant class who had to surrender a part of its produce in order to maintain access to the land.

The symbolic and imaginary connections to antiquity that persisted through the European Middle Ages were not merely a vestigial mentality, but a means of preserving statist organization on an imaginary plane, given its unfeasibility on the material plane, and a code or diffuse instruction manual for eventually recovering state formation, a sort of trail of breadcrumbs by which Hansel and Gretel could find their way out of the forest again.

Early medieval society was also characterized by a resurgent tripartite division that was universal at one point or another among Indo-European peoples. This division consisted of *"oratores, bellatores,* and *laboratores,* or clergy, warriors, and workers."[6] We should note, as Le Goff does with other terms and with another point in mind, that the linguistically inappropriate but semantically accurate translation of *laboratores* is "improvers." These were not toilers but landowners or independent farmers—those with their own land who were rarely self-sufficient laborwise but who made use of additional seasonal labor, eventually giving rise to the post-feudal class of landless or salaried peasants. Some of the techniques and instruments credited to these improvers were the product of their own initiatives and others no doubt were observed among and stolen from the peasants, who in their unregulated labor time experimented with labor-saving methods, bounty-amplifying devices, and creative, impressive, gratifying gadgets. We are thinking here of things like crop rotation, more extensive and less labor-intensive irrigation, asymmetrical plows, water wheels, and so forth.

These improvers were not primarily the ones who toiled to implement and manage their improvements, though many were probably poor enough that they had to work alongside their helpers, and some perhaps prefigured the Protestant work ethic

---

6   Ibid., 53.

by taking part and pleasure in the manual aspect of their labor. However, the early medieval attitude among the literate strata towards work—unambiguously negative—leaves no direct record of their enthusiasm.

What is curious is that these improvers were heretics, according to the letter of Church law, for disputing God's control of time, his prescription of asceticism, and his admonishments against the glorification or adornment of the earthly world; yet they were pious supporters of the Church and often won its admiration. We might surmise that the improvers simply tread roughshod over Church doctrine because it was the only way to increase their wealth and their power relative to the other castes. If this were the case, the ecclesiastical authorities would have treated them the same way they treated other heretics, or the way they treated the invisible fourth class, the peasants who carried out most of the actual labor. Church complicity with the improvers in the subversion of their own doctrine reveals a shared dream, a quest for a greater glory not present in the social structures of the day, and whose attainment would require the total transformation or liquidation of those structures.

By the time the *laboratores* established their hegemony, the tripartite system from which they arose had already disappeared. By advancing a new, scientific[7] conception of time and forcing the Church to reverse or at least modify its doctrines on labor, wages, usury, and the honor or dishonor inherent to a long list of professions, this caste helped create the surplus, the discipline, and the instruments that not only allowed the reemergence of the State, but of a more powerful state animated by a productive

---

7   As a demystifying aside, I would argue that the "scientific" conception should more accurately be labeled as "profane." Enlightenment science, as Christianity before it, also justified itself as "natural," though the Enlightenment's nature was mechanical rather than sacred, and the sacred was supernatural and exogenous rather than chthonic and immanent. One way to elucidate this difference can be found in Zlodey and Radegas's distinction between "production" and "creation," since this is not a difference that Enlightenment thinking itself is capable of expressing.

rather than parasitic logic.

The *oratores* placed limitations on the *bellatores*, creating the rudiments of a culture of internal peace and cooperation within Europe, in order to assert their divine importance over the more actionable power of the warriors, their obvious rivals in the tripartite system. The priests' activism as peace brokers also prevented their potential domain from being broken up into a collection of bickering fiefs each dominated by warlords. They supported the development of martial powers, as a way to increase their own power, but they also worked to see that those powers were subordinated to a political hierarchy legitimated by the Church rather than remaining in the hands of a knightly caste that could easily come to resent the Church. Hence the many days on which war making was forbidden, and the preeminent role of the Church as mediator. Elite historians, however, can easily forget the important role that peasants played in pressuring the Church to limit the power of the warlords, and thus assuage the ill effects that warfare had on the poor.

As for the heresies of work and wealth, the Church strove to have holy days respected, when many peasants apparently wanted to keep working. Material independence free from centralized spiritual values threatened the entire social hierarchy. So the Church rallied to make sure the improvers and laborers frequently left the fields in order to come pray, celebrate, and receive their moral instructions. When material poverty was the only option, the Church preached the holiness of poverty and urged independent-minded peasants to sustain themselves with spirituality. When the accumulation of wealth became a social possibility, and most importantly when the political structures to monopolize that wealth were coming into place, the Church began to urge the laborers to work harder, and they began sacralizing the values of their upper crust, the improvers. Even before the Protestant Reformation, wealth and accumulation had become signs of godliness. Although this change may have contradicted the clergy's narrow caste interests, it corresponded to the imaginary of a resurgent state.

The three castes competed for relative power in the evolving hierarchies, but at a more fundamental level they cooperated. In a typical chiefdom, certain castes resist the push by specific power-holders towards statist lines of development. The resurgence of the state in Europe cannot be chalked up to a traditionalist allegiance to mentalities and symbologies of the defunct Roman state. Too much time had passed for a memory, largely faded, to retain such power, and besides, the ideation of control, despite the conservatism of mentalities, was highly adaptable throughout the Middle Ages, eventually giving rise to a state model almost entirely distinct from the Roman predecessor, even as Renaissance statists claimed a direct pedigree in antiquity and opened the way for capitalism by restoring "Roman law," which allowed private ownership of land.

The key to this paradox lies in the imaginary. Even though the state fell on a material plane, European societies did not become tribes or chiefdoms because, in most areas, state organization was maintained in the imaginaries of dominant castes. Those communities that overthrew such castes, such as the heretics of Stedinger, the pagan rebels of the Spree and those of the nascent Polish state, put down by Kazimierz the Restorer, the free peasant communes of the Slavic hinterlands, and the Bogomils of the Balkans, had to be dealt with militarily by neighboring states or proto-states, because they had demonstrably rejected the statist imaginary. The fervor of the crusades against them, and the way they were so specifically and enthusiastically targeted, finds no parallel in the contemporary wars between Christian proto-states. The wars between hierarchical societies that held true to the dream of statehood were fraternal, whereas the wars against these rebellious anti-authoritarian societies were wars of colonization and extermination.

The statist mentality of the European Middle Ages was no vestige. It was a dynamic plane in which new state models could be developed and tested, nourished by a non-material continuity with past states. European statists did not reinvent the wheel, or start from scratch after a Dark Age, even though the state they reformulated after centuries of statelessness was a wholly new model of state. Theirs was the **projectual state**.

The available sources do not permit us to know if there existed a similar imaginary among priestly and other castes in the stateless interregnum between the Tiwanaku and Inca states in the Andes, but I would suggest it as another historical period in which a statist imaginary may have been at work. In any case, I can affirm that the overthrow of the Tiwanaku state is certainly an episode in the imaginary of anti-authoritarian indigenous rebels today.[8]

8   John Severino, "The Other Gods Were Crying," *theanarchist library.org*, 2010, https://theanarchistlibrary.org/library/john -severino-the-other-gods-were-crying.

V.
The Modern State:
A Revolutionary Hybrid

STATES CAN BE CONSERVATIVE—OR even lazy—institutions that seek stability and develop progressively when impelled to do so by resistance or adversity. European states stumbled upon a great advantage in the process of developing biopower and colonialism to fuel themselves, arguably as a response to a series of crises of governance. To the extent that capitalism provoked so much resistance and instability, any state seeking to ride this new force would constantly have to adapt, plot, spy, mobilize, militarize, and grow. Capitalism inaugurated an unending social war that has constituted a ceaseless learning process for states.

Rephrasing an essentially anarchist hypothesis[1] and backing it up with extensive research and novel analyses, Giovanni Arrighi argues for a dichotomous nature of the modern state, combining a commercial power that inhabits a space of flows with a territorial power that inhabits a space of places. In *The Long 20th Century*, he traces the evolution of this marriage expertly, from the city-states of northern Italy,[2] to its first prototype in the partnership between Genovese merchants and the Castilian Crown that began a global cycle of capitalist accumulation, to its perfection by the United Provinces of the Netherlands, authors of the Westphalia or

---

1   See Alex Gorrion, "Anarchy in World Systems: A Review of Giovanni Arrighi's *The Long 20th Century*," *The Anvil Review* (2014).

2   Given his Marxist influences, Arrighi generally tries to privilege economic actors, though such emphasis is in no way justified by his findings. Equally interesting would be research that explores the origins of the other pillar of this biped: the state that sought financing beyond its own jurisdiction.

interstate system, to its global expansion by Great Britain and its
intensification under the guidance of the United States.

We can complement a reading of Arrighi's detailed history
with a consideration of the factors that laid the groundwork for
the emergence of the modern state, some of which are glanced
over in his work and others of which fall outside its scope.

The lack of strong family ties and clan systems in most of
Western Europe, as will be discussed in another chapter, strongly
advantaged both the democratic militarism that was essential for
the development of a large number of Europe's early states, and
for the restructuring that the emergence of the modern state
required. There was no strong *structural* resistance to bureaucra-
tization and the emergence of a new paradigm of sovereignty: in
fact, the culture of individual advancement that may only arise in
a context of weak family ties was simultaneously instrumental to
the bourgeois supersession of the nobility, to the practices of education necessary for training a bureaucratic class closely complicit
with the commercial class (rather than unquestioningly loyal to
a despotic ruler, or "corrupted" by loyalty to kin), and to the new
labor ethic that had to be inculcated in the lower classes.

The war on heresy and the war on the commune were also
vital factors. The repressive institutions and methodologies necessary to the emergence of the modern state arose in the war
on heresy, the witch hunts, and the bloody legal and paralegal
campaigns that facilitated the enclosure of the commons. E.P.
Thompson's seminal study, *Whigs and Hunters*, on the application
of the Black Act to punish resistance to enclosure reveals the new
practice at work. Marcus Rediker and Peter Linebaugh, in *The
Many-Headed Hydra*, explore the origins and some of the parallel
lines of development of repressive methodologies related to the
private property regime, while Silvia Federici, in *Caliban and the
Witch*, and Arthur Evans, in *Witchcraft in the Gay Counterculture*,
dig even deeper, tracing the process farther back and revealing
a missing link—patriarchy—which has modulated the entire
repressive evolution. Christianity's previously mentioned preference for intolerance and for a separation of secular and ecclesiastical space, allowed this repressive evolution to take place.

R.I. Moore convincingly argues that the bonfire, though it

has become the very symbol for the state campaign against heretics, represented a failure for the authorities. Punishment of heresy was systematically designed to discipline, to gain repentance.
And though there were clearly exceptions to this, when political
enemies needed to be eliminated or elites judged it better to burn
"one to educate one hundred,"[3] the spectacle of supreme punishment was sometimes used by the heretics and witches themselves. Refusing to repent and facing execution was often a form
of insubordination: some heretics even threw themselves into the
bonfire as an ultimate act of defiance against the Church.[4]

Falling into the peculiarly postmodern, post-Holocaust error
of rating the relative importance of historical phenomena according to their body count, Silvia Federici exaggerates the number
of deaths in the witch hunts, claiming a million killed when the
true figure is almost certainly less than 100,000. But far more
important were those who weren't killed. Even if "only" 50,000
were executed[5] (a huge figure, relative to the population of early

---

3   The quote is not from the Church, but from Lenin, whose
     methods, and perhaps the man himself, would have been right
     at home in the Inquisition.

4   R.I. Moore, *The War on Heresy: Faith and Power in Medieval
     Europe* (London: Profile Books, 2012).

5   At this point, there does not seem to be any serious scholarly
     research suggesting more than 50,000–60,000 executions.
     However, new research by Catalan scholar Pau Castell, which
     has yet to be translated into English, has discovered documen-
     tation of "hundreds" of previously unpublished executions in
     Catalunya and the Pyrenees, starting already by the beginning
     of the fifteenth century. These findings add a new epicenter to
     the burnings, paint a picture of a more rapid and geographi-
     cally widespread beginning to the phenomenon, and also sug-
     gest a relation between the intensity of the witch hunts and the
     prevalence of municipal over centralized government, noting
     that royal courts were not as zealous as local governments and
     traveling preachers. David Marín, "Terra de Bruixes," *El Punt
     Avui*, January 2, 2016, http://www.elpuntavui.cat/societat/
     article/-/929459-terra-de-bruixes.html.

modern Europe), this also represents tens of thousands of communities traumatized and threatened, tens of thousands of people who received non-lethal punishment, and many more tens of
thousands of people who repented to avoid punishment.

Another criticism against her work and of *Witches, Midwives,
and Nurses* by Barbara Ehrenreich and Deirdre English disputes
the feminist hypothesis that the war on witches was in part a
patriarchal attempt to eradicate the tradition of women healers.
This criticism is demonstrably misguided. The argument[6] is based
on what appears to be a solid but completely misinterpreted fact:
the majority of the victims of the witch hunts were probably not
healers, and in fact a disproportionate number of state's witnesses
were officially licensed midwives and nurses. While it is true
that we must avoid a simplified, homogenous, and romanticized
vision of who these people were, it is also true, as Federici documents, that the witch burnings were complemented by a process
of increased state regulation of women and of feminine professions. The newly professionalized male doctors were appearing
on the scene and attempting to monopolize healing practices.
A place was reserved for women who were willing to subordinate themselves to the doctors as nurses, and to subordinate
themselves to the state by getting licensed. In other words, these
sellouts were also frequently snitches against their sisters who
continued to practice autonomously and without permission. On
consideration, this troublesome fact only reinforces the analysis
of Federici, Ehrenreich, and English. And the documents of the
witch trials demonstrate a direct link between the repression and
the Church and secular elite's fear of women healers; "No one
does more harm to the Catholic Church than midwives," as the
Malleus Maleficarum claims.[7]

---

6   Barbara Ehrenreich and Deirdre English, *Witches, Midwives,
     and Nurses: A History of Women Healers* (New York: The Femi-
     nist Press, 1993). Argument made by Diane Purkiss, *The Witch
     in History: Early Modern and Twentieth-Century Representa-
     tions* (Abingdon: Routledge, 1996).

7   Soraya Chemaly, "What witches have to do with women's
     health," *Salon.com*, October 31, 2013, https://www.salon

As Federici and Evans both amply demonstrate, in their ways, the emergence of the modern state was preceded by and in turn aided the renewal (a renaissance, if you will?) of patriarchal social relations, accomplished by the Church and other ruling institutions of the day. Roman patriarchy had been eroded to a large extent after the collapse of the Western Empire, first thanks to the relatively egalitarian gender relations among the Celtic, Germanic, and Slavic tribes, and later thanks to the resistance of women, queer people, trans people, and heretics or tradition-alists/pagans. First Christian philosophy and then, in a seamless transition, Enlightenment philosophy, served to coordinate the offensive that restored an absolute patriarchy utilizing a broad array of state and non-state institutions, from the municipal to the continental level.

Another important element of the interstate system the Dutch and their allies inaugurated with the Settlement of West-phalia was the nation. It's important to distinguish the European context, in which the term arose, and non-Western contexts, spanning a great variety of processes, in which some peoples subsequently chose to term themselves as nations. For the time being, however, I am referring to the Western context. Contrary to nationalist mythologies, nations in the West did not arise as part of a slow process of linguistic and cultural unification, nor did they even appear within their own borders. Confirming a plank of postmodern theory, this particular self was only defined when it came in contact with an other. Following Jacques Le Goff and Giovanni Arrighi, we can contend that nations arose between the twelfth and seventeenth centuries in the universi-ties and the trade posts, respectively. As Le Goff documents in *Time, Work, and Culture in the Middle Ages*, students at Europe's new universities organized themselves according to nation. They were, after all, an international body. And I would surmise that, while their own prior identities might have predisposed them to relate only with those of their own immediate city or polity (because of course, there were no Italians there, only Paduans,

.com/2013/10/31/what_witches_have_to_do_with _womens_health/Chemaly.

Bolognese, and so forth), their relatively reduced numbers pushed them to seek out other companions with whom they now saw similarities. Previously they would have only seen linguistic and cultural differences, but in contrast to other students who might hail from as far away as Brittany, Flanders, or Saxony, now they found a common identity. And the same process would play out in a university in Bologna, Paris, or Augsburg. Students, far away from home, organized themselves as Italians, Flemish, French, or Germans, whereas before they had been Genovese, Antwerpers, Provençals, Hannoverian, and so forth.

Similarly, at the trade posts that were popping up in Europe's hubs of commerce, and which in certain inchoate moments were indistinguishable from embassies, birds of a feather flocked together. In this instance, their ornithological affinity had less to do with the anxieties of young men away from home for the first time, and more to do with the need to trade reliable information with colleagues who could be more easily trusted and more easily communicated with, due to speaking similar dialects and broadcasting various cultural cues that could provide the basis for solidarity in a strange land. What's more, a businessman is more likely to treat someone with respect if they know they will likely coincide in the future, and though the merchants inhabited a space of flows and not a space of places, trade volume and thus interactions were at least somewhat proportional to distance. Proximity, therefore, also favored a common identity.

These two classes of people, students and traders, played a dynamic, essential role in the subsequent creation of nation-states. They had already formulated their nations in the special petri dish constituted by those hubs of education and commerce, and they transposed the same identities and etiquettes onto the state structures when they were called on to help govern, filling in functions of bureaucracy, social control, and productivity that were lacking in the feudal state.

R.I. Moore also highlights the need of the emerging modern state to dismantle the feudal system of dual power, which had been necessary to hold society together while the state was weak, but which constituted a major obstacle to the accumulation of power once productive, cultural, and repressive forces had evolved to the point where totalitarian states were feasible (and I would insist that all modern states are fundamentally totalitarian, differing by degree and strategies for disguising or celebrating this fact). This conflict with preexisting state structures was above all a process in which power was streamlined, centralized, and made more efficient. But it had profound impacts on the Western mentality and provided new tools for state control. Modernizing state elites could present themselves as rebels, and almost without exception they used marginalized and exploited elements of society to help them topple the old regime so they could institute a new one. For this reason, nearly every revolution in modern Western history is accompanied by aftershocks, from the *enragés* and peasant insurrections of France, to Shays' Rebellion, to Kronstadt, when the oppressed realize that though the forms of power have changed, they are still at the bottom of an even more potent social hierarchy.

Progressive movements systematically redirect popular rage, which is inspired by nothing less than the violence of being governed, at elements of power that are ineffective and potentially obsolete. The goal (at least of those who command such movements) and the result is to make power more powerful. Progressives' favorite whipping boy has long been corruption, but corruption is the last vestige of humanity in an increasingly inhuman system.

The organizational ambiguity of medieval democracy, which resulted in situations of dual or even triple power, presented opportunities for would-be state architects to play their rivals off one another. Forward-thinking monarchs often favored the commoners in order to use them against the feudal lords, similar to how the burgers would subsequently use the peasants and urban laborers against the monarchs in a number of democratic revolutions. After the collapse of the Western Roman Empire, a great number of towns, cities, and rural communities won their economic independence and defended it vigorously against the encroachments of different elites. The independence of the rural communities had a communal rather than commercial character, based in a universal access to the commons. Faced with the conflict between commoners and nobles, monarchs were sometimes forced and sometimes astutely chose to legally recognize and codify the rights of the commoners, either as "uses and customs" as regarded the commons, or as charters in the case of politically independent towns and cities.

The Church was able to wield its monopoly on spiritual rituals to impede the commoners' autonomy, imposing taxes in exchange for the rights to marry and bury community members. And the nobles used war and debt to gradually impose serfdom or land alienation on the peasant economy. Though peasant and urban militias meant that the nobles never had a true monopoly on military force, it was the nobles who were the recipients of land titles doled out by monarchs in exchange for fealty, participation in military campaigns, and other services. Title did not extinguish preexisting communal and usufructary rights of the peasant inhabitants, but it did give the nobles a claim for exacting payments in goods and services. In the Iberian Peninsula, as Christian warrior-kings pushed out the Muslim rulers of *al-Andalus*, the new elites were particularly opportunistic, declaring their conquest *terra nullis* even though it often came with peasant inhabitants attached. They were also able to monopolize the castles, which in many cases had been communally maintained and garrisoned. Because self-defense was seen as a collective obligation, nobles could use it as another excuse to impose levies and taxes.

Medieval monarchs won power as the arbiters of the conflicts that this increasing exploitation provoked, enacting legal compromises in response to the frequent lawsuits and rebellions with which nobles and commoners pressed their interests. They also intervened in the evolution of the institutions of medieval democracy. Free villages, towns, and cities made their decisions in open assemblies, often given legal recognition by the monarch, against the wishes of the nobles trying to extend their authority. But the political equality of the democratic structures served to mask the growing economic inequalities that were an inevitable consequence of the currency-based commerce subsidized by the elite. As guild masters, merchants, and peasant landowners grew in power, all of them using legal, monetary, and infrastructural devices created or defended by the monarch, the commoners were divided against themselves and could no longer pursue common interests that might have obstructed the growth of the State. The new commoner elite easily took over the democratic structures that once constituted the bulwark of their kind. It bears noting that majoritarian, centralized structures of unitary decision-making have never successfully prevented the emergence of an elite; to the contrary, they have generally been complicit in the process.

In 1265, the city of Barcelona created the *Consell de Cent,* the Council of One Hundred, a representative body composed of *probi homines* or first-class citizens selected primarily from among the guild masters and merchants of the city, which supplanted the power of the open assemblies of neighbors. King Jaume I was a direct instigator of this process. In 1284, King Pere III granted the Council the power to directly seize the goods and properties of those who did not pay their rents. In 1285, the inhabitants of Barcelona revolted against the patricians and attempted to recover control of the municipality, but the king intervened on the oligarchs' behalf. The model of rule by closed councils and magistrates spread throughout the rest of Catalunya, replacing the open assemblies in all but a few rural communities in the mountains. Urban merchants quickly became more important to the monarch than the landed nobility for funding the many wars by which he cemented his power, and by which the merchants expanded their trade networks. Wars between trade rivals Catalunya and Genova reflected this mercantile turn of logic. The oligarchs, in turn, quickly discovered the usefulness of *patriotism*, a key force in the birth of the nation and the modern state, in convincing the poor and middle-class commoners to support the wars and the taxes that accompanied them. Within a couple of centuries, municipalities small and large throughout Catalunya became mired in war-related debts. How did they resolve these? By selling off the commons.[8]

The Enlightenment, and the philosophy of scientific rationalism that accompanied it, were also a *sine qua non* for the

8   David Algarra Bascón, *El Comú Català* (Barcelona: Potlatch Ediciones, 2015).

development of the modern state. Silvia Federici illuminates some of the horrors perpetrated by the rational worldview and subsequently blamed by the dominant historiography on the "irrationality" of the Middle Ages. Going considerably further, Alex Gorrion writes that scientific rationalism is a mythical system directly descended from Christianity that unconsciously posits anthropocentrism, ecocide, a supremacist, unilineal progressivism, and a Cartesian worldview, and that functions at the service of the perpetual accumulation of power.[9]

There is also much to be said about the restoration of Roman law favoring private property and allowing land to be alienated, the development of new productive techniques and modes of production, and new forms of economic and political organization. On the one hand, these are the aspects of the transition that have already been most studied, and on the other hand, the latter of these aspects are more the flourishes rather than the driving forces of the process. I will, however, include one example that challenges the linear temporality of such progress, and illustrates the simultaneity of military development, scientific development, and historical identity Arrighi writes:

> By rediscovering and bringing to perfection long-forgotten Roman military techniques, Maurice of Nassau, Prince of Orange, achieved for the Dutch army in the early seventeenth century what scientific management would achieve for US industry two centuries later [...] Siege techniques were transformed (1) to increase the efficiency of military labor-power, (2) to cut costs in terms of casualties, and (3) to facilitate the maintenance of discipline in the army's ranks. Marching and the loading and firing of guns were standardized, and drilling was made a regular activity. The army was divided into smaller tactical units, the numbers of commissioned and non-commissioned officers were increased, and lines of command rationalized.[10]

---

9   Alex Gorrion, "Science," *The Anvil Review*, May 29, 2015, http://theanvilreview.org/print/science/.

10   Arrighi, *The Long 20ᵗʰ Century*, 47.

When Robert McNamara went from the Ford Motor Company to the Defense Department, he was coming full circle, completing a motion started by the Prince of Orange. In warfare, elite planners found the perfect terrain for developing the rational organization that is primarily associated with capitalist economics.

VI.
Zomia:
A Topography of Positionality

IT IS WORTH QUOTING the closing passages of Tacitus's *Germania* in full:

> Here Suebia ends. I do not know whether to class the tribes of the Peucini, Venedi, and Fenni with the Germans or with the Sarmatians. The Peucini, however, who are sometimes called Bastarnae [around present-day Slovakia or western Ukraine], are like Germans in their language, manner of life, and mode of settlement and habitation. Squalor is universal among them and their nobles are indolent. Mixed marriages are giving them something of the repulsive appearance of the Sarmatians. The Venedi [around present-day Belarus] have adopted many Sarmatian habits; for their plundering forays take them over all the wooded and mountainous highlands that lie between the Peucini and the Fenni. Nevertheless, they are on the whole to be classed as Germans; for they have settled homes, carry shields, and are fond of travelling—and travelling fast—on foot, differing in all these respects from the Sarmatians, who live in wagons or on horseback. The Fenni [around present-day Lithuania] are astonishingly savage and disgustingly poor. They have no proper weapons, no horses, no homes. They eat wild herbs, dress in skins, and sleep on the ground. Their only hope of getting better fare lies in their arrows, which, for lack of iron, they tip with bone. The women support themselves by hunting, exactly like the men; they accompany them everywhere and insist on taking their share in bringing down the game. The only way they

have of protecting their infants against wild beasts or
bad weather is to hide them under a makeshift covering
of interlaced branches. Such is the shelter to which the
young folk come back and in which the old must lie. Yet
they count their lot happier than that of others who groan
over field-labour, sweat over house-building, or hazard
their own and other men's fortunes in the hope of profit
and the fear of loss. Unafraid of anything that man or god
can do to them, they have reached a state that few human
beings can attain: for these men are so well content that
they do not even need to pray for anything. What comes
after them is the stuff of fables—Hellusii and Oxiones
with the face and features of men, the bodies and limbs
of animals. On such unverifiable stories I shall express
no opinion.[1]

As the Roman historian's gaze moves farther and farther
from the boundaries of the empire, passing through diminishing
rings of state influence, patriarchy, hierarchy, capitalist values,
and scientific certainty progressively disappear.

Environmental determinist explanations for state formation
tend to focus on original states. Because original states had the
cards stacked against them more than subsequent states, with
state formation being so actively resisted, we can accept that the
first states arose within a narrow range of ecological niches—
those that presented the fewest disadvantages—without assuming that the geography determined the state.

The inadequacy of the determinist lens becomes even more
evident when one examines secondary state formation. A map
alone—coded to indicate rainfall, soil type, elevation, and other
data—could not allow us to predict with high accuracy which
parts of northern Africa, Europe, and western Asia would be
stateless, and to what degree, in the first millennium of the
current era. Geographic conditions in the Baltic countries, the
plains to the northeast of the Carpathians, or the Maghreb were
no more hostile to state formation than they were in the Iberian

---

1   Tacitus, *The Agricola and the Germania*, 140–41.

Peninsula, England, or the original Russian territories. From the Cherusci to the Fenni, peoples across Europe responded to the pressures and influences exerted by the Roman Empire and subsequent states, and positioned themselves accordingly.

This is not to say that a state's influence diminishes smoothly with distance and that anarchy therefore is a reactive function of remoteness from existing states. Fiercely anarchic societies have existed and thrived directly next to or even in the midst of the claimed borders of powerful states. Speaking of Zomia, the highland area that extends across Southeast Asia, James C. Scott writes:

> After a demographic collapse following a famine, epidemic, or war [broadly speaking, state effects]—if one were lucky enough to have survived—swiddening [the practice of shifting and diversified agriculture generally associated with stateless peoples in the region] might become the norm, right there on the padi plain. State-resistant space was therefore not a place on the map but a position vis-à-vis power; it could be created by successful acts of defiance, by shifts in farming techniques, or by unanticipated acts of god. The same spot could oscillate between being heavily ruled or being relatively independent, depending on the reach of the padi state and the resistance of its would-be subjects.[2]

Additionally, "the choice between padi planting [necessary for state formation but not inevitably associated with it] and swiddening is more likely to be a political choice than a mere comparative calculation of calories per unit of labor."[3] Elsewhere, for example discussing Chin attempts to resist and avoid British domination, Scott drives home the point that the political choice of resistance, and the very construction of a society's fabric, often trumped economic considerations.

---

2   Scott, *The Art of Not Being Governed*, 162.
3   Ibid., 280. The subsequent example of the Chin is from page 212.

A stateless society in Zomia could practice padi [rice] planting as easily as swiddening, but the closer an anarchic society is to a state, the more it requires a wide range of defensive advantages—prominent among them, geography and subsistence techniques—in order to survive. Thus, as state power grows in history, the more it appears that inaccessible geography or supposedly primitive modes of production determine anarchic social organization, though in reality they are only enabling features often sought out by stateless societies as a reflection of their decision to resist state power.

States, then, usually arose in geographical settings where the massive, irrigated cultivation of the local cereal (rice, wheat, maize, etc.) was feasible, though they were often parasites to innovation rather than the original architects of irrigation, city-building, and agriculture. Once they had latched onto a subject population they certainly encouraged these activities and modulated them to encourage centralization. Presumably, societies that evolved to become anti-state rather than merely stateless, learned to reject such activities and develop others that would give them symbolic and technical advantages in their fight against state authority.

Many states collapsed due to problems of their own creation, such as famine, epidemics, and warfare.[4] But they usually came back, and over time, demonstrated their dominance within a narrow ecological niche. Peoples determined to be stateless therefore developed, with time, an identification with opposite subsistence practices, such as foraging, hunting, swiddening, and pastoralism, and with opposite ecological niches, such as mountains, deserts, forests, and swamps.

---

4   To be clear, I am not alleging that these three scourges were created by the State. However, the exploitation that accompanies states certainly makes famine more likely, and while epidemics are largely a function of population density that can, contrary to statist mythology, exist without states, state effects such as warfare and malnutrition in the majority lower classes sometimes provoke and always exacerbate epidemics. Stateless warfare tends to be qualitatively different, more a tradition of raiding or occasionally lethal sport.

To counteract this migration, both physical and philosophical, away from the realms of its domination, the early state had to develop organizational and ideological tools to retain its subjects. As Scott amply demonstrates, the states of Southeast Asia have historically been obsessed with captivating their own populations. He quotes dozens of adages and stratagems from all the states of the region, all similar to the following, taken from a "Chinese manual on governance" from over a thousand years ago: "If the multitudes scatter and cannot be retained, the city-state will become a mound of ruins."[5]

The Catholic Church, after the collapse of the Roman Empire, tried to accomplish the same objectives as the mandala states of Southeast Asia. Many early Catholic saints were civilizers and cultivators whose miracles are related to acts of settlement, deforestation, clearing, draining, and planting, taming the wilderness that had once again come to cover Europe in the freedom of the Dark Ages.[6] In the Iberian Peninsula, many pioneering villages corresponded to the *sagrera* model, in which a newly constructed church would automatically gain ownership over the lands within a certain distance from its walls. The peasants worked the church lands, and also carried out subsistence activities in the unclaimed forests and fields beyond the *sagrera*. The model was, fundamentally, a religious protection racket. By living within the *sagrera* (and working its fields), the peasants protected themselves from acts of raiding or usurpation by nobles (commoners were not, contrary to current misconceptions, powerless before nobles, but smaller groups of peasants might have a harder time getting their commune officially recognized by royal authority, which based much of its early power on its function of arbiter between the nobility and the commoners). Especially in more mountainous and rural regions throughout the early Middle Ages, a principal difference distinguishing Christian from pagan peasants was whether they submitted to the protection racket and agreed to live in the Church's shadow, or whether they tried to maintain autonomous communities. Their religious practices—consistently syncretic and

---

5   Scott, *The Art of Not Being Governed*, 66.
6   Le Goff, *Time, Work, and Culture in the Middle Ages*, 170–73.

often crossing the line into blasphemy, heresy, and polytheism—
were far from sufficient to qualify them as believers.

On the organizational plane, warfare was one of the first and
most common measures deployed to achieve and maintain the
labor-power states needed for their existence. This involved "forcibly resettling war captives by the tens of thousands and by buy-
ing and/or kidnapping slaves." But as captives ran off, states had
to develop complementary methods. Subsistence activities and
living outside of sanctioned villages were prohibited, and state
planners developed legal and economic mechanisms, with the
aim of forcing their subjects to choose between grain cultivation
and starvation. Tattooing or even branding of subjects became
common in certain places. The destruction of wild places was
another obvious tactic, if we accept the pathological mentality
of states and their agents. "Cut the forests, transform the forests
into fields, for then only will you become a true king," as a ruler
in ancient Mali was instructed.[7] Forests were cleared, herds were
exterminated, marshes were drained. In more recent times, states
have been able to add the wholesale destruction of mountains
to their repertoire (first with megadam projects and then with
mountaintop removal mining).

Contrary to the mythology of social peace, which would
have us believe that state evasion is a thing of the past, this
war on the world, this wholesale destruction of places that
favor ungovernability, is a preoccupation that has stayed with
states up until the present day. Scott notes that the marshes
on the lower Euphrates and the Pontian marshes near Rome,
each of them locations that have long harbored rebels, outlaws,
and state evaders right in the midst of two of the cradles of
civilization, were drained in the twentieth century by Saddam
Hussein and Benito Mussolini, respectively; he also mentions
the Great Dismal Swamp, one of the most important foci of
indigenous, African, and fugitive European resistance to colonization on North America's eastern seaboard.[8] And to this we

---

7   Scott, *The Art of Not Being Governed*, 67 and 72.
8   Ibid., 26. For an excellent discussion of resistance in the Great
     Dismal Swamp, see Saralee Stafford and Neal Shirley, *Dixie Be*

can add the destruction of another anarchic zone, the Appalachian Mountains, particularly the attempt to carry out mountaintop removal mining on Blair Mountain, the site of a short
war between an interracial group of coal miners and the US
government, in 1922.

Social conflict can also turn once civilized territory into
a liberated space of resistance, self-organization, and illegibil-
ity. At the end of the American Civil War, state power in the
South had collapsed, and through Reconstruction, the northern
bureaucracy and northern capitalists worked with the southern
planting aristocracy to put the former slaves back to work, either
as wage laborers or as enslaved chain gang prisoners. The overwhelming preference of the newly liberated Africans, however,
was to engage in illegible, non-monetary subsistence activities
like gardening, hunting, and fishing, to feed themselves as
communities rather than laboring for the production of cash
crops like rice and cotton. The State changed or broke its own
laws to dispossess Africans, Native Americans, and poor whites
of the newly expropriated plantations, drained the marshes and
cut down the pine barrens that often served as refuge for liberated communities, and instituted a reign of terror through the
indistinguishable forces of the police and white vigilantes like
the Ku Klux Klan to enforce racial separation and to teach the
citizenry that freedom was only granted to those who worked,
and "work" meant working for a rich person and never for one's
own self-sufficiency; whether the labor contract was negotiated
with whips and chains or with salaries and evictions proved
to be a mere detail. In places like the Ogeechee Neck, where
former slaves evicted the planter aristocracy and their overseers
and communalized the land, the military had to come in to
crush the rebellion.[9]

Urban zones of evasion have opened up in the cities of many
modern states, with subcultures, ethnic minorities, or large and
heterogeneous groups taking advantage of capitalist decadence to

Damned: 300 Years of Insurrection in the American South (Oakland: AK Press, 2015).

9   Stafford and Shirley, *Dixie Be Damned*, 53–86.

transform entire neighborhoods into areas where census-taking, tax- and rent-collecting, policing, the centralized control of popular culture, and the enforcement of labor discipline all become difficult or impossible. Police campaigns of criminalization and gentrification—which is instigated by state planners more often than is commonly recognized—are the main, and usually complementary, methods for demolishing resistant, autonomous, illegible neighborhoods and constructing pacified, striated, legible residential and commercial zones in their place. San Francisco's Mission District, Harlem and the Lower Eastside in New York, Kreuzberg in Berlin, Raval and Gràcia in Barcelona, and the Cabanyal in València, are all good examples of state evasion and the reimposition of state control.

A long-standing task of municipal police and bureaucracies has been the prohibition of street vending, the direct sale of their wares or produce by small-scale artisans, who liberate themselves of the costly, dependency-creating burdens of taxation, regulation, and rent. The primary purpose of such state mechanisms is neither quality control nor consumer protection, but the protection of shop owners and large producers, and the prohibition of self-sufficiency. Even poorer urban denizens might liberate themselves from the money economy and thus the slavery of wage labor through squatting and dumpster-diving, both of which are increasingly prohibited through legal and architectural means. The latter might include the demolition or semi-legal renting of vacant units, as commonly occurs in Spain and the Netherlands, respectively; and as far as dumpstering is concerned through the use of trash compactors or underground waste storage. Dumpstering, today, is the malnourished final heir of a once proud tradition of rural commoning that included gleaning in the fields after harvest or gathering brushwood in the forests enclosed by lords and landowners, a practice that came to be harshly punished by the UK's Black Act and other laws in the eighteenth century.[10]

From the beginning, architecture has been a principal means of exerting control, organizing the population so that it is

---

10   Thompson, *Whigs and Hunters*.

more comprehensible to state surveillance and more susceptible to state administration, and structuring certain forms of blackmail and coercion into the fabric of social life. I give an anarchist history tour where I currently live in Barcelona, and over several years of compiling radical histories and chronicling the development of social control, I have come across an important pattern.[11] A striking feature of all state interventions in urban architecture is the remarkable convergence between the strategic interest of exerting military control over the population, the sociocultural interest of breaking up autonomous lower-class neighborhoods, and the commercial interest of spurring legible economic growth, sometimes to the point that they become indistinguishable. I would argue that this dynamic reflects the essence of the social war and can be found even in the earliest state interventions, although the element of this trinity that is often posited as the foundation or fundamental cause, the profit motive, can in fact be considered extraneous in the short term. It is icing on the cake, a way for state planners to communicate shared interests with the economic elite, and in the long run, necessary for the state to fuel its processes of power accumulation and social control, but it is by no means the *sine qua non* of civilization. On the contrary, countless states have bankrupted themselves in pursuit of the social war, and not every state that has gone bankrupt has disappeared. Nor have all states held back from destroying the productive processes they feed off of, when it was a question of asserting social control.

This authoritarian convergence can also include non-state actors applying progressive values they believe will make the world a more equitable place, such as progressive environmental activists who help modern states to wipe out state-resistant

---

11   A good book in English for exploring this pattern is Chris Ealham's *Anarchism and the City* (Oakland: AK Press, 2010). The book contains a few minor but important flaws, which I discuss in my review (PG, "A Critical Review of Anarchism and the City," *The Anvil Review*, May 24, 2012, http://theanvilreview. org/print/criticalreviewanarchismcity/), which professor Ealham considered libelous.

practices like swiddening agriculture, which they hypocritically and myopically blame for larger environmental problems.[12]

A common example of architectural control is the near universal location (under non-modern states) of granaries within the city walls, where they will be under the control of the civilization's more privileged castes. Considering the city walls themselves, which frequently exhibit a structure of two or more tiers, we can intuit a few things about non-modern states' treatment of the middle classes, the artisans and merchants. They were privileged, sheltered, culturally separated from the peasants, but were also kept close, under the control of the rulers, and thus generally or partially prohibited from an independent or illegible economic activity.

Walls have also existed on a much greater scale. Contrary to popular belief, or rather, the belief inculcated by statist education, the Great Wall of China was constructed at least as much to keep the empire's citizens in as to keep the barbarians out.

Hadrian's Wall, built by the Romans in the British Isles, served the same dual purpose. Yet we are systematically taught that the only purpose of the wall was to keep out the barbarians, who always remain on the wrong side of history. The student is trained to view them from *this side* of the wall. The needs of state are privileged, whereas the stateless are presented as dangerous, opaque, and ultimately evil outsiders.

Such walls are also important as symbols, and complementary to the State's organizational efforts to capture and retain subjects is a whole array of ideological efforts that to this day shape what it means to be a state subject. Religion, history, citizenship, nationality, and identity as we know it all train us to be incapable of imagining our lives outside of state authority. All of us grow up believing that the State is an inevitable and universal evolution for humankind that improved the quality of our lives; only later are we given access to the information that conflicts with this narrative, once it already constitutes our fundamental worldview and sense of self. We grow up lacking information about contemporary or historical stateless peoples. The vast majority never

---

12   Scott, *The Art of Not Being Governed*, 190.

surpass this ignorance. States and their leaders are fed to us as the protagonists of history, and when the stateless cannot be symbolically suppressed as primitive, savage, obsolescent, ignorant, evil, or terrorist, they are relegated to the shadowy backdrop of a stage the State clearly commands.

Anticapitalists will often insist that the purpose of public education is to prepare workers. This is balderdash, a perfect example of dogma obviating reality. The vast majority of the lesson plan, once a pupil is literate and knows the most basic maths, is irrelevant to the tasks of the future worker, unless we count the abilities to follow orders, accept confinement, and complete meaningless tasks; however, those skills are required of all citizens, employed or unemployed, prole or petty-bourgeoisie. A typical worker has absolutely no need to know about ancient Egypt, William Shakespeare, or basic chemistry. No, the fundamental purpose of education is to civilize children, and a large part of this means filling their heads with the lies that are necessary to make them always view history and society from the perspective that privileges state power.

In recent literature, Hadrian's Wall has come back to us as the Wall in George R.R. Martin's *Songs of Ice and Fire*. An intelligent writer, Martin has incisively deconstructed the romantic aspects of state mythology. In his worldview, statecraft is a bloody, authoritarian, and cynical affair. Many of his most sympathetic characters are rebels who fight authority or tragic characters who are foolishly dedicated to the sham principles the State hypocritically espouses. Stateless people are often depicted in a positive light; the most prominent example call themselves the "Free Folk" and they refer to their statist neighbors as "kneelers." It is curious to see, at the vanguard of the popular imaginary, which aspects of state mythology can be dismantled, and which cannot. The stateless peoples in *Songs of Ice and Fire* are still kept to the margins of history, and do not have any voice capable of offering an anarchic solution to society. They remain a relic.

As for the Wall, as brutally honest as is the portrayal of statecraft in these novels, mass abandonment of the State is never brought up as an option. "Going savage" is not considered as a possibility.[13] The Wall does not exist to keep the kneelers in, but only to keep out the "wildlings," and an even greater evil: the Others. The Others are a completely unnatural monstrosity. What remains beyond the consciousness of these novels is that the origin of monsters within our collective imaginary is in the very margins of the State. Whether the source is the fables of ancient Greek travelers, the more scientific account of Tacitus, or the racialized fantasy of writers like J.R.R. Tolkien and C.S. Lewis, monsters may only thrive where civilization and state authority are weak. In other words, the monsters also represent stateless people (or more broadly, forms of life, since humanity as distinct from animality also blurs beyond the borders of the State). Evil, in our imaginary, owes its existence entirely to the ideological machinations of the State. (Making a similar point regarding the Early Middle Ages, Le Goff notes that peasant morality was characterized by an ambiguity between good and evil, in total contrast with the moralistic dualism of the clergy.[14]) In other words, Martin, though his vision is admirable, has done nothing more than give us a multicultural fantasy with good savages and evil savages, but in the end the narrative is the same one that has played out—no, that we have been forced to play out, and to swallow, and to play out again, until we believe it, until we cannot question it and are no longer aware of its existence— for thousands of years. In this context, it is tragically hilarious how liberals speak of freedom of expression, as though it were a meaningful concept. At a fundamental level, all expression in our civilization is saying the same thing.

What would change if everyone grew up knowing that states built walls to keep their subjects in, that a great motor of history was the state need to coerce people into being its subjects, that all

---

13 Individual cases of joining the wildlings are mentioned. The only one explored at any length is that of Mance Rayder, a civilized man who joined the wildlings in order to lead them, giving them the organizational and military capacity they ostensibly lacked, not to destroy the state, but to shelter behind its ramparts, escaping from the true evil.

14 Le Goff, *Time, Work, and Culture in the Middle Ages*, 162.

of us, in one way or another, are the descendants of slaves, and that the mechanisms of our enslavement have never disappeared, only been elaborated?

VII.
Chiefdoms and Megacommunities:
On the Stability of Non-State Hierarchies

FOR A LONG TIME, Western anthropologists accepted Elman Service's neo-evolutionist sequence of four stages for classifying social development, the pinnacle being the state, of course. The penultimate stage, the chiefdom, was generally argued to be an unstable political formation, lending more credence to the assumption that state evolution was inevitable, in this instance due to the inconveniences and imperfections of the previous stage of political organization.

In recent years, this sequence has been problematized; for one, because chiefdoms in many parts of the world have proven highly resilient in resisting the imposition of state power, remaining intact up until the present day, even though they nominally fall within the presumed borders of one or several states.

> Chiefdoms appear more durable and stable than was originally envisaged by neo-evolutionist thinking. Not only have they survived into the present age but, in countries where the state has collapsed or failed to discharge its most minimal responsibilities, chiefdoms are increasingly taking over a more overtly political function, buttressing the important social and cultural role they have always played. Not surprisingly, the partisans of chiefdom stress longevity and consensual patterns of decision-making as two of the most crucial characteristics of this form of political arrangement.[1]

---

1   Patrick Chabal, Gary Feinman, and Peter Skalník, "Beyond States and Empires: Chiefdoms and Informal Politics," in *The Early State, Its Alternatives and Analogues*, 53.

The false supposition of instability in chiefdoms can be chalked up to an unexamined ethnocentrism that causes scientists to place importance on an element that their own culture emphasizes. Westerners often make the mistake of assigning paramount importance to masculine, formal leaders, and many chiefdoms regularly produce political alliances that tend to fall apart, especially after their most charismatic figure dies. But perhaps the process of fission as much as that of fusion is an essential part of the society in question; perhaps structures and relationships that only exist at a village or local level are far more important in the actual functioning of the society than the figure of a paramount chief.

Not only are chiefdoms more durable than assumed, they also resist classification within a continuum that ends with the formation of a state. Many chiefdoms throughout history grew in size and complexity not by transitioning to statehood, but by forming "megacommunities" that could include millions of members, without relying on the centralized, coercive, and administrative structures that define statehood.

Understanding how and why some chiefdoms acted as stepping stones to state formation, whereas others experienced political growth without developing the states that supposedly accompany such growth, and still others resisted (and in some cases continue to resist) the transition to statehood or the development of state power, can shed some light on some of the dynamics of state formation.

In sum, and repeating what is now a common theme, it seems that it was less the outward forms (what could be traced as an organizational schema by an outside observer) and more the internal ethos that guided these transitions.

The Haudenosaunee, also known as the Iroquois or Six Nations, are organized in an intertribal confederation of six different nations (Mohawk, Oneida, Onondaga, Cayuga, Seneca, and Tuscarora). "This system incorporated six widely dispersed and unique nations of thousands of agricultural villages and hunting grounds from the Great Lakes and the St. Lawrence River to the Atlantic, and as far south as the Carolinas and inland Pennsylvania," in the words of Roxanne Dunbar-Ortiz.[2] Before colonization, the stateless confederation comprised complex forms of village, intervillage, and intertribal organization, preceding contact with Europeans by several centuries. During the period of colonization, the Haudenosaunee welcomed the Tuscarora, a coastal tribe fleeing warfare, and engaged in alternating strategies of trading, alliance, and armed resistance to keep the colonizers at bay. They were eventually forced to live on reservations and adopt tribal governments, though traditionalist members of the Six Nations continue to fight for autonomy, reclaiming their land and blockading different forms of economic exploitation.[3]

Gord Hill notes that Mohawk armed resistance at Oka, where Canadian settlers were trying to build a golf course on their land "set the tone for indigenous resistance all throughout the 90s."[4] Much of this resistance occurred in conflict with the "Indian Act chiefs" and tribal governments.

Before colonization, the confederation was "characterized by a complicated and efficient system of organization of the society, which functioned, however, without any bureaucratic government institutions, retaining its egalitarian traditions and having no pronounced hierarchy." The alliance that formed the "Iroquois League" preserved peace between the nations and gave them an advantage in warfare against hostile neighbors, a capacity that proved especially necessary after the arrival of the Europeans. Decisions concerning all the nations were made in a league council, celebrated periodically or irregularly. The council comprised a number of sachems, hereditary delegates from each tribe. The sachem could not propose or accept a decision without the approval of the population, and the council itself made decisions

---

2   Dunbar-Ortiz, *An Indigenous Peoples' History of the United States*, 24.

3   Gord Hill, "Never Idle: Gord Hill on Indigenous Resistance in Canada," *The Portland Radicle*, March 18, 2013, https://portlandradicle.wordpress.com/never-idle-gord-hill -on-indigenous-resistance-in-canada/.

4   Ibid.

by consensus. "A decision to be made was first discussed in a clan by the women, and then the warriors held a meeting."[5] A new sachem was first nominated by the women, based on his personal qualities, and then ratified by the chiefs and elders at a meeting of the whole tribe.

The sachem had no special authority in wartime, and the chiefs who functioned as military leaders enjoyed an authority "based on their military merits alone." The organization of groups of warriors was non-hierarchical. Villages also had their own councils, in which local elders (*Agokstenha* among the Mohawk) played a special role, though the councils were open and anyone could speak.[6]

Within the alliance, individual communities and tribes retained their autonomy, their traditions, and their decision-making practices. In addition to political unification for reasons of peace and warfare, the Haudenosaunee also engaged in a high level of coordination and exchange in cultural and economic matters, but the communities and households (the "lower levels" of the confederation, within a Western optic) retained their organizational powers in these affairs.

> The Haudenosaunee peoples avoided centralized power by means of a clan-village system of democracy based on collective stewardship of the land. Corn, the staple crop, was stored in granaries and distributed equitably in this matrilineal society by the clan mothers, the oldest women from every extended family.[7]

Extended families lived together in collective, matrilocal "longhouses."

The political unification of the Haudenosaunee, in large part for reasons of warfare, did not in any way constitute a step

5   Denis V. Vorobyov, "The Iroquois," in *Civilizational Models of Politogenesis*, 157, 159.

6   Ibid., "The Iroquois," 160.

7   Dunbar-Ortiz, *An Indigenous Peoples' History of the United States*, 24.

towards state formation or greater internal hierarchy. This fact disproves determinist theories about the organization of warfare provoking politogenesis. Warfare does not cause state formation, as I have already argued; rather, preexisting hierarchies can use warfare to justify and accelerate state formation. A resolutely anti-authoritarian society like the Six Nations can effectively organize itself for warfare without increasing internal hierarchies. Another demonstration of the anti-authoritarian character of their organization at all levels is the fact that the league council, the sachem, and other spaces or agents of political power did not evolve into the posterior tribal governments. On the contrary, British and American colonizers had to break the political unity of the Haudenosaunee and end the practice of the league council in order to fully subjugate and colonize the Six Nations. And in contradiction to Vorobyov, the white anthropologist I have quoted, the Haudenosaunee did not "fall in the late 18th century."[8] They continue to exist, practicing autonomous forms of existence where they can, and still fighting against the imposition of authority, as the quotations from Gord Hill indicate.

Nonetheless, they were subjected to genocidal policies, particularly by white settlers acting as paramilitaries for the colonizing states. George Washington, the foremost slave owner of Britain's colonies in North America, ordered an army under his command to sow "terror" and "lay waste" to all the Haudenosaunee towns, "that the country may not be merely overrun but destroyed" and he instructed his subordinate to refuse "any overture of peace before the total ruin of their settlements is effected."[9] Such are the tactics of the State.

In the sixteenth century, the Powhatan confederacy arose in the lands just west of the Chesapeake Bay. Powhatan was able to replace chiefs of lesser chiefdoms with his close relatives. Such a maneuver constituted a great coup, given that a chief appointed from without contradicts the logic of the chiefdom, which is ostensibly a group of related people tied to a specific community.

---

8   Vorobyov, "The Iroquois," 157.

9   Dunbar-Ortiz, *An Indigenous Peoples' History of the United States*, 77.

He was able to achieve this with the specter of his status and power as a ruler, in a context when the incursions of external enemies made the partial loss of autonomy seem preferable to the threat of extinction. One must also ask if within those subordinate chiefdoms, the people saw Powhatan's representatives as their rulers or as mere emissaries. The partial loss of autonomy of these subordinate chiefdoms, and the presence of a paramount chief, suggests that the Powhatan confederacy was following a different path than the Six Nations to the north. However, the different communities of the Chesapeake Bay were almost entirely annihilated by the insatiable English within a hundred years, making it impossible to know if in time they would have developed a state of their own.

All the nomadic empires of the Eurasian steppes—those of the Turks, the Huns, the Mongols, and the Uighurs—used a similar system. Lacking a bureaucratic principle of authority, paramount rulers sent their comrades-in-arms or their relatives to govern provinces, dependent tribes, and allied chiefdoms. Each of these groups was largely self-sufficient and autonomous, with their own structures of internal organization, but they presumably tolerated the representative of the central authority as a way to maintain their alliance and avoid hostilities. On the whole, the duties required by the central authority were mutual self-defense and military discipline: limiting raiding and offensive warfare to the enemies of the central polity. Such an alliance tended to come with few obligations beyond ritual gifts and obeisance, and provided the benefits of protection from powerful state neighbors and the booty from successful raiding.

All the "nomadic empires" (actually tribal confederations) formed as neighbors to large sedentary states: whether Han China, the Byzantine Empire, or the Roman Empire. The Turkic tribal confederation was born out of an independence struggle, whereas the Hsiung-nu, contemporaries of the Han dynasty, were composed in part of runaways and refugees from state power. The nomads achieved an autonomous subsistence in the steppes thanks to their large herds, which determined their nomadism, as they regularly had to move on to fresh pasture. However, nomadic communities that relied exclusively on their own pastoral products could not hope to escape material poverty. To complement their resources, they had to raid or trade with sedentary neighbors.[10] But when those sedentary neighbors were states, they tried to control commerce with the aim of dominating the nomads. Whereas raiding by nomads was not typically a factor in the formation of sedentary states, the expansionist tendencies of a powerful state did encourage an imperialistic evolution among the tribal confederations. The backbone of a nomadic empire was the extensive military hierarchy that definitively constituted a state at the point when the nomads took over a sedentary state, using clan representatives to quickly establish a bureaucracy. The post-nomadic bureaucracy, however, attached itself like a parasite to the preexisting bureaucracies of the sedentary state. Officials of the nomadic empire oversaw the continued functioning of the sedentary state, making sure that a part of already ongoing exploitative processes went to the enrichment of the nomadic military hierarchy.

Speaking of barbarian invasions of Europe, Tymowski writes:

> the transformation of the invaders' tribal organization into a state organization was relatively fast. This was because it took place in an area where a state organization had already been operating for a long time, and the local organization patterns, economic potential, and—despite the destruction—also the demographic potential, were all at hand, ready for use.[11]

The states of the great nomadic empires tended to be short-lived, perhaps in part due to the nomads' anti-civilizational imaginary, and their disdain for sedentary life and bureaucratic

---

10   Nikolay N. Kradin, "Early State Theory and the Evolution of Pastoral Nomads," in *Social Evolution and History*, 289.

11   Tymowski, "State and Tribe in the History of Medieval Europe and Black Africa," 173. He cites K.F. Werner, *Structures politiques du monde franc (VI – XII siècles)* (London: Ashgate-Variorum, 1979).

functions. "'All cities must be razed' Ghenghis Khan used to say, 'so that the world may once again become a great steppe in which Mongol mothers will suckle free and happy children.'"[12]

In Europe, many tribes resisted Christianization and the imposition of state authority for centuries, whereas tribes like the Franks that had undergone a process of militarization and adopted, at least in part, the culture of the Roman Empire, established states by suppressing the autonomous existence of different tribes, first subordinating and then replacing local chiefs, eventually abolishing the tribal customs to allow for bureaucratic administration.

Quite the contrary, in sub-Saharan Africa, states and tribes coexisted indefinitely Tymowski writes

> Many states in Black Africa disintegrated and collapsed not only as the result of invasions, but also due to internal processes. The phenomenon of state fragmentation, and return to tribal organizations in the former state's area was well known in Africa [...] The tribes, despite the existing possibilities, did not always transform themselves into states [...] Moreover, until the end of the pre-colonial period, the establishment and development of states was far from being a one-way process [...] On the contrary, this process was often reversible, and several states fell apart in tribal organizations.[13]

The Benin megacommunity of the Upper Guinea coast of western Africa began as a network of localized communities linked by a common language, Bini, and not by any formal relationships or administrative structures. Bini communities sustained themselves through communal agriculture, performed jointly by the extended family group, and by hunting and gathering, from the end of the first millennium BCE through the first millennium CE. The archaeological record suggests that the Kwa,

---

12   Maalouf, *The Crusades Through Arab Eyes*, 235–36.
13   Tymowski, "State and Tribe in the History of Medieval Europe and Black Africa," 176.

the ethno-linguistic predecessors of the Bini, were foragers at the beginning of the first millennium BCE when they moved into the region. The autochthonous inhabitants of the forest belt, whom they named the Efa, already practiced hoe agriculture and lived in stable villages, practices the proto-Bini eventually adopted. The two ethnolinguistic groups coexisted for centuries before the Bini integrated the Efa into a joint cultural system in which the Efa constituted a less prestigious tier. Eventually they were assimilated through intermarriage, though those who identify as descendants of the Efa "hold some quite important priestly posts within the Benin system" of religious and political institutions.[14]

Within this process arose the extended family system that has remained relatively constant throughout their social evolution. Perhaps the extended tracing of family ties allowed for both integration and differentiation in a dual-tiered ethnopolitical system characterized by a weak cultural hierarchy, intermarriage, and coexistence, that eventually led to assimilation. In other words, the further someone mapped their sanguinary relations, the more likely they could connect themselves to both Bini and Efa, whereas in a system of either nuclear families or delineated clans, each particular group could more effectively preserve the illusion of belonging to one ethnicity or the other. The family structure, however, was not a cause of this ethos of coexistence, since it seems to have arisen after the two groups came into contact.

In contrast, we can consider the evolution of Aryan society in the Indian subcontinent. Upon initial contact with the autochthonous inhabitants, the Aryans viewed the locals with disgust, and applied a practice of domination and subordination. In their case, the result of a dual-tiered ethnopolitical system was a complex caste society that encouraged the development of a powerful state.

What we do know is that the extended family system in Bini society was and continues to be closely linked to agricultural

14   Bondarenko, "From Local Communities to Megacommunity: Biniland in the 1st Millennium B.C. to the 19th Century A.D.," in *The Early State, Its Alternatives and Analogues*, 326.

practices. The extended family can better approach economic subsistence than a nuclear family, therefore not leaving *organizational gaps* that emerging administrative institutions could fill. On the other hand, it is not so large as a clan, and not so suited for a redistributive economy that would allow the concentration of wealth.

Bini families are divided into three age-grades, with male elders enjoying political leadership, backed by an ancestor cult (since elders are seen as the intermediaries with the ancestors). The elders form a community council and appoint the oldest member as a ceremonial leader. Significantly, no extended family amasses power over the other families, because membership in the council includes all families, and leadership in the council effectively rotates from one family to another. Extended families also have their own councils, and in communities of a single extended family, a member of every nuclear family is present in the council. The councils decide on the use of communal lands, preserve traditions, mediate infractions of community laws, and worship deities and ancestors on behalf of the entire community. In turn, they traditionally receive gifts of a "prestigious and ritual character" though for their subsistence they have to depend on their families. Public assemblies of all community members were probably also practiced in earlier centuries.[15]

The Bini experienced a concentration of political power beginning in the middle of the first century CE. Before that, multiple communities sometimes coordinated their activities with temporary councils presided over by the most senior elder; however, such unions were temporary and never infringed on the autonomy of individual communities. Subsequently, chiefdoms appeared in which a privileged family (and, most immediately, its leaders) had the prerogative of representing and thus governing other families. That family's community of origin thus gained preeminence over other communities in the alliance. In some cases, the leaders of a chiefdom extended their rule to a weaker chiefdom, though in general this was accomplished not through military conquest but by the paramount leader adopting

---

15   Ibid., 327–28.

"supernatural airs" and successfully arguing a divine right to rule. Significantly, independent communities and egalitarian community unions were able to coexist alongside the chiefdoms. Another mixture has also survived into the present day: in some communities, the position of priest to a specific deity is inherited (a characteristic typically associated with greater hierarchy and the accumulation of power) whereas other communities still hold to the traditional practice in which priests must be appointed their specific roles by the council.[16]

The rise of chiefdoms coincided with the appearance of iron-working technologies, an intensification of agriculture, and a rise in population leading to a population density potentially higher than in the present day. The material conditions of this explosion might lead some to expect a militaristic turn in social organization; however, though the clearing of forests and the hunger for arable land sometimes led to violent competitions, "the unification of the Bini communities was peaceful" and the population pressures did not provoke the development of a militarily effective system of political organization.[17]

These pressures did not, of course, lack consequences. The new chiefdoms began to legitimize a new figure of profane leadership, the *onogie*, who complemented the spiritual leadership of the council of elders. The first *enegie* were warriors from the second age-grade who distinguished themselves as leaders on the battlefield. "All this was a blow to the gerontocratic principle of management among the Bini."[18]

Cities arose as a consequence "and an aspect" of the rise of chiefdoms, in a complex process of mutually influencing factors. The leaders of a chiefdom privileged their community of origin over the other communities, and tried to organize the communities within an agricultural enclosure delineated by ditches and earthworks. Such an evolution both required and favored population growth and intensified agriculture, while also providing defensive advantages in warfare, which increased in tandem with the other

16   Ibid., 329.
17   Ibid., 332.
18   This and the subsequent quote are from ibid., 334.

factors (since Bini unification was peaceful, as mentioned, warfare was primarily waged against raiders from neighboring societies or groups of Efa that defied assimilation). The agricultural enclosure quickly filled in to constitute a city of up to a couple of thousand people, in the earlier period of this evolution. Subordinate family groups then went out to form settlements associated with the chiefdom-city, and these settlements grew in turn.

At least ten different proto-cities, backed by 130 chiefdoms "and a great many independent communities" aligning with one or another of these proto-cities, competed for cultural predominance and recognition as the "sacral-ritual center." In the first centuries of the second millennium CE Benin City won out and the other centers shrank back "down to the level of big villages." This marked the beginning of a monarchic period in which the many chiefdoms were politically united by a paramount ruler, claiming the title of *Ogiso* ("rulers from the sky"). These rulers were likely Yoruba warriors who came in raiding parties from the north. The son or grandson of the first *Ogiso*, Ere, is credited with many innovations and institutions, particularly "symbols of royalty and objects of the ancestor cult," with moving the seat of his government to Benin City, having a palace built there that measured a half mile by a quarter mile, and opening a central market in front of the palace. He and his brothers are credited with leading the formation of many new settlements. Forty craft unions were also said to have been initiated in his reign, and the leaders of the unions eventually played important roles in government administration. Ere's son, however, was the last ruler in the dynasty. After failing to impose his leadership, he abdicated and left the country, returning to Ife (the land of his forebears). However, two or three generations of rule by foreign war leaders was enough to establish the tradition of a paramount ruler governing the whole country. The next twenty *Ogiso* were "representatives of different local, Bini chiefdoms" who all failed to establish their own dynasty. The last of them died in misery after being banished for being autocratic and not "consulting his advisors."[19]

---

19   Ibid., 335, 338–39.

The leaders of this supra-chiefdom polity were typically leaders from specific communities who were able to govern on the basis of charisma but were never able to create the institutional framework and coercive authority necessary to centralize political power and establish a state. They were little more than *primus entre pares*, first among equals, although such an ethos would not be antithetical to state formation in the democratic pathway of politogenesis.

In fact, when the monarchy was abolished in the twelfth century, Benin City was governed as a republic, and the city itself almost broke up, as many people desired a return to the more egalitarian, albeit gerontocratic, system of community councils. Two symbolic leaders of the republic wished to found their own dynasties, one after the other. The first was prevented from doing so by popular pressure, but the second was enthroned and aided by the leaders of Benin City, who had succeeded in extending their authority well beyond the city and across all Benin during the earlier reign of the *Ogiso*, whom they used as a "screen" for their own authority. They desired "the restoration of the supreme all-Benin authority" and to this end they invited a foreign ruler from Ife to ascend the throne and bring "peace and concord." The heads of the Benin City chiefdom "hoped to control the foreigner" and to preserve the political unity of Benin, but under their own influence and not that of the heads of other Bini chiefdoms.[20]

In the end, they failed in this endeavor, though the ultimate danger came not from their traditional rivals, the other chiefdoms, but from their own weapon, the *Oba*, or monarch. The fourth *Oba* succeeded in violently subordinating the Benin City leaders who had styled themselves "king-makers." He deprived them of the right to bear symbols equal to those of the monarch or to confer titles, and restricted them to crowning each new king rather than choosing kings from among the royal family. He also "created a new category of title-holders as a counterbalance." Before, Benin was a complex chiefdom in which one segment, the chiefdom that controlled Benin City, held preeminent influence over the other chiefdoms. The new monarchy constituted

---

20   Ibid., 342–43.

a qualitative change in which a ritual and administrative center wielded a unique and increasingly coercive power over all the
segments, against them but also in concert with them, as each
segment was led by heads who enjoyed a good deal of privilege
and spiritual power.

The royal court employed a number of dignitaries and
office-holders who acted as intermediaries between the *Oba* and
the other people. In fact, the cross-culturally common taboo
against supreme leaders relating freely with common people seems
to be an effective mechanism, not only for creating a mystical status around a supreme leader, but also for ensuring the complexification of authority and the proliferation of courts (which are at
least partially the predecessors of bureaucracies), and to allow the
upper strata to isolate and control the supreme ruler.

On the other hand, the Benin megacommunity remained
relatively stable for about six centuries, until its invasion by the
British, without developing many characteristic features of the
state, even though the qualitatively different authority of the *Oba*
constituted a potential kernel of state power. The chiefs and paramount rulers did not generally interfere with subsistence activities, but on the contrary continued to favor communal values.
Related to this, the central authority never developed strong coercive powers, and no social group ever achieved total dominance
over the others. Most dignitaries and title-holders were officially
non-hereditary and appointed by the *Oba*, but in practice they
remained within the same families for centuries, thus they never
came to support the paramount ruler over the communities. And
in the communities, councils of elders continued to hold preeminence, though often balanced by the younger warriors, and so
the different families remained more or less equal, and thus subsistence practices remained egalitarian and communal. The *Oba*
had broken out of the constraints of a complex chiefdom—a type
of alliance among chiefdoms that is typically short-lived—yet he
did not develop state authority on other social fronts. The function of the paramount ruler remained religious, and his power
was primarily symbolic. It symbolized the unity of all the chiefdoms and independent communities, therefore lending itself to a
political stability that was spiritual rather than bureaucratic.

This peculiar balance, nonetheless, was arrived at by a power struggle between different loci of leadership, which is a dynamic that deserves further exploration. It is characteristic of state evolution that the emerging center of state authority must wage a bloody conflict against the power-holders in the preexisting political organization. Those prior leaders are generally complicit with politogenesis (sometimes unwittingly so) but in many specific instances will fight against state formation in order to hold onto their own power. Given such ambiguity, we can view non-state power-holders as conduits of the logic of power, which conditions them to push for innovations and forms of organization that encourage the further accumulation of power; at the same time they wish to hold onto power, even though the conditions that allow them to be power-holders must be superseded for power to accumulate further. Thus they favor the accumulation of power even as they oppose the organizational progress that higher intensities of power require.

In European history, the collaboration and conflict between monarchies and the bourgeoisie displays the same ambiguity. In this, we can see that the logic of power is both seductive and impersonal. As anarchists have long argued, though often hesitantly, metaphorically, or ambivalently, given the Western prejudice in favor of quantitative social science, power is a social force that must be analyzed as a protagonist of history. In fact, much of the behavior of capital as a social force is due to the extent to which it serves as a cover for power. Though it is more enticing as a subject of analysis due to its quantitative and objective pretensions, it derives its function from the symbolic value it is imbued with by a whole host of military, spiritual, administrative, and cultural institutions.

An analysis of power as an active value can also shed a clarifying light on other controversies regarding where to draw the line for the threshold of politogenesis. There is a debate among Early State anthropologists as to whether the ancient Greek poleis or "city-states" constituted states. Some, such as Moshe Berent, insist that they do not qualify, because they are structurally different from most other early states. Such argumentation puts definitions before phenomena and makes it harder to perceive

atypical innovations that open up new pathways of development.
The Greek poleis generated a great deal of theoretical and practical material that was drawn on by subsequent states and is still
drawn on by states today. I don't believe there was any similar
transference of organizational principles to stateless societies.
Therefore, if the Greek experience is more readily transferable to
states than to stateless entities, are certain elements of decentralization enough to justify the poleis as stateless societies? If the
supreme ruler in a typical early state wielded above all symbolic
power, what is the problem if in the poleis that symbolic center
were not occupied by a human claiming to represent the gods but
by a divine principle itself: law?

Other scholars refute the arguments of Greek statelessness,
pointing out that the proportion of bureaucrats in the poleis was
comparable to the early Chinese state; that the proportion of
slaves and other non-citizens was in fact a majority; that the private management of slaves is a commonplace in many states, and
that the state did in fact control slaves used in silver-mining, construction, and bureaucratic functions; that accumulation through
warfare rather than internal taxation was common in other early
states as well; as was the rotation of authority, for example in
Italian city-states and the Novgorod republic, which would even
invite foreign officials to come act as temporary rulers.[21]

The example of the poleis also encourages us to break out of
the artificially limited scope of analysis encouraged by the myopic
mythology of nation-states, which tends to ignore the margins of
a society and its neighbors. The commercial and military network of the Greeks constitutes the true terrain of each individual
city-state. Since a state's territorial boundaries are fictive in any
case, we shouldn't hesitate to look beyond Athens's walls, or even
beyond the plains of Attica, to measure the population and the
forms of exploitation linked into that particular state system. The
ancient Greek poleis organized their power in a space of flows

---

21   Leonid E. Grinin, "Early State and Democracy," in *The Early
      State, Its Alternatives and Analogues*, responding to Moshe Ber-
      ent, "Greece: The Stateless *Polis* (11th to 4th Centuries B.C.)" in
      The Early State, Its Alternatives and Analogues, 364–87.

rather than a space of places; therefore a systems analysis is best suited to understand the functioning of the states they created.

The Mediterranean provides an excellent terrain for such analysis, in fact. The fall of the Mycenaean state at the end of the Bronze Age opened up a specific socio-political space in which the Greek city-states later emerged. That collapse was part of a wave of invasions, revolutions, and catastrophes that spelled the end of a great many civilizations all across the eastern Mediterranean. The Late Bronze Age collapse occurred between 1206 and 1150 BCE and was marked by a sharp decline in trade, a widespread loss of written language, and the destruction of the overwhelming majority of cities in the region, from Phylos to Gaza, some of which were never resettled.

I believe the key to understanding this collapse is recognizing that all of these civilizations formed a shared world-system. Linguistics, as well as the Western inclination to break up reality into subjects (and corresponding objects or inert material) rather than understanding it as a question of fields and relationships, can prejudice us to view the region as being populated by "separate" cultures and polities: the Egyptians; the Assyrians; the Israelites; the Mycenaeans; and so forth. It is more accurate to understand these peoples and polities as different strands woven together in a complex fabric.

The Bronze Age collapse has been widely studied, and numerous causes have been proposed, from an increase in warfare and barbarian invasion, to climatic changes and volcanic eruptions, to economic collapse stemming from the exhaustion of the bronze supply (bronze-based industry, unlike the iron-based industry that followed it, required intense trade networks spanning a large geographic region). None of these explanations seems satisfying in its own right, and none enjoy a scientific consensus. Before suggesting another cause, I would like to problematize the concept of causation itself, at least in how it has traditionally been approached in scientific research.

Can we imagine that the periodic outbursts of insurrection, collapse, civil war, and revolution that at the present are occurring with an increasing frequency (Albania, Bolivia, Greece, Tunisia, Egypt, Libya, Syria, Brazil, etc.) eventually intensify to the point where they cause the collapse of the current world system? And what if ten thousand years went by, all electronic records were lost, and the only thing future researchers could uncover were climate data, some of the most basic chronologies of the major states, and some cursory information about economic practices?

Surely some would hypothesize that climate change were the cause of the collapse, others—unearthing cryptic references to the appearance of a bellicose class known as "terrorists" and discovering archaeological evidence of civil war in Ukraine, Iraq, Syria, Yemen, Afghanistan, Libya, and Colombia—would suggest invasion and warfare. Others might posit peak oil or currency inflation. From the current standpoint, all of these explanations should strike us as unsatisfactory, precisely because they are all interrelated and none of them, precisely, is the cause of the increasing systemic insecurity we can feel. At least not in the way a chemical reaction can be identified as having a clean, simple, concrete cause. On the contrary, all of these factors contribute to the insecurity of the world system, that great fabric we are all wrapped up in. Each of these factors shakes and pulls at the fabric, causing growing instability, until any structures built atop the fabric collapse (or until the fabric itself is torn). In complex systems, it is instability and turmoil that cause systemic collapse and the spontaneous emergence of new systems. But instability is not just the sum of discrete forces acting on a static equilibrium. On the contrary, the instability comes to constitute a force in itself that triggers more destabilizing events. It unifies the total array of forces that cause individuals and communities to reproduce the dynamic equilibrium of the system or to rebel against it. These forces are economic, ecological, technological, political (in terms of administrative structures, discourses of legitimacy, and also relations of war/peace between polities), spiritual, and also psychosocial. This last, often ignored, and approaching what George Katsiaficas terms the "eros effect," is undeniable on the ground: a society is most likely to rebel when the power structures that dominate it appear unstable, or when neighboring societies also rebel, no matter what their reasons. This explains why, starting at the end of 2008, social rebellions occurred with greater frequency, even in many countries where the economic crisis had only appeared in the news but not yet manifested in higher unemployment, or why there was a direct interplay and transference between insurrections and uprisings in Greece and Turkey—one country in economic recession and the other experiencing economic growth—or Greece and Bulgaria—one uprising inspired by anarchist values and the other by fascist values.

Assuming that we can understand systemic collapse in this light, I would like to suggest another factor (potentially the most important factor, although the data do not exist to prove this claim) for the Bronze Age collapse: internal rebellion and struggles for freedom.

I propose that we would attain a far more accurate view of history if, every time a state collapsed, we assumed rebellion was a principal cause, unless evidence existed for another cause. We know that states provoke resistance from their own subjects, and that struggles for freedom are universal (although visions of freedom and methods for attaining it are beyond any doubt historically and culturally specific). Too often, historians and archaeologists fabricate cheap mysteries, "Why did this great civilization suddenly collapse?," because they refuse to accept the obvious: that states are odious structures that their populations destroy whenever they get the opportunity, and sometimes even when they face impossible odds.

The scholars of power are staring Ozymandias in the face. Beyond the anarchist intuition, which has proven accurate in its historical predictions enough times that anyone whose psyche is not integrally wrapped up with bootlicking should have taken note, we have a number of facts to back up this assertion. To start with, there are numerous documented examples of societies that overthrow state structures in order to organize themselves horizontally. Such records are typically from places like Amazonia or sub-Saharan Africa where anti-authoritarian popular cultures are conducive to the preservation of such histories.

But in other parts of the world, a shortage of evidence is not evidence that popular rebellions were not a major force of history. It is precisely the one factor that is least likely to leave archaeological evidence. It leaves no trace in climate records, it need not be preceded or even accompanied by any dramatic change in technologies and material remains, and the literate classes of pre-modern states are unlikely to put it down in writing. In fact, the disappearance of writing is a likely result of an anti-authoritarian revolution in a society in which written language is controlled by the elite.[22] Neighboring states that witnessed such revolutions might also be unlikely to discuss and document a popular uprising because they themselves were assuredly afflicted by the same conflicts and dangers. Anyone who participates in radical movements today knows that revolutionary episodes are systematically downplayed or erased from the official histories, and this despite the fact that modern states command much more complicated means that allow them to recuperate radical histories, reframing them in a way that legitimates state power.[23] Bronze Age states did not have such means at their disposal. The principal way for them to avoid fanning the flames of transregional rebellion would be to suppress the news.

And what of the wars and barbarian invasions? Chronicles of the Egyptian state mention a series of seafaring raiders as well as land-based invaders whom modern researchers named as the "Sea Peoples." Probably originating from around the Aegean Sea, they warred with states in the areas of modern-day Turkey, Syria, Palestine, and Egypt. Their raiding was so calamitous that some scholars propose them as a cause for the Bronze Age collapse. It seems likely that some if not all of the Sea Peoples were stateless, and their warfare may have been in part motivated by hostility to the states of the region. The Egyptian, Hittite, and Mycenaean states, to name the principal players, were involved in a long-standing power play and scramble for resources that kept the region immersed in warfare, the worst consequences of which were born by the lower strata, the common people. And as we have seen, a major activity of state formation is slave-raiding and the capture of entire populations, which also leads to many people fleeing to zones of resistance (possibly in the mountains and

---

22   Scott, *The Art of Not Being Governed*, 226–34.
23   For example, see the discussion of Gandhi and King in Peter Gelderloos, *How Nonviolence Protects the State* (Harrisonburg, Virginia: Signalfire Press, 2005).

islands that made up the Aegean and its borders). As the states grew in power and the liberated zones filled up, there would be more pressure on fugitive populations to fight back.

Evidence for the statelessness of the Sea Peoples includes their use of oral history and their lack of writing, which also denotes a lack of bureaucracy; their nomadism and extreme mobility; their apparent use of confederal alliances between different peoples; their impressive military efficiency without a corresponding founding of dynasties or cities (state societies that are militarily effective are invariably prolific founders and builders); their oscillation between warring against neighboring states and hiring themselves out as mercenaries. All of these are characteristics of stateless peoples at the time, at least in areas devastated by state effects.

If this is the case, the appearance of the Sea Peoples would constitute ethnogenesis, the creation of a new people or ethnic group, in this case one constituted by runaway slaves and fragments of communities fleeing the warfare and slave-raiding of states. Such a process constituted the preeminent model for revolution at the time. Without internationalism, freedom would have been an ethnic property. Unfortunately, as in the case of the nomadic empires, we have seen how such ethnicities can eventually shift from being the antagonists of states to the founders of states. The relative strength of the values of anti-authoritarianism, on the one hand, and militarism, on the other, as well as the presence or absence of patriarchy, probably determine whether a liberated people become a new politogen.

In any case, population after the fall of the Mycenaean civilization was continuous, but palaces and many towns were burnt down, and people became more nomadic, living in shifting settlements and supporting themselves to a greater extent with herd animals, particularly cattle. After a few centuries the new poleis emerged, agriculture pushed animal husbandry to the margins, slavery returned in force, commerce flourished, and warfare increased. The great civilization from which the West claims descent had arrived.

A broad popular rebellion destroying the prior civilization may explain the particular relationship of the Greek city-states with power. The military basis of their power comprised egalitarian formations of foot soldiers who used innovative tight formations to overcome cavalry and larger but less motivated imperial armies, together with an effectively deployed naval power, the backbone of which—the rowers—were also granted political rights and thus given a stake in victory. Anti-authoritarian societies and those that result from popular rebellions tend to be innovative and adept when it comes to warfare, and this may explain the Greek developments.

Such a military organization dethrones the nobility, who otherwise could cement their political dominance over the middle strata through their ability to field mounted troops for warfare. Noble or high-status families still existed in the Greek poleis, since their economy allowed for the private accumulation of wealth, based as it was on monetary exchange, alienated wealth from livestock to slaves, the erosion of collective values in favor of private property adhering to households, and a patriarchal system whereby male heads controlled the households and all their wealth. (Note that such a regime—familial private property—was still a far cry from the regime of individual private property that liberal ideologues seek to naturalize. I believe that familial private property derives from degraded systems of collective property in which popular values of sharing and community solidarity have eroded, or when situations of forced migration and crisis have weakened the community and favored the atomized family as a survival institution.)

The important Greek political concept of *equality*, therefore, was an alienated political equality rather than a holistic social equality, the same as it is in the representative democracies of today. Political equality is an authoritarian concept that encourages the constitution of a broad elite (based on the inclusion of all potentially elite sectors rather than an exclusionary process by which elite factions compete for absolute dominance, often destabilizing the system in the process). Factions in this broad elite may compete economically but they all must collaborate in the wielding of political and cultural power, with the aim of advancing a unified statist projectuality.

The poleis, therefore, rejected monarchs but not the sort of power that monarchs accumulated and wielded. Nobles, in this system, might achieve dominance for a time, especially if they could mobilize the middle classes against their rivals, but on principle the presence of a single ruler, a tyrant, was culturally proscribed and discouraged.

On an ethical plane, we can classify this vision of equality—the slaver's equality—as hypocrisy, then and now. But in a historical light, we are looking at a very important governing strategy, and one that may reflect the reemergence of a state out of the ashes of the Mycenaean civilization. Successful popular rebellions often create an anti-authoritarian ethos. Perhaps, over three centuries, incipient elites used military brotherhoods and a resurgent patriarchy to establish a new kind of state authority. They did more than pay lip service to the anti-authoritarian ethos that may have thrived after the rebellion. They would have co-opted and modified it to protect their own interests as elites from the attempts of any single faction to achieve total domination, as in the prior despotic model. They also would have used it to mobilize a larger portion of their society—any candidate for "citizen" status, and thus the privileges of equality—to support the state project. After all, they would have needed a broader base of support at a time of material poverty and infrastructural weakness. And because "free" males are not the only agents of history, although reading most academic works you'd never guess, these conniving elites additionally had to protect themselves from a leveling rebellion by the others in their society who still championed the anti-authoritarian ethos. Therefore, they continued to vocally oppose a symbolic aspect of the prior state that was for them obsolete, the king, in order to cash in on and recuperate a rebellious popular culture. The leaders of the American and French revolutions did exactly that in order to create new states that were in the end far more authoritarian than the regimes they replaced.

The above is conjecture, but every element in the hypothesis has been documented in other processes of state formation. Whatever the trajectory, it was not universal. Much of the area remained stateless until invaded and conquered by the growing city-states.

Returning to the documented history and in particular to the anti-democratic figure of the tyrant, it is important to understand that a cultural proscription does not at all mean that what is proscribed will not be present in the society. Quite the contrary. Greek denigrations of tyranny tell us that it had no place in their ideal model of governance, but the historical record shows that in practice, the Greek democracies demonstrated a cyclical dependence on tyrants.

Majority rule requires an underlying consensus that whatever ritualized decision is produced will be respected by all. When this consensus breaks down, from the original democracies of the city-states to the representative democracies of today, a dictator steps in. Democratic mythology requires this dictator to be delegitimized, and indeed sometimes their motivation is personal power more than governmental stability, yet dictators provide institutional continuity where sometimes formal democracy cannot. They also have the extra-democratic ability to weaken or eliminate reformist factions that make the democratic consensus untenable, typically, those who stray too far from what is considered a centrist position. (Granted, this house-cleaning capacity is far more developed in modern dictatorships than it was in the Greek poleis.) Tyrants were like the paralegal Batman that every system of law and order needs to function; condemned and externalized to a marginal space of illegitimacy, but clearly present both in the imaginary and in the historical operation of the idealized model they shadow.

In the poleis, the tyrants made use of the same institutional forces as the assembly to mobilize resources and execute their decisions. To me, this interchangeability—take out the assembly, put the tyrant in its place, and the society keeps functioning—constitutes an important test: **compatibility**. The fact that the poleis pass this test proves that the assembly and the dictator function within the same democratic logic. On the contrary, truly stateless societies, saddled with a president, a chief, or an assembly of male, slave-owning citizens, will either ignore the addition (probably, the people would kill or exile them if they attempted to assert their authority), or the entire social fabric would have to be reengineered, because it contains no features or interfaces compatible with the operation of the statist institution. Give the !Kung a Department of Transportation, and there will

be a total disconnect, as the !Kung do not traditionally have taxation, or highways, or a cultural acceptance of bureaucratic chains
of command.

The compatibility test also works to differentiate states functioning according to mutually exclusive logics. Would a Han
bureaucracy function in Napoleonic France? The thought experiment could provide some useful analysis. The Catholic Church,
for certain, could not have replaced the religious institutions in an
African state based on ancestor cults; the former has no interface
with formal kinship systems. The fact of compatibility between
dictator and assembly in the ancient Greek poleis demonstrates
what most social scientists and historians, thanks to their condi-
tioning by democratic mythology, will never be able to see: that
these two institutions constitute part of the same political system, just as they do in parliamentary democracies today.

VIII.
They Ain't Got No Class:
Surpluses and the State

So far, we have focused on processes of secondary state formation: societies that formed states within world systems where other states had already been instituted, and thus constituted a model and an influence. We have begun to appreciate how a society's prior attitude towards authority has a critical impact on how it responds to state influence—whether with resistance or imitation. Placed in the same adverse situation, a society with anti-authoritarian, cooperative, and reciprocal values will find an anti-authoritarian solution, while a society that values hierarchy may likely form a state. We have also seen a number of non-state models for social evolution that enable anti-authoritarian societies to respond to those situations that supposedly cause states to form: warfare, population growth, internal complexification, trade expansions, technological development, et cetera.

Soon it will be time to turn our attention to the relatively rare process of primary state formation: societies that formed states in a stateless world system, without any guiding model or external statist pressures.

But first, I think it will be helpful to dedicate a chapter to the matter of economic accumulation, which some theories posit as the motor of state formation. The very notion of understanding (as distinct from analyzing) the economy as a distinct sphere of social life is problematic from the start. At this point, the illusion has long since become self-confirming, thanks to bureaucracies that produce statistics-based knowledge, patriarchal separations of social life, political expediency promoting an institutional division between the formal and informal areas of the State, and neo-Platonic/Christian dualisms that are still commonplace in scientific thought.

The concept of *social war*, an elaboration of anarchist theories of power, reveals how purportedly distinct maneuvers of politics and economy actually find their perfect synthesis within a permanent counterinsurgency strategy designed to accumulate power and to protect the State from all the resistance its accumulative process has generated to date.

The accumulation of capital can be usefully analyzed as *one of the means* a broadly understood State uses to accumulate power, both to provision itself with more resources and to transform the social terrain to facilitate authoritarian control. It can also be read as a special language that members of the elite use to communicate about shared interests.[1] But it only makes sense when understood as a part of the State's imperative to dominate the social body that gives it its perverse life. (Linebaugh and Rediker give us an indispensable example when they reveal the prototype of the factory to be the transatlantic ship, the perfect model of social control: a designed environment in which the needs of a site of production and the needs of authoritarian domination find a synthesis.)

It becomes apparent, on a long timeline that surpasses Marxism's narrow optic, that economic accumulation is inconceivable without the hierarchical structures and spiritual values that states and proto-states create. I believe all the available evidence confirms that economic accumulation is never a cause of state formation, although developing an effective strategy of economic accumulation can allow a state to grow rapidly.

How could the production of surpluses cause the formation of new political structures when a surplus cannot exist within a reciprocal economy? In a gift-based economy, bounty and abundance never manifest as surplus, since anything that is not used by an individual or her family is given away. The very concept of surplus does not exist; the pertinent categories would be "gift" and "waste."

Only a compound of structures of concentrated, coercive and metaphysical power can break the generalized practice of

---

1   Lev Zlodey and Jason Radegas, *Here at the Center of the World in Revolt* (Anonymous edition, 2011), 78.

reciprocity that is the foundation of every society, legitimize the concept of quantitative rather than social value, and achieve the institution of alienable property on the grave of the gift economy. Absent those radical social changes, economic accumulation is impossible. The paths by which the former can be accomplished will be explored in the subsequent chapters.

What forms of economic exploitation are available to early states? On the one hand, there is a weak parasitism on preexisting trade and agriculture. This could take the form of a tribute owed to the gods (and dispensed with by a priestly class), to a dominant lineage or clan that has effectively legitimized its claims to the territory and to the ancestors, or to the warrior caste of a neighboring community that has successfully instituted that age-old state-building mechanism, the protection racket. In a clear break with the voluntary character of reciprocity, non-payment of the tribute can be punished with spiritual ostracism, social exclusion, physical expulsion, or punitive raiding, kidnapping, murder, rape, and other acts of state-building.

On the other hand, early states invariably put their nascent authority to the test in the very kind of social reengineering and legibility-imposing architectures that capitalism, starting a mere five hundred years ago, has come to excel at. (Would it be too awkward to speak of *cratoforming*? Science fiction has given us the concept of *terraforming* to speak of the chemical, geological, and climactic transformation of other planets to allow more recognizable forms of colonization to take place. Likewise, *cratos*—state authority—transforms the environment at an elemental and ecosocial level to favor its own proliferation.)

Few early states were content with exacting tribute and skimming the top off of preexisting economic activities. To varying degrees, they pushed their subjects to augment production and to specialize in a single economic activity and thus become dependent on a distribution network controlled by the State; and they reorganized the social fabric, relocating people and developing new architectures, to cement and intensify these changes. In parallel, they captured slaves and manufactured ethnic or religious barriers to solidarity, allowing them to subject the slaves to levels of exploitation that the citizens would never abide.

Capitalism as a socioeconomic system[2] has thrived on making exploitive forms of economic activity profitable and efficient; however, the attempts of early states to impel economic production are generally marked by immiseration and inefficiency. Productivity, we could say, was until recently far less bountiful than subsistence (and continues to be much less effective, if measured in terms of energy input and ecological drain rather than labor power).

Referring to state-organized agriculture by pre-colonial states in Southeast Asia, Scott says: "They are rarely models of efficient or sustainable agriculture, but they are, and they are intended to be, models of legibility and appropriation."[3] Comparing early city-states in the Americas with those in Asia, Berezkin points out that hyper-urbanization was not efficient for production but was necessitated by administrative limitations of the state that attempted to monopolize and reorganize economic activity. "When the governmental tradition was firmly established, the proportion of urban population diminished."[4]

The Baluba, Bakunda, and Balunda states of the Congo basin, discussed in Chapter XI, can practically be considered original states, as they had little or no contact with the states of

---

2   I would agree with Fernand Braudel (*The Perspective of the World* [New York: Harper & Row, 1984]) and Giovanni Arrighi (*The Long 20th Century*) that capitalism, as a socioeconomic system, a strategy of accumulation adopted and expanded by states, emerged in the fifteenth to seventeenth centuries, though this marriage was preceded many centuries by a merchant class pursuing the same strategy on a much more limited scale. Arrighi (*The Long 20th Century,* 11) cites a study by Janet Abu-Lughod from *Before European Hegemony: The World System A.D. 1250–1350* (New York: Oxford University Press, 1989) showing that the principal markets of Eurasia and Africa were already connected in the thirteenth century.

3   Scott, *The Art of Not Being Governed,* 76.

4   Yuri E. Berezkin, "Alternative Models of Middle Range Society. 'Individualistic' Asia vs. 'Collectivistic' America?" in *The Early State, Its Alternatives and Analogues,* 69.

northern and eastern Africa, and until later only indirect influence from Middle Eastern and Mediterranean states. These states practiced the inalienability of land throughout their existence, and it was not among the first practices given up after European colonization. Economically, the obligations of statehood were equal to or less than those in many non-state societies: tribute and irregular obligatory collective labor.[5] Economically, the state structures supported themselves through foreign trade and thus constituted a minimal economic burden on their subjects. The glue and motor of state organization in these societies belong almost exclusively to what some would label the superstructure— the religious and ceremonial, in a word, symbolic, accoutrements to what was supposed to be the material base.

Though it is not always their primary source of sustenance, as in the Congo states, emerging states nearly always try to foment and control trade. The Zapotec and Mayan states centralized and monopolized the prestige sector of the economy (for example, the finest ceramics and the obsidian trade) and allowed other crafts to be decentralized and largely self-organized, though at the bottom of the economic hierarchy they forcibly relocated peasants in settlements dedicated to specialized, intensive agriculture. Curiously, many of the states that most effectively established trade empires organized networks of ceremonial centers in which spiritual and material commerce were overlaid. The Nile and the Andes states, which will be discussed more in a subsequent chapter, were both examples to that effect. The Inca state also assigned different sectors of the economy to specific towns, in a simple strategy that is nonetheless eloquent in demonstrating a synthesis of social control and economic accumulation. In the artificially heterogeneous map of their territory, individual towns were dependent rather than self-sufficient, hyper-specialization augmented innovation and output, and the entire population had to engage in intensified trade, which was more legible and taxable than localized production.

---

5   Lvova, "The Formation and Development of States in the Congo Basin," 289.

States can organize trade networks, but trade networks themselves do not generate states. The Indus Valley civilization, one of the oldest in the world, is an interesting example. At its height (between 2600 and 1900 BCE), the civilization had a population of some five million people living in half a dozen cities—such as Harappa and Mohenjo-Daro—and over a thousand towns and villages. It made up a world system together with its trading partners, ancient Egypt and Mesopotamia. Of these, the Indus Valley civilization was the largest. And in contrast to the other two, it was probably stateless. No solid evidence has been found of kings, priests, armies, temples, or palaces. Some of the largest buildings in the urban centers were public baths; the urban planning, sewage, and hygienic systems were the best in the ancient world; and the relative equality of housing size suggests an egalitarian, non-stratified society. However, some inequalities may have existed, given a high rate of disease and injury found among human remains. The disease can be accounted for by a dense urban population, although it seems that some of the sick and injured received no medical care. With the probable lack of an army, it is unlikely that the Indus Valley civilization practiced any form of slavery extreme enough to result in a high injury rate. Other possible social divisions might have existed between urban citizens (who seemed to be exclusively craftspeople and merchants) and rural inhabitants, the latter possibly excluded from urban healthcare, though the lack of military structures suggests that the rural population traded their surplus more or less voluntarily with the artisans of the towns and cities; without a military, the cities could not subjugate the countryside or do anything worse than impose mildly unfavorable balances of trade.

If this is indeed a case of an anarchic society with a high population density, it might be possible that collectively (and violently) enforced social norms were in place, leading to a decentralized practice of killing authoritarian would-be leaders as well as people engaging in behaviors perceived as anti-social, such as murder, rape, or theft; or that the civilization substituted warfare with ritualized or informal but in any case violent sport competitions (for which there exist numerous precedents among stateless societies).

In any case, there is no positive evidence for social inequality, as the disease and injury rate have multiple possible explanations, and no evidence for the corresponding military, religious, and economic structures that enable social inequality.

Preceding the Indus Valley civilization were farming settlements like Mehrgarh, a small agricultural village going back to 6500 BCE, which between 5500 and 2600 experienced a crafts and trade explosion. Doubtless it was one of multiple villages in the region, allowing us to imagine the following timeline. In a fertile ecosystem of multiple river valleys, neolithic (advanced stone-tool-using) hunter-gatherers eventually adopted sedentary settlements based on the cultivation of multiple grains and other plants, which they domesticated over time to favor characteristics that met their dietary and technical needs. Soon after, they also began domesticating a few animal species. Networks of such settlements, still practicing a good deal of hunting and gathering and still surrounded by pure hunter-gatherers, with whom they may have maintained relations, existed in relative stability for thousands of years, which is to say hundreds of generations, which in human terms might as well be an eternity.

After this eternity, copper working gave rise to bronze technology, a multiplication in the available tools and techniques, and a diversification of crafts, intensifying trade and interdependency within the village network. Increases in trade and in agricultural efficiency led to a population increase, which after another couple thousand years led to the emergence of cities. But in this case, the cities had no religion, no armies, only the most modest forms of warfare, if any, and no rulers. For another seven hundred years, they carried out their crafts and their trade, and organized their cities with some form of council or assembly of inhabitants. Such a degree of stability is rare in state timelines. Constituting another achievement for statelessness, the Indus Valley civilization was in many ways the most technologically advanced of the ancient world, they distributed their wealth in a relatively equal manner, and evidently they did not resort to slavery, religion, or aggressive warfare.

Eventually the cities were abandoned, perhaps due to the environmental impacts or the deterioration in living standards wrought by high population densities, though the towns and agricultural settlements thrived for many centuries more until their eventual conquest by Aryan invaders.

Stateless societies also existed at the heart of one of the most intensive, high-value trade networks in world history, in the Banda islands of the Maluku archipelago. The islanders participated in the spice trade for centuries, occupying an essential productive niche, while preserving their statelessness.

Social organization throughout the Maluku archipelago was localized and largely horizontal, though there was also a council of wealthy male elders—*orang kaya*—each one representing a district. The majority of local affairs were self-organized, with the *orang kaya* primarily dealing with, and deriving their power from, the spice trade, which was organized by Malay, Arab, and Chinese traders. Islam arrived peacefully to the islands in the fourteenth century, providing a shared social fabric with the dominant trade networks and helping to unite outside traders with local merchants. Traditional forms of animism continued to be practiced in the interior, away from the ports.

When the VOC (the Dutch East India Company) arrived in the seventeenth century and tried to impose a trade monopoly with unfavorable terms, the islanders revolted and killed the interlopers. After militarily defeating the English in a series of battles, ending the major subversion of their monopoly, the Dutch returned and forced the *orang kaya* to sign a new treaty. Citing perceived violations of the treaty, the Dutch company instituted a policy of genocide, killing or expelling the natives and repopulating the islands with slaves or forced immigrants. This was the beginning of state authority in the archipelago.

Elsewhere in the East Indies, local societies alternated between states and statelessness until they were definitively colonized. Periods of high-intensity trade availed more resources to state-building projects, but they did not make them inevitable. On the important island of Java, at the center of the pepper trade, we see the same cycles of state-formation and state collapse as we see elsewhere, with mildly hierarchical but stateless societies proving their resilience over centuries. In the end, it was not endogenous processes of class stratification that brought enduring state structures to Java, but military imposition by external powers—first Muslim and then European traders.

The first contender for statehood in Java might be the Tarumanagara kingdom, though the available evidence suggests that the kingdom lacked coercive powers, institutional continuity, and non-charismatic authority (in other words, it might have been what anthropologists classify as a chiefdom and not a state). King Purnawarman was the most famous ruler, his reign lasting from 395–434. The kingdom's founder was his grandfather, a refugee from India who possibly came from a ruling-class family, who fled the expansion of the Gupta empire and married a woman the founding myths refer to as a local Javanese princess, probably the daughter of a high-status family.

(Curiously, a similar story exists about the founding of Salakanagara, the first Indianized society of West Java. Though no direct information on the society exists, later accounts claim that Salakanagara was founded by an Indian trade emissary who married, again, a local princess. Though impossible to verify, the story suggests the status that serving as the representative of a foreign state can bring, especially in a hierarchical but non-state society. It also shows one of the ways that a state's control over and promotion of trade can spread the state model.)

Purnawarman was said to have subordinated forty-eight smaller kingdoms, which may have been semi-autonomous clans or communities, each with their own chief. Monumental inscriptions that Purnawarman commissioned suggest that he won the alliance of lesser kings (or chiefs), and that the forty-eight kingdoms were therefore not administrative units under his direct control. The Tugu inscription speaks of "his intelligence and wisdom" and notes that he "has become the royal flag of all kings."[6] Other inscriptions speak of loyal allies fighting at his side being rewarded with honorable receptions, rather than subordinates under his command simply following orders.

A typical state-building figure, Purnawarman oversaw irrigation works and spread Hinduism, using the Brahmans—the

---

6   Wikipedia "Tarumanagara," https://en.wikipedia.org/wiki/ Tarumanagara (accessed February 20, 2016).

priest class—to legitimate his rule. Two years into his reign, he established a new capital, another common event in state-formation, as a new configuration of power (usually assembled around a skilled statesman) demonstrates and cements its strength by creating a new center and breaking the old networks of power.

Many of Tarumanagara's later rulers, like the most famous king, bore the Sanskrit word *warman* in their names, meaning "protector" or "shield." That symbolism, and the military history of the region, suggests that many hierarchical but non-state societies in the area developed states as a way to protect themselves from more aggressive neighboring states, though just how defensive the Tarumanagara kingdom was is uncertain (monumental inscriptions speak of Purnawarman destroying enemy fortresses, for example). The strategy, in the end, was unsuccessful for the kingdom, though it did allow the elites to wield greater power for a time. Around 650, an invasion by the Srivijaya Empire put an end to the polity. The latter was a Buddhist maritime empire based on Sumatra that profited from trade agreements and cultural ties with China and the Buddhist Pala Empire of Bengal; its trade network stretched all the way to the Islamic Caliphate in the Middle East.

The evidence that Tarumanagara might not have crossed the state threshold is, in part, the lack of evidence or information regarding its subsequent leaders. Few of them erected monuments, as Purnawarman did (the strange obsession with monument-building is nearly universal among states), and while it is unknown whether subsequent leaders came from the same dynasty, it is clear that central authority fractured and faltered, as the capital changed location often. Note that the founding of new capitals tends to be a one-time and not a repetitive event in state formation. A new capital demonstrates that authority has undergone a qualitative change, breaking with the relatively free confederation of chiefdoms or communities that preceded it. A constantly changing capital demonstrates a lack of continuity and stability, values that all states attempt to project.

The kingdom maintained diplomatic relations with China, an important trade partner, and this contact remained stable even after the reign of Purnawarman, though trade networks do not necessarily collapse when states do.

In any case, the Hindu polity that succeeded Tarumanagara was almost certainly not stratified or institutionalized enough to qualify as a state. The Sunda kingdom of western Java hovered around the state threshold from around the seventh to sixteenth centuries. Chinese and later Portuguese merchants described the territory as "lawless" in this time period, and the diplomatic relationship with the Chinese court was not maintained. The capital changed frequently, schismatic centers of power competed with one another, borders were unstable and shifting, and the succession of authority was irregular at best. Within the sphere of influence of the Srivijaya Empire, Sunda guaranteed its survival through alliances and acts of submission to powerful neighbors. Nonetheless, the society was hierarchically organized, and while it sought to preserve its political autonomy, its resistance to neighboring states was not anti-authoritarian.

In the sixteenth century, the Sunda kingdom made an alliance with Portuguese spice traders to protect themselves from the Muslim sultanates that were growing in power in the region. The sultanates were often aided by local elites who used conversion to a new religion as a tool to launch rebellions against the previous rulers. The Portuguese got free access to the highly valued Sunda pepper, but they only profited off the alliance for five years before the Sultanate of Demak expelled them, in 1527, and took over the key port of Sunda Kelapa, which they renamed Jayakarta. It subsequently became part of the Banten Sultanate. From that point on, the territory was the property of one state or another, each fighting to control the trade networks.

In the early-seventeenth century, Prince Jayawikarta, a vassal of the Sultanate of Banten, granted permission to the English and Dutch to build trading houses in the port city. He tried to play the European powers off one another to keep either one from gaining too much power, but in doing so lost the support of Banten, which by that time was fully in the pocket of the Dutch. The Dutch VOC razed Jayakarta and built their regional capital, Batavia, on its ashes, banishing the local population and importing Chinese and other non-Javanese to populate the area to prevent an insurrection.

The initial strategy of the Portuguese, English, French, and Dutch colonists was to occupy and control preexisting trade hubs, as when the Portuguese conquered Malacca in 1511. But as their power and the extension of their network expanded, their activities reached a whole new scale, as the VOC operation at Jayakarta/Batavia illustrates. No longer content to profit off of or even monopolize trade, they began to reengineer the terrain, destroying and remaking entire societies, in the symmetrical interests of social control and productivity. The Dutch East India Company was peerless in this regard.

A chartered company, the first with publicly traded stocks, and—within a few decades of its foundation—the richest company in the world, the VOC was not merely a business interest. It constituted a politogen, even a state in itself. By 1669, it commanded over two hundred ships, a quarter of them warships, and ten thousand soldiers. The Dutch state had granted the VOC law-making, war-making, and judicial authority. It founded colonies that proved to be fully functioning, if not fully independent, states that lasted for centuries. It deported and imported populations to build new societies dedicated to a productive economy, it annihilated horizontal communities, and toppled preexisting local states. It was not, however, omnipotent, as it lost several wars against the most powerful Southeast Asian states, such as Vietnam, Cambodia, and Ming dynasty China.

One of the VOC's most groundbreaking achievements was to organize, practically alone, an intercontinental cycle of accumulation that was vital to the emergence of global capitalism and the modern state. In the sixteenth and seventeenth centuries, Europe produced practically nothing that the economically advanced societies of Asia wanted. Only Spain and Portugal had any abundance of gold and silver, so to avoid unfavorable if not impossible balances of trade, the VOC initiated intra-Asian trade circuits in order to fund its spice shipments to Europe. Securing an exclusive trade contract with the isolationist Japanese shogunate for two hundred years, the VOC got silver and copper from Japan for silk and porcelain from China, which the company acquired with cotton from India, opium from Bengal, and tea from Ceylon. The revenue and the trade goods generated from this circuit allowed them to acquire the spices in the Indies that sold for such astronomical prices in Europe.

But the VOC quickly learned not to let short-term considerations predominate. They stockpiled spices and made sure not to let prices get too high, to keep commercial ventures aiming to break their monopoly from becoming too profitable. And in their position as both a state body and a trade company, they learned to win the wars with commerce that they could not win with bullets. The opium trade to China provided an important example of how economics—and addiction—could bring to its knees a country that European powers had been unable to defeat militarily. Their need for military and state-making power, however, was evident from the very beginning as a prerequisite for any economic accumulation.

The history of the Minoans and the Mycenaeans suggests some basic parallels with that of the Sunda and VOC. The Minoans, more accurately referred to as the Cretan civilization, were in all probability a stateless people who organized an important trade network spanning the eastern Mediterranean over more than a thousand years. They were a peaceful society with a minimum of defensive infrastructure and no record of involvement in offensive warfare. They were, if not matriarchal, non-patriarchal, with almost exclusively female deities and female or trans priestesses.

The Cretan civilization is best known for its large ceremonial centers, which archaeologists termed "palaces," the most famous one located at Knossos. However, these palaces were not the seats of political rulers, and in fact there is no evidence of such rulers. The palaces served as warehouses, redistribution centers, collective housing for priestesses and administrators, archives, and religious sites. In the Cretan society, all of these functions were probably mixed to the point of being indistinguishable.

Scientists and historiographers have proposed these palaces as the lynchpin in an exploitative economy, wherein the agricultural surplus was hoarded and redistributed to the upper classes. And while archaeological evidence does suggest economic stratification, with artisans dealing in more high-prestige crafts enjoying more wealth than farmers and herders, this vision is probably inaccurate and almost certainly unfaithful to how the Cretans themselves saw their "palace economy." On the one hand, the Cretan diet was too rich, too diversified to suggest a hyper-exploited, enslaved lower class. Put simply, enslaved workers do not have the resources for a healthy diet, and they lack the time to dedicate to multiple forms of subsistence. Nor is there evidence of a Cretan army or other mechanisms capable of imposing the sort of work-or-starve, blackmail economy so common in other city-states. The very diversity of Cretan food production (spanning multicrop agriculture, apiculture, silvaculture, aquaculture, fishing, and hunting, a diversity that would be impossible for a weak state to surveil and control), paired with the lack of evidence of a police or military structure makes the proposal of a coerced or dependent peasant population ludicrous. In the worst case, merchant-priests controlling the palaces might have been able to impose an unfavorable exchange rate making it difficult or impossible for the peasants to acquire luxury goods, but the peasants would still have been more or less self-sufficient, autonomous, and healthy.

The Cretan civilization did have a written language, at the time a common sign of state authority, although nearly all the decoded fragments of Linear B are simple trade records and lists of resources, with a few religious references thrown in. Universally, early states with written languages used the written record to preserve laws, chronicles, and accounts of the power and grandeur of their supreme leaders.

In practice, the palace economy was probably a network of religious centers where farmers, artisans, and merchants brought their produce or their trade goods, sometimes in the spirit of a gift, an offering to the gods that would be redistributed, and sometimes in the spirit of exchange. Mask-wearing priestesses represented the gods in important ceremonies, ano-nymizing spiritual power rather than concentrating it in any individual or family. They also specialized in the occult knowledge, like math and writing, which allowed them to administer a large trade network.

The symbolic importance of Knossos was so great that the warlike and patriarchal Mycenaeans, who occupied Crete

around 1420 BCE, left it intact, apparently using it as a cultural and bureaucratic center, even as they burned the rest of
the Cretan palaces. They were unable to build something as
grandiose, so they kept it, ostensibly in order to co-opt its spiritual and cultural power and perhaps also as a monument to
their conquest. For centuries, a flourishing trade network did
not cause the Cretans to develop a state. It was, in fact, a less
technologically sophisticated society that espoused patriarchal
and militaristic values distinct from those of the Cretan civilization that succeeded in bringing state authority to the island.
The Mycenaeans did their best to take over the eastern Mediterranean trade network. Once again, economic accumulation
was a prize that a pre-existing state captured, and not the cause
of state-formation.

Two thousand years later in Central Europe, the tribal centers of sedentary agriculturalists were often located in places of
symbolic, spiritual importance. These settlements were fortified
over time, some of them giving rise to towns between the eighth
and tenth centuries that occupied an important productive niche
in preexisting trade networks. They were sites of production in
agriculture, animal husbandry, metallurgy, construction, fortification, and jewelry making. "These newly emerging urban centers, however, appeared independently from the state-formative
process and their existence does not indicate the necessary occurrence of state societies." In the two centuries prior to the emergence of these towns, the construction of both forts and open
settlements had increased 50 percent, creating a density more
favorable to trade.[7]

The Polanie state that emerged between the ninth and tenth
centuries abandoned many of the old tribal centers early in the
process of politogenesis. A centralized confederation of chiefs
was able to aggressively redraw the social map in order to favor
administrative concerns and a centralized military strategy. In
other words, short-term economic concerns were trumped by
politico-military concerns that allowed a new economic paradigm

7   Ludomir R. Lozny, "The Transition to Statehood in Central
     Europe," in *The Early State, its Alternatives and Analogues*, 283.

to be born. The old, abandoned centers had been founded on a spiritual or economic logic, e.g. sacred gathering places and good settlement locations close to well watered fields or fertile pastures. The new settlements established by the Polanie state were fortified administrative-military centers at regular intervals (about every fourteen kilometers).

The new towns displayed a bimodal division: a heavily fortified section for the ruler and nobility, and a moderately fortified section for merchants, artisans, and minor knights. The fact that the nobility reserved for themselves not only buildings of greater monumental status but also greater military effect demonstrates an antagonism not only between the inhabitants of these settlements and outsiders (exploited peasants as well as hostile foreign polities) but also between the middle and upper strata.

The artisans, in fact, were initially prisoners of a sort, forcibly relocated to privileged, central towns that state planners wanted to turn into centers of artisanal production. These towns tended to be the seats of political authority, and the craftspeople made to settle there included war-captives as well as compatriots brought in from their villages or towns of origin.

At a stroke, the emerging class of military administrators galvanized processes of economic production and accumulation, and also monopolized them. Their control over the growth in economic activity allowed them to pay more retainers and field larger armies, as well as to expand their construction works. In all likelihood they regularly invaded their neighbors to "provide a constant growth of labor and keep the positive balance between the growth of population and food production."[8]

A hundred years into this process, "multicomponent forts with monumental architecture, surrounded by a number of open habitations [...] named by the Medieval chronicles as *sedes regni principals*—the seats of royal representatives" appeared at intervals of twenty-five to thirty kilometers, "usually on the long distance trade trails." By the end of the tenth century there were six of these regional capitals, none of which were distinguished as the exclusive seat of the monarch, suggesting that increasing

---

8   Ibid., 285.

centralization still had not overcome some kind of confederal equality among the nobility.[9]

To summarize, a growing population and the interrelated improvements in agricultural and metallurgical techniques, which probably arrived in Central Europe as decentralized (one might say "anarchic") innovations, together with a context of neighborly warfare, provided an opportunity for hierarchical, non-state chiefdoms in Central Europe to develop a state. The pathway, following well-known models practiced by the neighboring Germanic states, involved convincing preexisting nobility and local leaders to centralize their power, first in some form of confederation, to administer construction, production, and warfare. This state-building activity spurred a cycle of accumulation and a paradigm shift in the economic mode of production, seen not only in the quantitative increase in trade and population (outstripping the earlier population increase) and the qualitative improvement in agricultural and metallurgical techniques, but also in the (re)appearance of such significant and game-changing elements as currency.

Significantly, all the chiefdoms and tribes in the region experienced the conditions identified with the first stage (pertaining to the seventh and eighth centuries), and the archaeological record shows that they also increased their participation in trade, fortification construction, and aggressive warfare in the ninth and tenth centuries, but only one of these groups, the Polanie, created a state. Presumably, all of these societies were culturally and economically similar. They had the same material opportunities, and they tolerated the existence of elites; these elites, in turn, applied hierarchical solutions to social problems, increasing their wealth and carrying out aggressive warfare. Still, for politogenesis to occur, something else was needed: an ambitious plan to reorganize society. State-formation was a strategic act of elite will.

The Polanie state was the most proactive force in establishing a new economic mode based on monetization, competitive rather than reciprocal trade, alienated production, noble prerogatives,

9   Ibid., 283–84.

and accumulation. And the new mode of production, always closely administered and monopolized by the emerging state, fueled and financed the political class as they transitioned from proto-state, to early state, to a centralized monarchy. In other words, we have a complex process with demographic, cultural, political, commercial, and technological factors all interrelating simultaneously, but among these multiple threads, the first to develop self-consciousness and a strategic projectuality, the first to become a proactive agent capable of pushing the other threads in a given direction, was the political class that built up a state around themselves.

Confirming the *social war* concept of anarchist theory, the kind of economic accumulation that would eventually give rise to capitalism was originally conceived by the political class as a strategic means for increasing their power, another maneuver in their unifying strategic activity: warfare. In its origins and in its essence, the economy is but one moment in the war the State constantly wages against society.

IX.
All in the Family:
Kinship and Statehood

THROUGHOUT A BROAD SWATH of human history, the accumulation of status was more feasible than the accumulation of material wealth. It is possible that in some, if not many, societies, the family structure evolved to enable the inheritance of status and charisma before it was put in use to facilitate the inheritance of property. In fact, alienable property (the liberal "private property") long postdates familial descent groups, therefore the kind of property passed on by the family would be usufruct property, the right to use a piece of land belonging to the community. The two kinds of inheritance potentially went hand in hand. A high-status family claiming descent from a charismatic, mythologized personality or from the original founders of a community might claim exclusive access to important roles in community rituals, cementing their status, as well as exclusive access to the best of the commons (the best fields or fishing spots, first pick in a harvest), availing themselves of prime opportunities for the most lavish gift-giving, further producing status within the community.

Two persistent examples that have carried over to modern times illustrate how families can function as mechanisms for the accumulation of status. In the Patum festival in Berga, to name just one of the popular festivals that occur in every town, village, and neighborhood throughout Catalunya, many of the most important functions—who bears which mythical animal in the processional dances, who gets to dress up as what—are hereditary. Nowadays, these roles are a mark of pride, but in stateless, non-industrial societies in which spiritual rituals were one of the most important guarantors of social cohesion, acquiring and maintaining such a role was the contemporary equivalent of sitting on a goldmine.

In his magisterial history of the French Revolution, Kropotkin notes the important class division in the rural villages between *citizens* and *inhabitants*. Those who identified as *citizens*, thus projecting themselves into the same class as the burghers or bourgeoisie of the towns and cities (and in all three etymologies, linguistically attaching themselves to the cities), were the better-off farmers who claimed descent from the original founders of the community. These, in their overwhelming majority, favored the alienation—in privatized, individualized lots—of the village commons: the fields, the forests, the pastures and waste lands, that the peasants collectively tended for their subsistence. The others, the *inhabitants*, who were often more numerous, were said to be recent arrivals given permission to settle in the community by the magnanimous citizens, though they may have been living there for generations. They overwhelmingly favored the preservation of the commons.

The relationship here expressed pulls us in two interesting directions. Going back, we can imagine how interested parties in an agricultural society, in which communal relations were predominant and hierarchies had little or no material backing, could produce an important development on the path towards greater hierarchy. Against the ceaseless movements of human history, they could insist that outsiders (wanderers or refugees of war, famine, or political domination) be allowed to settle in the community only if they were granted fewer rights to the commons than the native-born community members. Such a social consensus, even though it would lay the basis for an unprecedented level of inequality, could be easily won in a horizontal society. On the one hand, it appeals to the commonsense notion of "first come, first serve" and takes advantage of the fact that the newcomers are asking a favor (acceptance in the community) and are therefore not in a good position to negotiate the conditions of their acceptance.

Clearly, a community that emphasized solidarity and mutual aid would never be so stingy; unless the stream of newcomers were too great to absorb, they would welcome them to form a part of the community with no strings attached. But a community that did not undertake constant efforts to inculcate feelings of generosity would look on newcomers with misgiving and avarice, while the authoritarian-minded would look for a way to profit from the new arrangement. Again we see how important the cultural values of a society are in determining how it evolves.

In the case of the stingy society, the new proto-caste of dependents would be allowed to work the communal lands, but only if they gave away a part of their produce as an obligatory gift. Additionally, they could be appropriated as the dependents of one or another family, as a way to administer their integration into the community. Such a social structure would not break with the communal economy or enable the accumulation of material wealth, but it would accustom members of the society to inequalities in rights and in quality of living, and it would enable the production of even greater inequalities of status as the big families redistributed a part of the production of their dependents. It would also provide a ready mechanism for the accumulation of wealth (productive dependents) once the communal relation were set aside. All of these features depend on the family structure in order to be realized.

And to digress a moment and trace this relationship forward to the present, we unmask an important fraud in the democratic ideology. Rights, as we know, pertain to adult citizens. We are taught that they are universal, and simultaneously trained to ignore the excluded categories as exceptional, minute, and inconsequential. Immigrants may not enjoy all these rights, but we are meant to think of them as a tiny sector, who, in any case, are on the way to attaining their full inclusion.

In reality, democracy in its origins (as much its mythical origins in Greece and Rome as its institutional origins in England, the United States, and France) has always relied on the exploitation of a substantial underclass. In revolutionary France, the citizens were the well-to-do part of the population. The others, mere inhabitants, were intended to be excluded from the new social contract. In other words, the category of citizen, from the beginning, was intended to be exclusionary, not inclusionary. The fact that it attains a universal aura is only due to the disappearance of that which has been excluded, a process of invisibilization that only intensifies the original exclusion. Such a revelation further affirms the emphasis that anarchist theory places on the marginal as more important than what a society holds to be central in the development of systemic languages, cultures, and logics.[1]

Returning to the question of status and family, we need to work out what kind of family structures enable the accumulation of status, the stratification of society, and the formation of states. We can start by looking at the family structures of resolutely anti-authoritarian societies. They tend to be non-patriarchal, though both matrilocal and patrilocal examples abound.[2] Collective homes, consisting of large extended families,[3] are common among the sedentary, indigenous inhabitants of eastern North America and the Amazon Basin in South America.

---

1   See, for example, Alex Gorrion ("You don't really care for music, do ya?," *The Anvil Review*, July 21, 2011, http://thean-vilreview.org/print/you-dont-really-care-for-music-do-ya/) on the importance of marginalized sectors of the population, immigrants and children, in the creation of language; John McWorter, *Our Magnificent Bastard Tongue: The Untold History of English* (New York: Gotham, 2009) on language; or "Fire Extinguishers and Fire Starters" and more recently "From 15M to Podemos: The Regeneration of Spanish Democracy and the Maligned Promise of Chaos" (Anonymous, *CrimethInc.*, March 3, 2016, http://crimethinc.com/texts/r/podemos/) on anarchist debates about a marginal or central participation in the occupation of Plaça Catalunya, Barcelona.

2   Meaning a married couple goes to live with the woman's family or with the man's family, respectively.

3   As Pierre Clastres noted, these are not strictly "extended families" in the Western sense, containing three generations descended from two common ancestors, but larger groupings in which blood relations might be loose or even fictive. To denote such a grouping, Clastres uses the term *demos*, suggested by Murdock, *Society Against the State*, 58–63.

We can find an exception among the present-day Mapuche. Traditional communities are resolutely anti-authoritarian and as stateless as conditions permit, and they tend to live in separate residences of nuclear families. Bilineal kinship is a common feature, meaning individuals trace their descent and their relations through both the mother and the father (the matriline and the patriline). Within Mapuche communities, there are traditional positions of status, but they do not adhere to kinship lineages nor do they function as hierarchical status. If we only had the accounts of Western observers, we might have assumed the Mapuche to be another primitive hierarchical society ruled over by chiefs, the *longko*, but for the resistance and the preservation of their traditions by the Mapuche themselves. In addition to the *longko*, there are also the *werken*, who play the role of messengers and organizers in community works and in relations between communities; the *machi*, a medicine man or woman; the *lawentuchefe*, who specializes in a knowledge of plants; the *gütamchefe*, who specializes in the skeletal systems of humans and other animals; *pelon*, a diviner; the *weupife*, a community historian; and others.[4] All of these roles bring special recognition and status, but they carry neither coercive authority nor material privileges. In traditional Mapuche communities today, one can observe how being a *longko* or a *werken* above all means having responsibilities and working extra hard for the good of the community. Through a Eurocentric, cratocentric ethnology, we would only be familiar with the figure of the chief, and it would be harder to envision the reciprocal, complementary,

---

4   José Millalén Paillal, "La Sociedad Mapuche Prehispánica: *Kimün*, Arqueología y Etnohistoria," in Pablo Marimán, Sergio Caniuqueo, José Millalén, and Rodrigo Levil, *¡...Escucha, winka...! Cuatro ensayos de Historia Nacional Mapuche y un epílogo sobre el futuro* (Santiago de Chile: LOM Ediciones, 2006), 34. The subsequent observation about responsibilities comes from John Severino, "With Land, Without the State," *theanarchistlibrary.org*, 2010, https://theanarchistlibrary.org/library/john-severino-with-land-without-the-state-anarchy-in -wallmapu.

"circular" ways in which power is shared in anti-authoritarian societies. Though Mapuche family structures may not be the most typical of such societies, the multiplicity and complementarity of power probably is.

In his writings on the various societies of the Amazon Basin, Clastres discusses how these horizontal, anti-authoritarian societies preserve their bilineal tracing of kinship and the separate identity of extended families within a community, as a way to prevent the centralization of the residential community or the emergence of separate lineages and clans (kinship structures associated with greater hierarchy). Adults tend to live in a single community, and they have little contact with the original community of their mother or father (depending on whether they are patrilocal or matrilocal), meaning it would be easy for them to only trace one line of kinship—through the matriline if they are matrilocal and through the patriline if they are patrilocal. Their insistence on a more expansive view of kinship can be read as a method for creating more numerous horizontal ties and preventing the centralization of society in atomized communities or separate lineages.[5]

Referring to the stateless societies of Southeast Asia, James C. Scott describes families that are so expansive and multilinear that many individuals can not only claim kinship with a large number of families and communities, they can even claim multiple ethnicities, a useful resource for peoples who need to assure their survival through horizontal relations, who often have to flee state armies and slave-raiding parties, and who constantly resist state efforts to homogenize potential subjects.

Among nomadic Mbuti communities, Colin Turnbull described the habit of claiming kinship relations with every other member of the community, as well as with neighboring communities, regardless of whether common ancestors or blood relations were a genetic "fact." Traditionally, kinship relations were deliberately ambiguous, all the adults of a community were parents to all the children, and all the children of the same age group were siblings. In fact, the anthropologist reports that the Mbuti got annoyed when he tried to map out a "factual" family tree of the

---

5   Clastres, *Society Against the State*, 62–65.

community to ascertain who, within a Western conception, was related and who was not.[6]

Societies without an anti-authoritarian ethos, we can surmise, treated relations not as an opportunity for everyone's mutual enrichment, but as a resource to be controlled. And for someone to gain power from access to a resource, they first must make that resource artificially scarce. In fact, the whole Western concept of an "objective" kinship based on shared genetic material, or in earlier terms, "blood," is little more than a massive mythical justification for limiting familial relations.

Unilineal descent enables a society to break into distinct lineages or clans, and these lineages can attempt to accumulate status until one lineage wins a privileged position. Referring to the hierarchical Lua in Southeast Asia, Scott writes: "lineages are ranked; they jockey for status; and part of the jockeying rests on claims to superiority based on different, and fabricated, origin myths and genealogies."[7]

Through the unequal accumulation of hereditary status, an authoritarian society can subdivide into multiple ranked lineages, forming a complex hierarchy. With outsiders being given permission to live on the society's territory on the condition that they accept fewer rights, a caste of dependents could also arise, giving even more privileges, status, and economic benefits to the higher-ranked lineages.

But before such a society could sustain state formation, it would need to undergo other transformations. A society accustomed to inequality and with a hierarchical distribution of privileges still has not sunk low enough to legitimize and normalize coercion, organized violence, against the lowest ranked members of society or to break the fundamental idea of reciprocity or the practice of communal or collective property. The society's territory still belongs to everyone, and the status of the highest-ranked lineages still depends on their generosity. If they begin to act in an autocratic way, they could feasibly lose their status and drop in the rankings.

---

6   Colin M. Turnbull, *The Forest People* (New York: Simon & Schuster, 1961).

7   Scott, *The Art of Not Being Governed*, 276.

There exists a critical difference between a ranked society and a stratified society.[8] A ranked society is still, in many ways, a meritocracy. Whatever the criteria for status, the lineages still have to earn it. Ranked status can and does change, and such a hierarchy is too flexible and unstable a base to support the unwieldy weight of a state. A stratified society, on the other hand, posits an essential and therefore an ostensibly unchangeable difference between the different clans or other social groupings, thus creating a stable, layered organization of castes, classes, or orders.[9] Such an arrangement allows the concept of *nobility* to emerge, permitting the permanent division of society into nobles and commoners.

What does such a transformation require? The only possible factor I have been able to identify is warfare. The irreparable division of society can only be achieved on the grave of reciprocity. The only way to break the living connection between members of a community is through cold, calculated murder; only such a level of psychological distance could permit one to forcibly change another's conditions of existence. Permanently dividing society demands the organized spilling of blood and the vanquishing of those populations that will make up the lower orders.

Such a society, in theory, would still practice communal or collective property, though the commoners, as dependents, would be expected to give a part of their produce to the nobles in that distorted, asymmetrical, and coerced version of reciprocity that becomes the basis for the state relationship.

---

8   Morton H. Fried, *The Evolution of Political Society* (New York: Random House, 1967).

9   We can also consider another model of social stratification, as found in capitalist societies. Without strong family groups or cultural cohesiveness within a class—which is to say, within an atomized society—capitalism must allow *individuals* the possibility of social mobility (not every individual, contrary to capitalist dogma, but many individuals). What is essentialized and naturalized in this model are not the social strata themselves (a member of the bourgeoisie, in theory, could end up being a proletarian, and vice versa) but the productive means that generate stratification and inequality.

Now, the nobility must advance in their political organization if they are to achieve state formation, for their ability to exercise coercion and to extend their power beyond a single community or town will probably still be limited.

The lineage competition can provide a solution. A charismatic man from a leading lineage, usually both a skilled military commander, an effective orator, and a lucid organizer, can unite multiple chiefdoms into a single confederation (or, just as often, he can create a position of central leadership within a preexisting confederation). Historically, the most likely outcome of such alliances is dissolution and fragmentation, after or even before the death of the charismatic leader. But if his closest collaborators can succeed in creating an effective court of advisors, dignitaries, and functionaries, that court can assure the institutional transition of power, potentially denoting the transition to statehood.

An effective transition may be aided by, or it may produce, a certain innovation that facilitated many processes of state formation: the further subdivision of the nobility with the emergence of a royal lineage, a family group that the other noble lineages legitimize and consider uniquely endowed to rule the entire society. The innovation of royalty brings new stability to the social hierarchy, potentially ending or at least limiting the continued jockeying for rank and status between the different elite lineages.

European royalty were simply noble families, themselves just the evolution of the warrior class in a tripartite system, who succeeded in uniting a large territory (i.e. one that included multiple less effective chiefs or kings) over multiple generations. Among the nomadic Scythians, the founders of the first "nomadic empire," the clan of the Royal Scyths claimed descent from the most prestigious of the three brothers remembered in legend as the founders of the Scythian tribes. The Royal Scyths not only claimed the best pasture lands, they also furnished the ruling classes in times when the nomads occupied and administered sedentary civilizations they had conquered.

We can call this the **royal court state**. This model brings us to the cusp of a new category, primary state formation, processes of politogenesis that societies underwent without the guidance or pressure of any preexisting state. The Aryan states in the Indian subcontinent display many characteristics of this model, though it is uncertain if those qualify as primary states or if the Aryans were familiar with the states that had already formed farther west. Given the transformative function of warfare within this model and the expediency of conquering other populations to create underclasses, the royal court state has much in common with the conquest state, already discussed. However, the former tends to be a slower, more fragmented and halting process than the latter. In the case of the conquest state, the warrior class that constitutes the politogen has already received some kind of cultural tutelage from a preexisting state, which allows them to erect their own state more quickly.

The service of an effective warrior class is not the only way a dominant lineage can cement its power. One important source of status in the ranking competition is claimed descent from famous ancestors. These ancestors can be entirely mythical figures or real people whose achievements take on added symbolic importance after their deaths, such as forefathers of the lineage, founders of cities, tamers of wilderness, builders of irrigation or monuments, deliverers from slavery or hardship, conquerors of territory, vanquishers of enemies. They are nearly always men, given that as far as we know, all states and proto-states have arisen from patriarchal societies.

Ancestor worship creates an important circuit in the concentration of power. To increase its own prestige, a lineage that has been able to claim a certain ancestor will intensify their worship of that ancestor, which also means they must make the ancestor ever more worshipable. The result augments both the lineage and the ancestor. It seems almost inevitable that the ancestors eventually attain divinity, either as a god's favorite mortal, the son of a god, or a god in his own right. It is highly plausible that in at least some pathways of social evolution, the very concept of gods is a civilization effect and a relatively recent invention, resulting from the multigenerational ritual exaggeration surrounding famous ancestors.

Once the prestigious ancestors become divine, the lineage that claims them will need highly specialized, elaborate rituals to maintain their monopoly. And this almost certainly will require specialized priests to honor the ancestors, maintain their favor, and secure their blessings. Powerful ancestors can be credited with bringing rain, fertility, good fortune in trade and warfare, and protection from enemies.

The necessary centralization of power for state formation can be achieved when one lineage and one ancestor (or a limited group of ancestors) easily leads the rankings, and when the male head of that lineage becomes a supreme ruler by transforming into some kind of symbolic reincarnation or exclusive link to the divine ancestor. The society itself may not have made the transition from ranking to stratification, but through the monopolization of a divine ancestor, the god-king and his court of priest helpers have created another impermeable social division: between the divine and the profane. This is the **holy father state**.

It is unclear to what extent the holy father state and the royal court state constitute separate models. Though processes of warfare and the monopolization of ancestor worship might vary in their relative importance, in all the well documented examples I am aware of—such as the Congo basin states, the early Mayan states, and the Shang and Zhou states in ancient China—religion and warfare both played fundamental roles.

In the Congo basin states, "While the tombs of the paramounts were the objects of special reverence, the priests-keepers of 'king's tombs' were among the most important courtiers."[10] Symmetrical to the hierarchy of priests and spiritual courtiers who attend to the god-king, a hierarchy evolves among the divine ancestors and natural spirits, such that the supreme divinity gains his own court that serves to naturalize the earthly political institution. The result is a simultaneously mystical and bureaucratic pantheon and social apparatus that transforms power from charismatic, ceremonial performances into a distributive mechanism that successfully delinks power from a set of localized and limited familial relations and binds it to an expansive, mobile, and monopolized claim to the divine. It is expansive and mobile because a revered ancestor has an exclusive relationship

10   L'vova, "The Formation and Development of States in the Congo Basin," 293.

to his descendants, whereas an ancestor-turned-god can exercise supremacy and therefore also serve the symbolic half of domination over people of other lineages or other societies. The claim is monopolized because a common person can no longer access it by simply calling on their ancestors, as the king-priest and lesser priests mediate access to the tombs, relics, and energies of the ancestor spirits.

In the Mayan states, where the elite ideology was based on a cyclical view of time,

> all the mythological events [...] had their exact dates [...] organically included into the history of the ruling dynasty [...] The key figure which united the myth and history was the ruler. In the ideal model it was the supreme ruler which represented all the polity and as the eldest person in the eldest lineage kept the relations between this world and the supernatural one, between ancestors and the living.[11]

Within this new apparatus, the ruler himself is captive to the intensified symbolic relationships:

> A "king-priest" [among the early states of the Congo basin] was believed to be closely connected with the forces of nature and to influence the good things of life. His mode of life was controlled by means of a number of special taboos. Such a sacred ruler must also be physically perfect. There were special trials for his health. When he was found unhealthy during the trial, ritual killing was used.[12]

And in ancient China, Richard Baum writes:

> Though he was *ex officio* Son of Heaven, the king nevertheless had to constantly demonstrate, affirm, and renew

11   Dmitri D. Beliaev, "Classic Lowland Maya (AD 250–900)" in *Civilizational Models of Politogenesis*, 135.

12   L'vova, "The Formation and Development of States in the Congo Basin," 233.

his own charisma. And if, in spite of his conscientious attention to duty, the rivers overflowed their dikes or the rains failed to fall, this was *prima facie* evidence that the emperor lacked the charismatic qualities demanded by Heaven. In such cases the emperor was expected to perform public penitence for his failings. In extreme cases [..."failure to perform appropriate sacrifices" or "excessive taxation or persistent neglect of irrigation works"...] the Son of Heaven might even forfeit his claim [...] Such forfeiture carried with it the implied "legitimate" right to rebel against—and overthrow—a reigning monarch.[13]

Another limit to the intensive production of spiritual power is described by Max Weber. Not only do spiritual rituals lose their effect over time (paralleling the modern phenomenon of saturation that causes advertisers to lose so much sleep), but, according to Weber, "charismatic authority may be said to exist only in the process of originating. It cannot remain stable, but becomes either traditionalized or rationalized, or a combination of both."[14] A state that did not wisely reinvest its spiritual capital in military, administrative, and infrastructural capital, would most likely collapse. The Chinese state of the Shang and Zhou dynasties pursued aggressive military and administrative expansions, and during the Warring States period, Confucian scholars secularized what had been an intensely religious conception of power. Mencius conceived the vital Mandate of Heaven in almost entirely secular terms: divine intervention was limited to the investiture of new rulers, who simply had to renew their charisma through good governance.

Hierarchical kinship structures attached to the monopolization of spirituality, as seen in the model of the holy father

13   Richard Baum, "Ritual and Rationality: Religious Roots of the Bureaucratic State in Ancient China" in *The Early State, Its Alternatives and Analogue*, 199.

14   Max Weber, *The Theory of Social and Economic Organization* (New York: The Free Press, 1947), 364, quoted in Baum, "Ritual and Rationality," 205. Data in the rest of the paragraph is from Baum, "Ritual and Rationality," 205–206.

state, provide a well trodden path to politogenesis. Paradoxically, hierarchical kinship structures also constitute a barrier.[15] We have already looked at examples of states forming in societies with weak kinship organization, such as the Greek city-states, Rome, and the Germanic states. One of the characteristics typical of states is a territorial rather than familial basis for organization. Territory can be more easily used to delimit and unify a society when the state or proto-state results from conquest, most frequently in the case of nomadic groups that take over sedentary societies. But when a stratification process is entirely endogenous, arising from a society's own kinship structures, family-based ties often prevent the institutional loyalties that states need to function. Often, it is clan elites who foil the designs of state-making elites.

Would-be state-makers need to rupture, at least in part, with the kinship logic so that their claims of sovereignty and authority transcend familial relations and can be extended to a potentially infinite pool of subjects. They also need to use their power to override or supplant the community-level relations of reciprocity that typically remain intact through the reign of chiefdoms and other non-state hierarchies. Weakening community forms of existence can provoke resistance that might spell disaster for the fledgling state, but failing to do so will often lead it to disintegrate back into a non-state society with pronounced hierarchies but only weak forms of coercion and centralized organization. This seems to have been the case with many early states in the Near East in the third and second centuries BCE.[16]

Another sort of collapse related to the limitations of power based in kinship organization occurred in China with the expansion of the Shang and Zhou dynasties. Familial relations were important in the organization of power even before the Shang dynasty. Already in the late neolithic period (ca. 2000 BCE), proto-Chinese cultures used family names (a statist invention that did not reach the part of Europe my patriline hails from until the

---

15   Bondarenko, "Kinship, Territoriality and the Early State Lower Limit," 21.

16   Ibid., 25.

early-nineteenth century CE).[17] At this time, the Longshan culture flourished in what is now northern and central China. Technologically similar, at a political level, Longshan constituted multiple cultural variants. Warfare seems to have been common between polities, which tended to be grouped together in economically integrated units of larger and smaller settlements. Some of these polities were stratified, with up to three social classes, as at the large walled settlement of Taosi (three hundred hectares in area). The relatively egalitarian Shangdong settlements contained multiple regional centers engaged in production and trade in pottery, jade, textiles, stone tools, fermented beverages, and agriculture.

Though economic stratification and settlement integration varied, these polities can generally be described as "military democracies" with councils of lineage chiefs, popular assemblies, and a supreme military leader who may have been chosen by the chiefs.[18]

The Longshan sites declined dramatically in population around 1900 BCE, shortly before the spread of bronze technology. The strongest polity to arise in the aftermath of this collapse was the Erlitou culture, which probably corresponds to the Xia dynasty referred to in subsequent Shang texts. The Erlitou, which developed from the Wangwang III subset of the Longshan culture, constructed a city of up to thirty-thousand residents on the Yi river, erected multiple palaces, and monopolized bronze smelting in the region. Around the time of urbanization (one hundred years into the culture), it is feasible that a dominant lineage secured a royal status and consolidated its rule over

---

17 In my father's family's case, the event was the conquest of northern Netherlands by Napoleonic France. Previously, the farmers of the Groningen region only used first names. Well aware that the purpose of last names was social control, most obviously taxation, they registered a faint protest in their choice of surname: *Penniless*. In the even more rural province of Friesland, scatological and other joke names were a common choice by the peasants.

18 Jianping Yi, "Non-Autocracy in Pre-Qin China," in *Social Evolution and History*, 224–25.

other hierarchically ranked lineages. From 1900 to 1500 BCE, the Erlitou culture existed somewhere on the cusp of statehood, until its quick decline with the establishment of the Erligang city at Zhengzhou, and the rise of the Shang dynasty; however, especially if the documentary account is correct, the Erlitou culture was already defeated and subordinated to the Shang dynasty in 1600 BCE, when King Tang ordered the construction of the city Yanshi just six kilometers from the Erlitou capital.

In any case, the Erligang culture and the corresponding Shang dynasty are well known to have organized on the basis of hierarchically ordered kinship lineages that centralized and monopolized access to divine rites. The kinship system was instrumental to the Shang state's territorial expansion. Younger male relatives of the dominant lineage or inferior elite lineages (e.g. lineages said to be descended from younger brothers of the mythical ancestor-king, or younger brothers from subsequent kings in the dominant line) would be sent out from the royal capital to found new settlements as a way to secure military frontiers, expand agricultural production, and encourage population growth. Each of these elite males, sent out with blessings from the king and "ritual paraphernalia and ceremonial regalia," would become the founder not only of a new town but also a new branch of the royal lineage.

> In his new settlement, the royal benefice holder would erect an ancestral temple, in which his own lineage tablet would eventually be placed as a founder of a branch clan. In time, new segments would hive off from this branch, forming secondary (and then tertiary) territorial sublineages which were ranked in a sequential hierarchy of descending political and ritual statuses. In this manner, the system of Shang patrimonial benefices—the earliest known form of institutionalized territorial governance in China—reflected gradations of kinship status within a segmented royal lineage, gradations which had themselves been patterned in the first instance after the patriarchy of ancestral spirits.[19]

---

19   Baum, "Ritual and Rationality," 209.

But when military successes allowed the Shang state and the Zhou dynasty that followed it to continue expanding, this kinship system of territorial administration became "diluted" and "the king was unable personally to conduct all the manifold ceremonial rituals that, as Son of Heaven, he was called upon to perform in each of the central state's territorial domains." Ever more degrees of authority had to be delegated to elites who symbolically were inferior but in practice came to exercise supreme power. Additionally, the strategic interests of territorial expansion convinced the king to grant hereditary administrative mandates to unrelated but allied tribes on the periphery who performed military service and swore fealty.

Eventually, growth of the state led to a feudal form of organization in the Zhou period, with hereditary enfeoffment granted to lesser nobles who promised obedience. Unsurprisingly, such a system could not support a strong centralized power, and the unified state disintegrated, giving rise to an efficient empire only after the centuries-long Warring States period. Curiously, though a kinship-based system of state power had seen its collapse in that period of internecine conflict between embattled mini-states struggling "for imperial supremacy, the legitimizing principle of ancestral lineage became so significant as to provide full-time employment for a bevy of itinerant scholar-genealogists."[20] During the Warring States period, "Confucian ideologists" laid the groundwork for the subsequent Han empire by fusing "the three worlds of ancestral spirits, kinship groups, and the imperial bureaucracy into a single, integrated system of hierarchical social and political authority."[21]

Subsequently, lines of command were stronger and the monarch could exercise despotic rule, whereas in the Shang dynasty the king could only rule by consulting other priests or the heads of the clans, and in Zhou times the king had to seek the counsel of the Guoren and the Daifu, a popular assembly and a council of elite elders, respectively.[22]

---

20   Ibid., 210.

21   Ibid., 211.

22   Yi, "Non-Autocracy in Pre-Qin China," 229.

Rulers in the Mayan civilization also used genealogies, as well as titles, claims of divinity, and special forms of clothing and headdresses to assert their legitimacy and compete for status relative to one another. The basis for social organization in Classic Maya were hierarchical communities of three to six nuclear families with a common origin, led by the head of the "eldest" family, who had the privilege of polygamy and monopolized the ancestor cult. Around the seventh and eighth centuries CE, the Maya changed from a system of vassal kings (*yahaw*) ruling subordinate but semi-autonomous kingdoms in obedience to a divine supreme ruler, to a system of provincial lords (*sahal*) controlled directly by the supreme ruler. Multiple such early states existed across the Mayan cultural area, competing for dominance and unifying through conquest.[23]

The Polynesian societies of the Pacific provide other histories of state formation in which kinship lineages exercise a key function. The spread of the proto-Polynesian culture across many hundreds of islands at diverse latitudes, from tiny to large, isolated atolls and extensive archipelagos, each of them a laboratory of social evolution, presents a unique theoretical opportunity (although the academic fetish of phenomena *in isolation* is perhaps out of touch with how things work in the living world, especially if the mythical-scientific belief that a complex system can be understood by understanding its separate components is not entirely accurate). The proto-Polynesian culture that spread to all these islands included a hierarchical social organization led by chiefs, divided by lineages, and fixed genealogically.

It would be an elucidating field for further research, but with the limited data I have access to, it seems that Polynesians developed states on any island that was large enough. This data set, it must be cautioned, does not give us any absolute lower size-limit for politogenesis. The Polynesian pathway for state formation was particular, reflecting one strategy of hierarchical social organization and not any universal human truths. What would be interesting to confirm is whether one common cultural

---

23   Beliaev, "Classic Lowland Maya (AD 250–900)," 136–38.

model *always* evolved into a state, given a land base able to support a sufficient population for complex political hierarchies; what alternatives developed on islands that could not support a large population; and under what conditions, if any, horizontal or non-authoritarian social forms triumphed (for example, on small and isolated islands that could not engage in competitive warfare or cater to chiefly ambitions, and therefore had to re-center cooperative and egalitarian values).

The Hawaiian Islands, the largest population and the most isolated archipelago within the Polynesian diaspora, presents a good case study for state formation through kinship hierarchies. The islands were settled sometime around 400 CE by a flotilla of canoes loaded down with pigs, dogs, and chickens; domesticated plants like "taro, sweet potato, sugarcane, and bananas, and a full assortment of seeds, nuts, and cuttings for coconut, candlenut, medical plants, and fiber plants that would be encouraged to go feral."[24] As their "transported environment" took root, the new Hawaiians lived largely off of seafood and the flightless birds that populated the islands. Then they dedicated themselves to cultivation, clearing the fertile lowlands and gradually augmenting their population, which by 800 CE numbered in the thousands (at European contact in 1778, it was estimated at 240,000–400,000). Population grew rapidly between 1200 and 1500 CE, when it peaked. Around 1400 CE, settlers began moving upland, clearing forests on steep mountainsides to open up new territory for planting. The new cultivation did not last. Erosion carried the mountain soil down to the refertilized lowlands, highland cultivation was partially abandoned, and population growth stabilized.

Prior to 1400, societies on the islands were materially egalitarian, with little differentiation in wealth. Chiefs probably had to work to feed themselves, same as everyone else. But in the first two centuries of rapid population growth, "chiefdoms expanded in scale," and in the Consolidation Period (1400–1500 CE), mutually hostile regional chiefdoms divided some of the

---

24   Timothy K. Earle, "Hawaiian Islands (AD 800–1824)" in *Civilizational Models of Politogenesis*, 77.

islands, such as Maui and Hawai'i. Despite the shortage of arable land, uninhabited buffer zones sprang up between them, a consequence of warfare. Also in the fifteenth century, just as chiefly residences "with elaborate terraces and enclosing walls" appeared, there was a "dramatic" increase in the "construction of religious monuments."[25] After 1500, when the population stabilized, irrigation and other productive infrastructures were expanded and intensified. At this point, political structures on the archipelago could be classified as states, though others (e.g. Earle) consider them very large complex chiefdoms. In any case, the technological reorganization of Hawaiian society was subsequent to the political transformation that took place between 1400 and 1500.

I would hypothesize that the flight to the mountains seen around 1400 was both a demographic effect and a state effect. Those with least status and least access to land would have comprised the refugees who headed upland to begin the arduous task of clearing forests and planting new gardens. But they also would have been people who wanted to gain distance from the increasing arrogance, exploitation, and warfare of the chiefs. These were probably free settlements, since at that time the chiefs likely lacked coercive authority or ownership over unsettled forests.

Flight and abandonment are some of the most common strategies of resistance against emerging states, and each has its analogue in modern states, which are now global and cannot be fled in the proper sense (analogues include emigration to less authoritarian states, clandestinity, and drop-out culture or other forms of voluntary marginality). These strategies are among the easiest, but they are not the most effective at stopping the rise of authority, and today humanity as a whole is paying the price for social rebels' historic preference for the easy way out. In the Hawaiian Islands, abandonment probably constituted an extremely useful release valve at a time when chiefly authority would have been particularly unstable. The runaways evidently lacked erosion-resistant horticultural techniques (such as those perfected by the stateless societies in the New Guinea

---

25   Ibid., 80.

highlands).[26] When they lost their gardens to erosion, they had to go back to the lowland settlements, which ironically had been refertilized by the eroded mountain soil, and this time they had no leverage to protest growing authoritarianism but presumably had to request permission for access to land, accepting the new property regime that may have come into force around that time. After that point, the basis of power was military effectiveness and access to land, and Hawaiian chiefs did not have to expend as much effort in symbolic production and the building of monuments, though ceremonial performances continued to hold great importance.

Within Hawaiian society, "Ranking is based on the measured distance from the senior line, whereby the highest ranked individual is the eldest son in the direct line of eldest sons."[27] The majority of the population was made up of commoners who were prohibited from keeping genealogies, which was a privilege of the chiefs, now considered distinct as members of a noble bloodline. In practice, chiefs competed for rank and position relative to the paramount ruler, though "in theory, a chief's genealogical distance from the paramount determined rights to an office."[28] A chief governed each community. Other chiefs attended to the paramount ruler, fought in his retinue, or managed the paramount's lands and labor projects, also organizing the feasts with which laborers were rewarded when work was done.

Land was divided between that belonging to the chiefs and subsistence plots conceded to the commoners. All land was considered to belong to the supreme ruler; in effect, commoners had to periodically work the chiefs' lands and give annual goods to the paramount in exchange for rights to subsistence plots. Surpluses derived from the new property system were used to feed not only the chiefs but also the chiefs' retainers: artisans, warriors, and priests. The paramount ruler, for his part, had the privilege and

---

26   For more on the New Guinea highlanders or modern-day drop-out societies, see Gelderloos, *Anarchy Works*, particularly the chapter on technology.

27   Earle, "Hawaiian Islands," 79.

28   Ibid., 74.

obligation of representing the god Lono, and he had to periodically visit local community shrines and make charismatic performances on monumental stages.

Between 1500 and 1650, dominant rulers on Maui and on Hawai'i unified their respective islands through military conquest. Later, these two islands "fought repeatedly with each other in an attempt to fashion inter-island politics," a project the Hawaiian monarch continued successfully with access to European weapons and ships.[29] We can hypothesize that if colonization by the United States had not interrupted this process, state power would have soon disintegrated and then reorganized in the Hawaiian Islands, as kinship hierarchies proved insufficient to project centralized political power across multiple islands.

The Aryan peoples who migrated into the Indian subcontinent in the centuries after the decline of the Indus Valley civilization provide an interesting example of caste structures giving rise to a proto-state hierarchy, with military conquest constituting something of a catalyst. Their process shows elements of both the conquest state and the royal court state.

The Aryans arrived as stateless, semi-nomadic herders, their livestock consisting primarily of cows. They wandered or lived in villages, and did not practice agriculture or build cities. Before their migration they were no doubt influenced by state effects, with warfare and slave-raiding from the state formation process in Mesopotamia having far-reaching consequences, but it is unknown if they had any firsthand knowledge of states. In any case they had not received any detailed tutelage in statecraft, which would make them atypical among conquest states.

In a tripartite division typical of the Indo-Europeans, which as we have seen also left its mark on state formation in the European subcontinent, Aryan society was divided into warriors, priests, and laborers. The latter included herders and craftspeople, such as copper or bronze smiths, pottery makers, carpenters, and weavers. Rather than constituting the bottom of a hierarchy, the laborers were one of three complementary pillars. Some of them were highly honored, such as the smiths or the carpenters,

---

29   Ibid., 80.

who made chariots and later plows.[30] Before the emergence of the caste system, professions were not hereditary and there was no taboo on mixing; at this point it seems that Aryan family structures were not divided into hierarchical lineages. If this was in fact the case, it shows that there are multiple pathways for the evolution of castes (out of professional divisions or out of kinship and clan divisions), just as there are multiple pathways for the evolution of states.

The Aryan tribes had an elected chief or king, but power remained with two tribal assemblies, the *sabha*, which was the council of the elders, and the *samiti* or general assembly. Some tribes had only these two assemblies, and no elected monarch. The tribes were bellicose and, if not patriarchal, patrilocal (with women joining the families of their husbands). The chief was primarily a war leader. Early wars basically consisted of cattle-raiding and related disputes, or aggressive takeovers of territory from the indigenous inhabitants.

The Aryans gradually adopted agriculture, which would have already been well known in the plains and the Ganges River Valley where they settled. Their priests composed the Vedas, which depict their spiritual universe, record histories of gods and of Aryan wars with neighboring societies, explain rituals, and preserve mantras. They were first recorded orally, starting around 1700 BCE, and written down at the end of the millennium.

The Aryans warred with the Dasas and the Panis, the indigenous inhabitants of their new territory. The former, they eventually incorporated as slaves, turning their tripartite labor division into a caste system. The Aryans felt a well documented contempt for the darker-skinned indigenous inhabitants, and promoted taboos against intermarriage. In fact, "the Sanskrit word for caste, *varna*, actually means color."[31]

It might be important to note that there was nothing inevitable about this hierarchical development. We can contrast the Aryan example with that of the Bini, mentioned in Chapter VII,

---

30   Romila Thapar, *A History of India*, Vol. I. (New York: Penguin Books, 1966).

31   Ibid., 38.

who, even though they were militarily superior to the Efa who
preceded them in the territory that they took as their home, promoted an ethos of coexistence and mixing.

Initially, the caste system was arranged as follows: the *Kshatriyas* were warriors and aristocracy; the *Brahmans* were priests;
the *Vashiyas* were cultivators; and the *Shudras* were Dasas and
mixed race people. Each caste also allows for a good deal of internal hierarchy (between a young, unproven warrior and an elder of
an aristocratic family; between an unimportant village priest and
a priest who advises the king; between a landless peasant and an
honored craftsperson; between pure Dasas and people with one
Aryan parent).

Gradually, the Vashiyas became traders and landowners and
the Shudras moved up to become cultivators. This allowed new
conquered ethnic groups to assume a place at the bottom of the
caste system.

With sedentary agriculture and political expansion (tribes
growing, uniting, or taking slaves) the king, helped by the
priests, became divine and then hereditary. The important role
of the priests in legitimating the authority of the chief aristo-
crat/warrior would play a key role in altering the caste hierarchy and also separating the monarch from the Kshatriya caste he
had come from, creating a royal family separate from the general
nobility. This shows a curious evolution in which the military
power of the warrior caste declines in relative importance, and a
priest class bestows divinity on a king, without the king having
to be a priest himself. Ancestor worship was important among
the Aryans, as were genealogies, but lineages did not evolve into
castes, or ancestors into gods, as in the holy father state. Rather,
in an effective campaign of class war, the Brahmans developed
the tools to augment their power in a changing environment,
to make themselves indispensable to the project of social control, and to divide the caste that had stood above them through
strategic alliances. In proto-state Roman society, by contrast,
which bears fundamental organizational and cultural similarities to Aryan society, the priests were never so dynamic, and
it was the warriors who became the architects of the new state.
Among the Aryans, the Brahmans also played the decisive role

in increasing patriarchy in Aryan society, a vital accompaniment to state formation.

At this point, the structure of the Aryan polity was as follows:

> The tribal kingdom (*rashtra*) contained tribes (*jana*), tribal units (*vish*), and villages (*grama*). The nucleus was the family (*kula*) with the eldest male member as its head (*kulapa*). The king was assisted by a court of the elders of the tribe and by the village headmen. Even closer to him were two officers: the *purohita* or chief priest, who combined the function of priest, astrologer, and adviser; and the *senani* or military commander.[32]

The royal court also contained spies, messengers, and later the royal charioteer, treasurer, steward, and superintendent of dicing—gambling being very important to the Aryans. As noted above, once the chief became a divine royal figure, he no longer served as the military commander, that role having been specialized and subordinated to him.

Aryan society at the local level had still not undergone such dramatic changes. The *grama* was originally a grouping of three generations of related families, in which brothers lived together accompanied by their wives and children. With sedentary living and agriculture, the grama grew to encompass more families. Land was the communal property of the entire village, though over time a part of the land came to be the property of the chief, who hired out laborers to work his share. "The house was a large all-inclusive structure with family and animals living under the same roof."[33] The hearth, which was always kept burning, was important economically and symbolically.

Before the emergence of the state, marriages were freely chosen, and women enjoyed a decent status. Female deities tended to lack importance, though some of the most important deities were hermaphroditic.

---

32   Ibid., 37.
33   Ibid., 40, 41.

Initially, the Aryan religious pantheon was similar to the general Indo-European archetype. The Indus Valley civilization probably left an important mark, as seen in the popular worship of the Mother Goddess, the Bull, the Horned Deity, and sacred trees, elements that later worked their way into Hindu worship. On the other hand, "the more abstract brahman system of belief, founded on the Vedas, appealed to a limited few."[34] In other words, there was an elite religion and a popular religion. It was the former that would become the state religion, Hinduism.

Animal sacrifice, encouraged by the Brahmans, came to play a vital role in religious life, winning the support of the economic elite, given that those who had the most cattle were the ones who could acquire the most spiritual capital. It is no surprise, then, that the heterodox Buddhists later did away with sacrifices.

Before the caste system opened the door to state formation, Aryan law was purely customary, with disputes mediated by elders or leaders, and reconciled with reparations (i.e. the payment of cows), even in cases of murder. The death penalty came later, as did codified laws in which people were punished differently according to their caste. Subsequently, "Judicial procedure was extremely elaborate."[35]

Codified and differentiated (unequal) laws were also the fundamental features of Hammurabi's law code (1754 BCE). In reflecting on the formation of the modern state—a more relevant problem for today's readers—it is worth noting that the liberal ideology demands "equality before the law" but keeps a complicit silence regarding the codification of law, even though written law (as opposed to community mediation) signifies the professionalization of justice and an authoritarian transformation of power relations at least as extreme as the results of differentiated law. There may no longer be one law for slaves, another law for masters, but the liberal principal of equal yet codified law is still a farce. Democratic formalism, combined with a capitalist economy, allows extreme judicial differentiation to exist

34   Ibid., 43.
35   Ibid., 52.

side by side with an ideology of equality. As Anatole France wrote, "In its majestic equality, the law forbids rich and poor alike to sleep under bridges, beg in the streets, and steal loaves of bread." Private property and states inevitably produce social inequality, whereas the codification of law professionalizes the reproduction of morality and excludes communities from conflict resolution, ensuring the reproduction of hierarchy through authoritarian punishment regimes. However, philosophers, historians, researchers, and educators continuously subject us to the insincerely naïve belief that writing is an unqualified good.

In the emerging monarchies on the Ganges plain, the Brahmans became the top caste, overtaking the Kshatriyas and authoring the new ideological system in alliance with the king. The key role of the priests becomes evident if we compare the monarchies that constituted early states with the largely stateless "republics" of the highlands. In the latter, the Kshatriyas remained the dominant caste.

The republics and monarchies that arose in north India before 600 BCE comprised single tribes or tribal confederations. The republics retained the idea of organization by assembly, and preserved more tribal customs in general. These republics were frequently founded by illegitimate or displaced members of royal lineages from neighboring states. At least, that is the version preserved in their mythical histories, demonstrating a curious relationship with the symbolic value of the monarchies. On the one hand they ascribed to the same status symbols, like royalty, and on the other hand they seemed to broadcast a perverse adulteration or a defiance of the monarchical values: their semi-mythical founders were not eldest sons but bastards and black sheep.

The republics tended to have a capital where the representatives of the tribes and heads of family would meet in assembly, presided over by the *raja*, who was chosen from among the representatives. In the case of the Vriji confederacy the tribes retained independent and equal status. They had an administration by officials such as a treasurer, assistants to the chief or raja, and a military commander. Emerging towns specialized in specific crafts, like pottery, or they became trading centers.

Kshatriyas lived in the towns and "probably encouraged the activities of the artisans."[36]

The Aryan republics tolerated unorthodox views, as seen in the subsequent appearance of Buddhism and Jainism; the founders of both those cults came from republican tribes, and they spread most quickly in the republican areas. Buddhists in particular supported the republics by replacing the Hindu myth of the divine origin of states with the myth of the social contract.

Power-holders within the tribes also defended the republican form of organization with its weaker hierarchies, whereas the monarchies had to subvert tribal loyalty and replace it with caste loyalty and loyalty to the monarch. The tribal republics lasted until the fourth century CE. Demonstrating the multi-lineal nature of social evolution, some monarchies like Kamboja morphed into republics, though in the Ganges plain the monarchies remained predominant.[37]

Before 500 BCE, four polities (three monarchies and the stateless Vriji confederacy) competed for control of the Ganges plain, controlling river traffic, fighting for access to trade with east India and Burma. By then, kingship was hereditary among the monarchies, royal families of different states intermarried, and the states that would prove victorious emphasized efficient administration with handpicked ministers (as opposed to hereditary ministers). Village headmen collected and delivered taxes. Most land was communal, worked by Shudras. Villages were stockaded, surrounded by fields and pastures. Beyond was forest and wasteland, and only the king could sanction the clearing of new lands. His prerogative was to receive one-sixth of their produce. The "untouchables" came into existence in this period; they were probably former hunter-gatherers who were partially assimilated and forced to live by rush-weaving or hunting, both of which were disparaged activities within the dominant culture.

Between 493 and 461 BCE, Magadha became preeminent on the Ganges plain, dominating neighboring states through warfare. The stateless Vriji confederacy was able to resist the

---

36   Ibid.
37   Ibid., 53.

longest: sixteen years. Once that fell, Magadha monopolized regional trade. A later ruling dynasty of Magadha, the Nandas, in power until 321 BCE, were the ones to amass an army so huge that they dissuaded Alexander of Macedonia from continuing his conquests past Punjab. Interestingly, the first Nanda was of Shudra origin, though his ascension to power only solidified— rather than upset—the caste system. In this history we can see another similarity between the caste state and the democratic modern state, suggesting (and not for the first time in our study) the contours of a logic of power capable of transcending the structural and ideological limitations it develops to express itself.

X.
Building the Walls Higher:
From Raiding to Warfare

"THE ACCUMULATION OF POPULATION by war and slave-raiding is often seen as the origin of the social hierarchy and centralization typical of the earliest states."[1] We have already looked at the process of militarization as a motor of state-formation, but I think it is also necessary to underscore that the role of warfare can be overstated. Randolph Bourne was not exaggerating when he said "war is the health of the state."[2] Nonetheless, warfare does not necessitate state formation and states do not need to favor military over non-military expansion.

The conquest state model that has cropped up so frequently in this study is, let's not forget, a model of secondary state formation and not primary state formation. The militaristic Indo-European warrior brotherhoods—whose legacy can be seen in multiple Aryan, Mediterranean, and Germanic states—may have been a consequence of the resistance of stateless societies to the slave-raiding and territorial conquests of the early states of Mesopotamia, as Fredy Perlman argues.[3] In the royal court and holy father states, warfare can play an accessory role as a catalyst in a process that is decidedly non-militaristic. In the **sacred commerce states** of Mesopotamia, which will be discussed in the next chapter, warfare made its decisive appearance not at the beginning but at an intermediate stage of politogenesis.

---

1   R.L. Carneiro, "A Theory of the Origin of the State," *Science* No. 169 (1970): 733–38, cited in Scott, *The Art of Not Being Governed*, 67.

2   Randolph Bourne, *The State*, 1918, http://www.antiwar.com/bourne.php (accessed October 13, 2016).

3   Fredy Perlman, *Against His-story, Against Leviathan* (Detroit: Black and Red, 1983), 66–68.

It might be fair to claim that a statist worldview traditionally privileges essentialism and the symbolic stability that accompanies it. States often tend towards conservatism and seek stability, but they are driven to develop and progress by the adversity they provoke.

Within a stateless system of sedentary settlements, where a hierarchical, patriarchal, and bellicose culture predominates, raiding and eventually warfare can provide a pathway for politogenesis: the **raider state**. In a mutually reinforcing cycle of militarization, neighboring communities raid one another to steal resources, capture slaves, and force weaker villages to pay tribute and pledge obedience. Over time, elites impose more efficient means of economic exploitation in order to improve their town's defenses, to sustain a larger warrior class, and to subsidize war-oriented technologies. To repeat an important point, state organization does not inherently give a society a military advantage; in fact decentralized societies tend to be the most effective at resisting invasion and conquest. But where an autochthonous elite already holds power, they will use situations of warfare to enact "security programs" that enhance their own power first and foremost, whether they are a stone-tool-using society in the Yucatan in 1000 CE or a nuclear society in North America in the twenty-first century.

Instead of protecting them, such security programs tend to put the population in even more danger, but as long as they believe the hype and don't notice that it's the fox who is guarding the henhouse, the policy will be successful. Just look at the anti-terrorism wars of Bush and Blair beginning in 2001: they exposed the populations of Europe and the United States to a huge increase in terrorist attacks, but rather than simply killing their leaders and being done with the whole circus, as reasonable people have done countless times throughout history, they were convinced to accept even more security measures and more supposedly defensive wars. States have been using the same trick for at least four thousand years.

Among stateless societies, constant raiding does not necessarily create greater levels of hierarchy. The indigenous inhabitants of the Amazon basin—a complex range of sedentary and nomadic societies of multiple ethno-linguistic groups, some living in tiny bands and others in huge villages, and nearly all of them resolutely stateless—were noted for their near-constant warfare. However, their practice of warfare, which was also complemented by a less visible practice of intermarriage and friendly trade, helped preserve the independence of individual communities and prevented state formation. Once again, the specific cultural values reproduced by a society—the *intentions* and the *projectuality* of its political actors—can cause the same situation to manifest in processes of state formation or state resistance.

The Aryan settlements of northern India might have given us an example of the raider state; certainly dynamics of a bellicose feedback loop established stronger hierarchies in a then-stateless society, but the Brahmans' ambitious use of the emergent caste system caused politogenesis in India to take a different path. A process of mutual hostility clearly transformed and accelerated the process of state formation in Mesopotamia, fitting Spencer and Redmond's "Rival Polity Model" in which conflict between neighboring societies spurs politogenesis; however, the intensification of warfare came after the emergence of multiple city-states following a religious pathway of development. Instead, we can turn to the early Zapotec state for our example.

The Zapotec state, with its capital at Monte Albán in the Oaxaca Valley, Mexico, was organized around 300 BCE. The capital city appeared as a regional center two hundred years earlier, in 500 BCE. The intervening years were times of raiding that gradually developed into territorial warfare, as Monte Albán subjugated its neighbors, constructed palaces and temples, and consolidated a four-tier settlement hierarchy of regional organization that spanned the Oaxaca Valley and beyond.[4]

The Monte Albán elite placed great symbolic importance on their military exploits. In the period from 500–300 BCE, when the city was hierarchically organized—though perhaps not

---

4   Charles S. Spencer and Elsa M. Redmond, "Conquest Warfare, Strategies of Resistance, and the Rise of the Zapotec Early State," in *The Early State, Its Alternatives and Analogues*, 220–61.

enough to qualify as a state—the elite commissioned the engraving of hundreds of slabs and monumental stones with depictions of what seem to be slain and mutilated enemies, some of them leaders of neighboring settlements and others simple warriors or captives. Probably to remind their own people of their power (as a threat or a source of pride, or more likely both, given that patriotism in the present day can be seen to serve both functions), the city elite had the stones placed in the central plaza. In the second period (300–100 BCE), there appeared dozens of "conquest slabs" that "refer not to raiding but to a more complex form of warfare: the taking and holding of territory."[5]

Curiously, some of the earliest conquests of the Zapotec occurred relatively far away from their capital, such as their 300 BCE takeover of the canyon Cañada de Cuicatlán, eighty kilometers to the north. Previously "the Cañada was occupied by 12 Perdido phase (750–300 [BCE]) villages," which were burned to the ground, replaced by new sites dedicated exclusively to intensive agriculture and lacking the rich ceremonial life of the earlier society, and by a heavily fortified complex of seven sites that controlled the northern entrance of the Cañada.[6] It was only several hundred years later that the Zapotec state conquered and incorporated the much closer Ocotlán, Zimatlán, and Tlacolula localities within the Oaxaca Valley. Charles Spencer and Elsa Redmond argue that the settlements neighboring Monte Albán were conquered later because they resisted more effectively, evolving simultaneously and thus deploying defensive military technologies from the start.

Starting before 1000 BCE, in the locality where Monte Albán was later founded, there was a large agricultural settlement that would eventually grow to a population of around one thousand people. In the subsequent period, 700–500 BCE, changes in settlement patterns suggest increased warfare; raiding and the burning of settlements became common between the different localities of the Oaxaca Valley, and an uninhabited

5   Ibid., 223.
6   Ibid., 224.

buffer zone appeared at their center.[7] Monte Albán may have been founded by survivors who either abandoned or fled the destruction of some of these earlier settlements, which for centuries dominated the region and later disappeared from the archaeological record.[8]

From 500–300 BCE, Monte Albán's main rival in the Oaxaca Valley also took several steps towards state formation, possibly in response to increased raiding and hostilities. These included "population growth and nucleation, a more centralized community organization with a sizable public plaza, a three-level settlement-size hierarchy in the Ocotlán Zimatlán subregion, and restricted interaction" as seen by minimal trade with Monte Albán.[9]

The main settlement of that rival polity, El Mogote (also a rival of the abandoned settlement whose survivors possibly founded Monte Albán, suggesting a long-lasting hostility), seems to have been raided and torched around 330 BCE. Subsequently, the inhabitants rebuilt their central plaza thirty meters upslope in a more defensive location, with a protective stone wall. Despite the setback, the settlement grew by over one-third in the period between 300–100 BCE, when Monte Albán had already organized a state and begun its territorial expansion. Architectural and ceramic styles suggest that the rebuilt El Mogote (El Palenque) maintained its independence from Monte Albán and continued to develop in the direction of a state, as seen in the construction of a multi-room temple and a palatial dwelling for the leader or leaders. Hostility with Monte Albán seems to have been continuous, including a trade embargo; obsidian from central Mexico regularly made it as far as Monte Albán, but not to El Palenque, neither do Monte Albán's fine ceramics appear in the archaeological record at El Palenque. There are also signs of increased warfare in this period, with the rebuilt settlement being

---

7   Ibid., 226–27.

8   J. Marcus and K.V. Flannery, *Zapotec Civilization: How Urban Society Evolved in Mexico's Oaxaca Valley*, (London: Thames and Hudson, 1996), 139–40.

9   Spencer and Redmond, "Conquest Warfare," 230.

completely burned and abandoned around 30 BCE.[10] Before its demise, the polity with its capital at El Palenque also developed the four-level settlement hierarchy that archaeologists consider definitive for qualification as a state.

The same process of politogenesis as the mutually hostile militarization of rival polities might also have occurred in the Yegüih polity in Tlacolula, to the east.

To summarize this chronology, several hundred years after the founding of sedentary agricultural communities, an increase in raiding led to changes in settlement patterns. Caught in a sort of feedback loop, the raiding became more violent. Reflecting the very bellicose culture that probably initiated the raiding and grew in response to it, communities imbued military actions with a central symbolic importance, as seen in the monumental engravings depicting vanquished foes, and in the burning of other settlements, an economically wasteful activity that goes beyond raiding for slaves or resources. There was a differentiation, at this time, between elite and non-elite members of the society, as seen in differences of material wealth and housing size. Nonetheless, neither trade and economic expansion nor religion seem to have been the motors of politogenesis. Less hierarchical societies in the region also experienced trade and growth. The construction of larger temples accompanied state formation, probably as a means for the new rulers to legitimate and augment their rule, but it was the plazas adorned with monuments to raiding and conquest—possible mustering grounds for the warriors—and not the temples that comprised the physical and symbolic center of the settlements.

Early on in this process, a mildly hierarchical society could win social consensus for a policy of constant warfare—despite the high social cost in casualties and the burning of settlements—by encouraging values of bravery and demonizing non-participation as cowardice. The competitive spirit that appeals to warriors even in stateless societies could intensify, given a tolerance for hierarchy. Elders who distinguished themselves in raiding would come to inhabit a privileged position,

10   Ibid., 234–35.

which they could use to encourage patriarchal and militaristic values. Non-warrior dependents (women, captives, non-participating men) could then be subjected to higher levels of exploitation and prevented from encouraging peaceful activities or reciprocal values. Priests or high-status families, together with elder warriors, could spur the young men into ever more violent and domineering forms of warfare, enabling economic accumulation, conquest, and the institutionalization of hierarchy, even though only a small minority would benefit from such developments. The cultural, psychological wage of constant opportunities for glory in battle was enough to harness an intermediate stratum—the warriors—to break social solidarity and avail the new elite with coercive powers.

An external or supra-local process accompanied the changes occurring at the community level. Smaller settlements quickly subordinated themselves to powerful neighbors, paying tribute and presumably participating in the military activities. This led to the emergence of regional powerhouses like Monte Albán and El Mogote, which reorganized the subordinate settlements in order to increase population, submit them to a hierarchical administration and economic exploitation, and increase their own defensive advantages. Parallel and interlinked processes of state formation in at least two subregions of the Oaxaca Valley acted as barriers to the expansionist desires of each polity, but these barriers were in fact a catalyst that spurred each polity to seek competitive advantages. The winner was the Monte Albán state, which militarized most rapidly, developing the administrative complexity that allowed it to conquer and occupy a weaker society a full eighty kilometers away, subsequently reorganizing its victim to support the exploitive and militaristic processes of state formation.

Within this model, growth is neither gradual nor geometrical, but a result of the political policies and military campaigns organized by the elite. Population growth is not the inevitable result of technological progress but an intentional strategy to foster defensive advantages. Intensified agriculture with irrigation, as at Cañada, was not an innovation by locals looking to improve their efficiency, but an imposition by the conquerors looking to increase output and steal all the surplus. In fact, we can imagine that the locals enjoyed a more leisurely existence when they practiced the supposedly more primitive agricultural method of alluvial flooding, and for them, the technological progress to fixed irrigation was accompanied by a dramatic increase in their labor requirements and a decrease in their quality of living.

JUST AS WE HAVE seen that status accumulation was more important than economic accumulation in the social hierarchies that developed into states, symbolic power was a question of vital importance for proto-states. Lacking a reliable degree of coercive power, the earliest states and the non-state hierarchies that preceded them had to concern themselves with the centralization and expansion of symbolic production, in order to unify and pacify their subjects, supplant the social practice of reciprocity, engineer a rupture with the old model of order, and establish a new model of authority.

The idea that "political power flows from the barrel of a gun" is largely true in a modern state, but in early states, though examples abound of political power descending from the edge of a blade, it most commonly flowed from the gods. Symbolic production was, above all, a religious activity, to the point that it becomes hard to imagine an early state without religion. A well developed, hierarchical religion seems to be almost as important as a patriarchal social organization and value system in the role of companion and motor to state formation.

Is there, inversely, a relation between atheism and statelessness? In Tacitus's survey, beyond the boundaries of Schwabia, we come upon the people who do not pray, "unafraid of anything that man or god can do to them."[1] Among hunter-gatherer societies, all of which have been stateless and egalitarian if not outright anti-authoritarian, the presence of gods is debatable. All documented examples traditionally believe in a living force connecting the entire world, such that no strong distinctions are

---

1   Tacitus, *The Agricola and the Germania*, 141.

made where Western thought deploys the mutually exclusive categories "human" and "animal" or "animate" and "inanimate." Some hunter-gatherer belief systems hold this force to be impersonal—an energy or an immanent spirit—and others hold it to be personal—named and distinct spirits inhabiting every natural phenomenon, from a rock to a cloud to an insect. I would argue that it is a misnomer to categorize these spirits as gods, given that a horizontal, reciprocal relationship exists between them, and a person's spirit, after death, can go on to inhabit another natural phenomenon. It is well documented how shamans or entire communities might insult or deprive a spirit who misbehaves. For example, an Ainu medicine man might withhold offerings of beer or call an unresponsive spirit an "idiot," whereas the Mbuti would traditionally use the noisy *molimo* ritual to wake up the forest— seen as a spirit in its own right—if things were going wrong.[2]

Perhaps it is most accurate to understand these hunter-gatherer non-religions as the opposite of the Western scientific non-religion, which arbitrarily views the universe as being made up of dead matter and energy, and tends to negate such concepts as spirit or will. On balance, this can be described as an ultimately non-falsifiable belief that is just as mystical as hunter-gatherer belief systems, with its rituals of dissection and categorization instead of rituals of transformation and reciprocity. Empirical evidence on its side certainly includes proof of a chemical difference between a rock and a toad (something of a non sequitur within a hunter-gatherer worldview), whereas empirical evidence against it, to be fair, should include the way scientific belief systems and the social structures they animate are interrupting and destroying the planetary life support systems, or the inferior record with regards to human health that scientific societies have in comparison, not to statist monotheistic societies, but to nomadic animist societies.[3]

---

2   H.T. Wright, "Recent Research on the Origin of the State," *Annual Review of Anthropology* 6 (2009): 379–97; and Turnbull, *The Forest People*, Chapter 8.

3   Just as the anti-globalization movement rightfully insisted that poverty should be measured with a complex array of factors and

However, even if we accept a distinction between spirituality and religion, the correlation between atheism and statelessness ends with hunter-gatherer societies. Numerous stateless societies that have practiced sedentary agriculture, from Crete to Southeast Asia, have worshiped gods, though heterodox beliefs, female deities, localized deities, or non-hierarchical pantheons distinguish them from the ordered, patriarchal religions of states.

The fact that the spiritual grammar of hunter-gatherers has typically been incompatible with that of sedentary states might present another reason why state conduct towards hunter-gatherers is more often than not exterminatory whereas their policy towards stateless agriculturalists tends to be one of conquest and absorption. Surrounded by spiritually unintelligible hunter-gatherers, a proto-state with limited coercive powers has few options other than to displace them or respect their autonomy. Surrounded by stateless but sedentary and god-worshiping communities, the proto-state might easily devise the innovation of a system of symbolic production as a way to attract and convert its neighbors. The godless, nature-worshiping spirituality of hunter-gatherers, therefore, is not the only egalitarian belief system, but it is the most state-resistant.

The necropolis of the Mycenaeans, in this light, was not a "dead city" but a vital site of production. Whereas the commoners were buried in anonymous pits or shafts, the elite were buried in special tombs with descending paths of access that brought

---

measurements that reflect well-being, as a way of disarming the manipulative metrics used by the World Bank, based only on monetary income, as true a measurement of human health as is possible with quantitative data cannot be reduced to mere lifespan but must also include frequency of disease and discomfort, mental health data, suicide rates, et cetera. Nonetheless, even if we only look at lifespan, pre-colonization hunter-gatherer societies probably still come out ahead if they are compared against the average for all modern scientific societies, and not only the richest of these, given that the relative good health (physical, not emotional) of the wealthiest countries is based on the exploitation and contamination of the poorest.

one closer to the underworld. Such architectural works, a short walk away from the settlements of the living, would be necessary to turn elite ancestors into intermediaries with the gods.

The building of pyramids and ziggurats in the Andes, in Egypt, and in Sumer attests to the organization of mass labor. However, the history of infrastructure development in both state and stateless societies leaves no doubt that such labor organization could be horizontal or vertical, an inconvenient fact most historians leave out. For our present purposes, the most relevant feature of these state-forming construction projects is what they tell us about the nature of power in early states.

A brief jaunt through the progression of state architecture is telling. When the bourgeoisie wrested control of the Western state away from the aristocracy, they financed the construction of gaudy yet beautiful buildings in the city centers—town halls, parliaments, train stations, opera houses, stock exchanges, and so forth—to demonstrate their greatness and their legitimacy, manufacturing a pedigree pointing back to the mythical origins of Western civilization in ancient Greece and Rome. Nowadays, when the state capacity for surveillance, domination, and coercive force is unequaled in the entire history of our species, the state in particular and the ruling class in general are incapable of constructing anything beautiful. Though more people than ever before go to train as architects, institutional buildings are insultingly ugly while the buildings of the rich are at best tacky and tasteless. The only impressive things present-day states are capable of building, things like supermax prisons or pit mines the size of cities, are kept out of view because the mere sight of them would tempt any sane, healthy person to go on a shooting rampage.

On the contrary, though I find power and its ostentation to be disgusting, I have to admit that elite architecture from earlier eras is both impressive and beautiful. This attention to effect speaks volumes about the weak grasp early states had on coercive power, and the relative importance of symbolic power. With few exceptions, early states built monuments that tended to impress viewers.

In Sumer, as in the Andes, proto-states built great pyramids that were initially open structures used in spectacular public rituals. It seems that in at least some cases, these pyramids preceded the cities that grew up around them, meaning that a concentration of spiritual power enabled a concentration of political and economic power. In 3000 BCE at the Sumerian city-state of Uruk, elites ordered the building of the White Temple on the ruins of an earlier temple, atop the ziggurat dedicated to the Sky God. This temple was covered in precious gypsum stone, which reflects sunlight, and positioned so that it would be visible from across the Sumerian plain. It was a master stroke of status competition with other city-states, attraction of subjects from independent farming settlements, assertion of a privileged relationship with divinity, and a legitimation of its owners' claims of privilege; in a phrase, it enabled the production of symbolic power. What's more, the construction of closed temples for elite use allowed public religion to take on a secretive character, necessary for the professionalization of a priestly class and conducive to maintaining the privileges of a hierarchical society's upper strata. Deprived of the full exercise or knowledge of their society's spirituality, the lower strata could not hope to fully exercise or understand political power.

In the pre-Warring States era of ancient China (1100–500 BCE), the growing bureaucracy was complemented by a bureaucratic religion. Just as there was a detailed hierarchy of greater and lesser functionaries and officials, there was a hierarchy of greater and lesser gods and spirits; just as every legal process required a specific bureaucratic ritual, every spiritual supplication had its corresponding sacred ritual. In this way, the Chinese state naturalized its structures and also trained its subjects to honor and participate in them.[4] The divine state and its procedures were a mirror of the earthly state and its procedures; both were organized in formal bureaucratic hierarchies.[5] This is a striking iteration of religion as a state-building spectacle, a mechanism we will see repeated in other examples in this chapter.

But more than just a spectacle, Chinese state religion was also a system of organization. Joseph Needham argues that the

---

4   Baum, "Ritual and Rationality," 199.
5   Emily Ahern, *Chinese Ritual and Politics* (Cambridge: Cambridge University Press, 1981).

I Ching, which apparently contradicts the scientific tendency of administrative thought in the ancient Chinese states, was useful because:

> its symbolic system of ritualized divinations closely mirrored the administrative organization of neo-Confucian bureaucracy [...and] constituted a structural framework for organizing and classifying diverse phenomena, a "giant filing system" that enabled all ideas and concepts to be neatly stylised and "fitted in to the [bureaucratic] system without difficulty."[6]

Religion also gave the ancient Chinese states the rupture they needed to break with the earlier family and clan system of hierarchical but non-state social organization. Local spirits and divine ancestors were preserved and honored within the state religion; they were included, but at a lower ranking. "Psychologically, then, the relationship of the people to their ancestral spirits closely resembled the contractual bond of interdependency linking clients to their patrons."[7]

Communities or family groups could appeal to their village spirits and ancestors to act as protectors or intermediaries *vis-à-vis* the more powerful, distant, and impersonal gods and spirits that form an intermediate strata, corresponding to administrative organs linking the districts to the imperial court, which found its own parallel in the court of the Jade Emperor. Though markedly hierarchical, the Chinese pantheon was not static; on the contrary it was itself a site of power plays. The earthly emperor recognized specific deities as deserving

---

6   Baum, "Ritual and Rationality," 200. Baum is quoting C.A. Ronan and J. Needham, *The Shorter Science and Civilization in China*, Vol. 1 (Cambridge: Cambridge University Press, 1978), 187.

7   Baum, "Ritual and Rationality," 202, citing F.L.K. Hsu, *Americans and Chinese: Passage to Differences, Americans and Chinese: Passage to Differences* (Honolulu: The University Press of Hawaii, 1981), 250–51.

worship, "bestowed title and rank upon them and occasionally demoted them again."[8]

In the Shang dynasty (ca. 1600–1000 BCE), state power was consolidated in ancient China. The "hereditary theocrats," ruling "under a conditional grant of divine authority," eventually secured an absolute monopoly on access to the sacred and established fixed rules for the secession of power.[9] In subsequent dynasties, the monarchs cemented their absolute right to rule, and the rituals of order and the concept of the Mandate of Heaven were secularized, as discussed previously.

The example of the Roman early state provides another interesting example. The Romans seemed to observe a strict formalism, a duty in the observance of rituals, sacrifices, and celebrations. Theirs was a spirituality of numbers and binaries that took on a simultaneously religious and administrative significance. The symbolic preference for the number thirty even determined an ideal social organization in thirty *curiae*. It would be easy to dismiss their fetishization of certain numbers and binaries, their insistent adherence to rites and observances, as a primitive anomaly within an otherwise efficient and militaristic social organization. It can only be explained by superstition. Yet the concept of superstition is inappropriately applied in the study of other societies, because it amounts to a voluntary blindness, an arrogant faith that all one's own practices and beliefs are reasonable, and that any divergent practices and beliefs in another society can be immediately chalked up to error, rather than functional and reasonable elements of their particular history.

In the case of the Romans, theirs was not an irrational, intuitive faith in the signs of the world. Rather, Roman superstition and hierurgy had a disciplined, administrative character. Though empathetic speculation may be decidedly unscientific, it can also help us break the Otherness of different cultures and, at the risk of projecting, shed a little light on practices that to us seem alien and to their practitioners were perfectly reasonable. Hypotheses

---

8   Max Weber, *The Religion of China* (New York: The Free Press, 1951), 30.

9   Baum, "Ritual and Rationality," 204–205.

must be tested and abandoned as the evidence requires; none-theless, much-maligned imagination is a driving force of theory.

Reading up on the early Romans, one gets the sense that their symbolic traditions and religious observances were adhered to with an iron will, as though they were subconsciously aware that they lacked other social glues. And the fervor with which it seems, from this great distance, they dedicated themselves to sacrifices and bacchanalia reminds me of frat boys, each trying to be the loudest in singing the school fight song, observing all the rituals unquestioningly, getting drunk every weekend as though it's their duty, subsuming traumas received and most of all inflicted, becoming effective trauma machines. In the end, they were probably not so different from us, and their adherence to seemingly arbitrary symbolic and spiritual rituals probably gave them a great advantage in surviving a world of growing political conflicts, and founding a new society that would quickly grow far beyond the scales that kinship and other traditional systems could hope to organize.

Spiritual power played a role in engineering a rupture with the value systems of earlier, non-state societies. The bellicose, patriarchal Mycenaeans give us a dramatic example of this. Con-quering the Cretans but preserving their most important spiri-tual and commercial centers, like the temple complex at Knossos, the Mycenaeans communicated their dominance with the sym-bol of a warhorse placing its hoof on the head of the cosmic bull, which for the Cretans was a hermaphroditic symbol of fertility. The ritual killing of bulls in the Iberian Peninsula may represent a similar symbolic rupture, an intentional offense against an ear-lier society. The pre-Indo-European Basques preserve alternate, bull-centered rituals in which the animals are the protagonists and not the victims, though after centuries of co-optation by a patriarchal society, the running of the bulls is now just another form of testosterone tourism devoid of any respect for the beasts.

Ecocentric and matrifocal peoples who inhabited the lands the Indo-Europeans would come to conquer, such as the Naga tribe in India, frequently worshiped snakes, which the Indo-Europeans generally held to be evil. Consequently, a negative snake symbol-ism is common throughout Indo-European cultures.

Symbolic inversions relating to femininity and maternity also have a special place in processes of state formation. As mentioned in Chapter IX, divine ancestors who were worshiped in order to legitimate earthly hierarchies were nearly always men. The father as founder and creator is a symbolic replacement for the mother creator commonly worshiped in stateless societies (though it must be mentioned that, contrary to the assertions of essentialist feminist historians, earth mothers and great spirits were frequently hermaphroditic, in the first case, or impersonal and genderless in the second). Given the frequency with which divine male ancestors are creators of some kind (founders of cities, progenitors of lineages, discoverers of fire or metallurgy), patriarchal ancestor cults allow men to co-opt and monopolize the symbolic realm of creation.

Men's monopolization of spirituality usually did not occur in a clean break with earlier belief systems, just as the Catholic Church could not abolish pagan gods, but had to turn them into saints. Many statist priestly classes co-opted the feminine symbols of earlier spiritualities.[10] The priest's gown reflects a forgotten evolution by which men, to act as spiritual intermediaries in certain societies, dressed as women.

The early states of the Congo basin developed a unique pathway for the patriarchal co-optation of feminine symbolic power, with female co-rulers legitimizing the power of the male paramount rulers.

> One of the characteristic features of the Congo basin early states was the institute of women-corulers [...] True, they had lost their influence rather considerably by the end of the 19th century. But their reverence persisted, and women-corulers had their own courts and guards. As for the Balunda, the lukokesha had even her own villages, which were not under the rule of the mwata-yamvo [male paramount ruler]. Her word was crucial in nominating a new paramount ruler and

---

10   For example Evans, *Witchcraft and the Gay Counterculture*; Moira Donald and Linda Hurcombe, eds., *Representations of Gender from Prehistory to Present* (New York: St. Martin's Press, 2000).

in many other cases. During ceremonies she was seated in
the most honorary place and had the first word.[11]

Such an institution reflects the relative weakness of patriarchy in the Congo states. In fact, here we glimpse a phenomenon
that deserves further investigation: why were the pre-colonial
states of sub-Saharan Africa so soft and non-imperialistic in
comparison to other states? Were other early states—most of
which disappeared or progressed before they could be documented by outside observers—equally soft? Is it an ethnocentric
reading of the archaeological evidence that has given us a more
patriarchal, brutal, and autocratic image? Did the well-known
anarchic character of many sub-Saharan African societies hold
developing states in check, forcing them to sustain themselves
through the organization of trade rather than engineering the
exploitation of their own subjects?

In any case, the gender complementarity[12] of many African

---

11   L'vova, "The Formation and Development of States," 294.
12   Because the concept of equality is in its origins democratic,
      and as such patriarchal, and because it is also applied to patri-
      archal societies that have equalized access to power between
      men and women, I refer to the antithesis of a patriarchy as
      complementary gendered society. Ideally, the antithesis of
      patriarchy would be a society with absolutely no differentiation
      of gender or with a gender performativity that is constantly in
      flux. Clearly, gender differentiation is a prerequisite to patri-
      archy, and it seems that societies that make gender immutable
      are more likely to develop as patriarchies. However, this ideal
      seems to reach an incorporeal extreme that does not find expres-
      sion in human history. Even societies with gender mutability
      and more than two gender categories were based, it seems, on
      the two primary genders common throughout the world. Even
      though the roles and characteristics of the genders differ, and
      postmodernism has long since problematized the assumption
      that categories are translatable, the two primary categories of
      gender seem to be universal. The characteristic that seems to be
      common in societies that are not patriarchal (including those

societies was eroded by European colonial influence.[13] British, French, Portuguese, and other colonizers saw patriarchies where none existed. By only dealing with male institutions and leaders, and ignoring or even annihilating female institutions and leaders, they gradually created the very societies they had projected.

Another method of symbolic rupture concerns the figure of foreign rulers. Multiple West African states were founded by members of the royal families of neighboring societies, or by expatriates, who lived for a time with the royal families of neighboring societies.[14] These neighboring societies may or may not have themselves been states, and the royal families referenced in so many legends of politogenesis may have been ruling dynasties, or simply families with a high status. It is also perfectly feasible that returning expatriates or traveling foreigners might have claimed connection to distant royalty in order to awe locals and justify a special position of leadership not supported by kinship relations. Multiple legends mention state founders who arrive with royal devices or other symbols of divine grace and leadership. These may have been symbols endowed with that exact meaning in the neighboring society (in which an elite or ruling family was sending out franchise-makers with their blessings), or they may have been strange tokens, the meaning of which the errant state-makers exaggerated or invented.

---

that have been dubiously classified as matriarchal, even though they do not exhibit analogous control structures and customs) is a complementarity between the two gender categories, a balance based in respect and mutual autonomy, and possibly one or more additional categories that allow movement from the gender assigned at birth. This historical limitation, however, says nothing about the possibility of establishing a society with no gender differentiation now.

13 Judith Van Allen, "Sitting On a Man," *Canadian Journal of African Studies* II (1972): 211–19.

14 Examples include Benin and Nupe kingdoms. Moses, the mythical figure important in the creation of Israelite states, who was according to different versions fostered by or a son of an Egyptian noble family, makes for a striking parallel.

The operative factor is the mystification of legitimacy. Most societies produce and justify status as a direct relationship to autochthonous power structures. Yet the expatriate or foreign would-be ruler has no immediate power or claim to social status within the society they come to rule. Instead they enjoy the same mystique as an "Indian princess" or the King of Siam might have in the West. By claiming a royalty status that is foreign, and thus exotic, and thus boundless, such a ruler can effectively win the loyalty of the preexisting hierarchies that would otherwise resist state formation. His lack of status becomes a stroke of good luck from a statist viewpoint. Lacking a role in the existing hierarchies, he can place himself atop all the lesser leaders, who would never tolerate their competitors (other chiefs, other high-status families) gaining power over them, and who are also prevented from amassing power by traditional inverse hierarchies. Such hierarchies, common to stateless societies, allow low-status people to keep their leaders in check. But they might have limited effect on someone completely external to the social structure. With the help of a symbolic interruption that exotic tokens of royalty might provide, a foreign ruler can justify the new position that they occupy at the top of a social pyramid. In fact, it might be the masses or the lesser leaders themselves who put the new king on the throne, in order to gain an advantage in their own power struggles.

For such a pyramid to morph into a state, however, the ruler would need a bureaucracy and a legion of officials, appointed from the top, capable of reworking and controlling the entire social hierarchy. Such an evolution might take generations, and usually requires another factor (warfare, an increase in trade, the arrival or development of a new religion) for the ruler to overcome the autonomy that other layers in the hierarchy preserve. Or, the pyramid might never become a state, either persevering as a stable weak hierarchy or shedding its upper layers to return to a relatively anti-authoritarian social organization.

The Bini provide a good example of why statist religion needed to enable the centralization of spiritual power. Among the Benin chiefdoms, senior leaders of the community councils were limited by their sacral and ritual duties, which prevented them from acting effectively as profane leaders (organizing military and administrative tasks). In the more powerful chiefdoms, therefore, *enigie* appeared to perform the profane administrative and militaristic functions that the *edionwere*, the spiritual leaders, could not. However, there remained an ambiguity between the two types of leadership, and the Bini society never developed a successful military engine that might have opened a path to politogenesis. The *odionwere*, the spiritual powers he mobilized, and the ancestors he represented, were tied to his local community, and therefore were not effective for complementing or surpassing the profane power of the *onigie* at the chiefdom-wide or macropolitical levels.[15] The two types of leadership, organized at different scales, could not complement each other; given the relative importance of religion over warfare, the profane leaders lacked the legitimacy to surpass the spiritual leaders; and given the decentralization of ritual practices in individual communities, the spiritual leaders lacked the scale of organization to surpass the profane leaders. A localized spirituality, therefore, amounted to a fatal barrier to state formation.

Changes in the organization of political power were often accompanied by changes in cosmologies and divine pantheons. On multiple continents, from Sumer to the Nile to the Andes, the figure of the Sun God reflects the growth of state authority. From a diverse and potentially horizontal pantheon of deities, the Sun God emerges as a supreme god, parallel to multiple political and spiritual processes: the centralization of state authority with supreme rulers dominating lesser rulers; the monopolization of spirituality by a professional priestly class, who need to streamline the pantheon and dilute the importance of localized deities outside their control; and the alienation of spirituality, with the ascendance of a supreme god who is apart from and above the earth and his worshipers. In Southeast Asia, the Buddha played this role, and state formation was in part the process of subordinating local deities to this supreme symbol of enlightenment.[16]

---

15   Bondarenko, "From Local Communities to Megacommunity," 329–30.
16   Scott, *The Art of Not Being Governed*, 275.

In other historical moments, a single god replaces a diverse pantheon to achieve the same effect, as when the Egyptian pharaoh
Akhenaten promulgated the worship of a single deity, Aten.
Though the figure of a sun god certainly lends itself to a statist
mentality, there is no essential or intrinsic symbolic relationship.
Divine hierarchies frequently change as different factions gain
power over the state apparatus. Even a goddess can be used by
a state-building project, as when Isis became preeminent in the
Egyptian pantheon. The common feature is the establishment of
a supreme figure that can order the spiritual universe in a hierarchical fashion.

According to Andean oral culture, the Tiwanaku state was
abandoned or overthrown in part because "the other gods were
crying," which is to say people decided to decentralize their
spiritual practices so as to again honor the localized deities who
had been abandoned in favor of the Sun God controlled by the
state.[17]

In the stateless, horizontal model, shamans, witches, and
medicine men were generally responding to a calling; to exercise
their office they had to demonstrate some talent and be recognized by the community. Their primary activity was in relation to
the community and not in relation to other shamans. In contrast,
a professionalized priestly class could be self-regulating, and was
probably hierarchical from the beginning. At sites of spiritual
accumulation—settlements built around sacred shrines or monuments—holy men could come together in larger numbers, they
could write the rules of their own conduct, and they could determine the norms of the sacred site and eventually of the surrounding settlement. They could also determine who could be included
within their cult, enabling the creation of elaborate hierarchies
that new initiates would accept in exchange for access to privilege
and status.

The concentration of spiritual power enabled the centralization of political power, putting a vital component of state formation in place. A professionalized class of priests, supported by

---

17   Yawar Nina, quoted in Severino, "The Other Gods Were
      Crying."

donations, sacrifices, and religious offerings but lacking anything beyond symbolic and spiritual power over the rest of society, created a ritual arena in which greater levels of hierarchy could be performed. Professional rituals were a stage that accustomed profane spectators to the leadership roles that played out among the priests. Those priests, within their closed cult, could enact far more intense expressions of authority and obedience than they could ever impose on the rest of the community. But because religion is spectacle, their very performance of internal authority ended up reshaping ideas of hierarchy reproduced in the society at large.

It is no coincidence that supreme rulers in many early states were also the heads of religious hierarchies. In the proto-city-states of Sumer, the rulers were priest-kings. In the Baluba, Bakunda, and Bakuba states of Central Africa, "The paramount ruler was both an embodiment of a divine spirit and a priest."[18] We find another example in East Asia:

> As the principal earthly diviner of heavenly intent, the king himself was the supreme high priest of ancient China. He was Son of Heaven, *Tianzi*, ordained by the God on High, Shang Di; and it was his duty to offer appropriate, timely sacrifices to the various deities as well as to accurately read and react to heavenly portents so as to ensure the well-being of his people.[19]

Written languages and number systems play a special role in state formation. Though they are not always linked to states, writing and mathematics are most likely to appear in statist societies, whereas societies in resistance to state domination, though they are perfectly capable of developing or maintaining both, are most likely to give them up, using illiteracy as a preventive tactic against bureaucracy and the hierarchy that accompanies it.[20]

18 L'vova, "The Formation and Development of States in the Congo Basin," 293.

19 Baum, "Ritual and Rationality," 198–99.

20 Scott, *The Art of Not Being Governed*, 226–34.

What is most curious, within the considerations of the present chapter, is that in early states on multiple continents, writing and number systems played a dual purpose, finding their greatest use in both religion and trade.

In Sumer, Egypt, the Andes, and China, early writing systems recorded religious beliefs and trade balances. In the case of Sumer, Mesoamerica, Crete, and continental Europe, writing was developed before the emergence of supreme leaders and before the prolific use of writing to record their deeds—the predominant notion of history up until the present day. Written records may be seen as a simple convenience from the standpoint of a merchant, and the existence of writing in the stateless, mercantile civilizations of the Indus River Valley and ancient Crete attest to this pragmatism. But as far as religion was concerned, writing gave priests the possibility to "classify" cult beliefs, to develop a measurable body of knowledge that could be systematically imparted to novices, and to secure a special role within emerging power structures as scribes and chroniclers.

We might assume that number systems and early mathematics were exclusively pragmatic in their social usage, but in fact, in early states they enjoyed a mystical status and a considerable symbolic power. If we accept what might appear to be a commonsense division between religion and commerce, then we can again assume that for the merchants, numbers were but a pragmatic means for measuring debt and production. However, the other principal use of early mathematics was in complex architecture, which in the case of Sumer, Egypt, the Andes, and perhaps to a lesser extent China, meant almost exclusively the construction of buildings of religious significance. The figure of the architect as public servant building secular buildings as a trade emerged much later. Many of the first state-employed architects may have been priests and religious men. The priest-architect who designed Egypt's first pyramid, Imhotep, is better remembered than the pharaoh who was buried there; in fact, Imhotep was immortalized as a god.

In Tiwanaku, a pre-Incan civilization in the Andes, numerology was fundamental to the religious order. Three was an important number, because it enumerated the elements (water, earth, and sky). Four was important for the four directions. Their sum is seven, another important number for the Tiwanaku priests. Seven times seven is forty-nine. Tiwanaku religious architecture often includes rectangles of forty-eight elements, a nice round number, the product of twelve times four (or three times four times four). Forty-eight reaches its perfection at forty-nine, representing the forty-eight leaders of Tiwanaku's ideal spiritual/political organizational scheme, plus the supreme leader or god.

The Mayan calendar is another iteration of the spiritual importance that states place on numbers. The cosmological belief that time was cyclical and that the same events occurred on the same dates of different calendar cycles was a driving force in how Mayan states recorded—and fought over—history. For the Mayan elite, recording events ensured a "perpetual cycle in the future and on the contrary, to destroy a monument signified to destroy the future." When one Mayan kingdom was defeated by two rivals, they engraved the story of their victory in a hieroglyphic stairway. When the first kingdom got its revenge fifty years later, they rearranged the engraved stones "to create a historical and chronological nonsense." In sum, "It was very important for [the Mayans] not only to connect a contemporary fact with its mythological prototype but also to set an exact chronological distance between them."[21]

Calendars were important to the early state in China as well.

> Even such ostensibly secularized, scientific activities as calendrical calculation and meteorological observation had profound political implications. Thus the promulgation of China's earliest lunar calendar—reputedly fixed by Shang dynasty rulers—was aimed less at responding to the immediate economic needs of farmers (who in any event continued to regulate their activities primarily by the onset of floods, the coming of rains, and the helical rising of certain stars) than at satisfying the ritual requirements of charismatic, sacrally-oriented dynastic elites.[22]

---

21   Beliaev, "Classic Lowland Maya (AD 250–900)," 135.
22   Baum, "Ritual and Rationality," 203–204.

What if the overlap between the interests of merchants and priests in multiple early states is no coincidence? I believe that what may be the most common model of primary state formation is based on the consolidation and centralization of interregional networks in which no practical distinction existed between spiritual and material commerce. This is the **sacred commerce state**. In such a model, commerce cannot be characterized as a mercantile concern motivated principally by profit. To understand the model, we have to imagine a world in which the pilgrimage and the trade venture are potentially indistinguishable; in which priests are also scribes, accountants, surveyors, architects, insurance agents, and brokers; in which holy sites are also meccas of artistic and artisanal production; the most valuable goods are those with spiritual and symbolic significance; and temples or temple grounds also serve as markets for trade goods.

The sacred commerce state is the one that captures such a network of spiritual and material commerce, instrumentalizes and bureaucratizes the professional religious order that already exists within the network (the ruling class and the instigators of politogenesis will probably emerge from the priestly order, or otherwise be a charismatic warrior-king and entourage who obtain its good graces), centralizes the network and its productive processes, and impels an expansion of symbolic production. Some of the best-known early states may be examples of this model.

Dating to around 4000 BCE, Uruk was the first city in the world. Prior and also contemporaneous to Uruk, the Fertile Crescent was filled with small farming settlements going back several thousand years to the development of agriculture in the region between 10,000 and 8000 BCE. In the centuries before and after the founding of Uruk, these settlements tended to contain small shrines, governed over by *ensi*, or priest-kings, assisted by a council of elders. They constituted a weak central power with a primarily religious authority, probably backed by age and lineage hierarchies.

Around 4000 BCE, a ziggurat or pyramid was built to the Sun God An at Uruk, parallel or even previous to the growth of that settlement as a city. Other cities arose in the region, such as Eridu. Between 3400 and 3000 BCE, increasingly elaborate temples were built, often atop the ziggurats and often atop the ruins of old temples. The presence of ruined or demolished temples suggests changing and even opposing religious beliefs, whereas the growing prevalence of closed structures of worship (temples commanding the previously open platforms of the ziggurats) suggests the development of professionalized, elite, and secretive religious institutions. Temple construction, using stones quarried as far as sixty kilometers away, suggests regional trade and a costly emphasis on religious power. Simultaneously, writing was developed, with the first engraved tablets dating to around 3500 BCE, and a functional ideographic writing system dating to 3100 BCE. Early writing in Sumer was used to record religious and commercial information, and later to record the histories of supreme rulers.

Around 2900 BCE, great changes took place in the Fertile Crescent. Many earlier buildings were destroyed, and the new, fortress-like buildings suggest conditions of warfare. A nine kilometer city wall was built at Uruk, whose dominance was undermined by other emerging city-states. The first historically attested supreme ruler in Sumer, Enmebaragesi, who ruled from the city of Kish, appeared in 2600 BCE. From this time forward, though probably starting earlier, the polities of Mesopotamia were slave societies based on the hyper-exploitation of agricultural laborers and the capture of workers from rival polities. At the time of Hammurabi's law code (1780 BCE), Mesopotamian society is divided into men (full citizens), free men (dependents lacking full rights), and slaves (with the status of property). Within each of these categories were invisibilized subsets with few or no rights: women and children.

State power was increasingly secularized after 2900 BCE, as was the case in other states where power was initially almost exclusively spiritual in nature. *Ensi*, now the heads of city-states, were elected by national assemblies and had profane military duties in addition to ritual ones. The *lugal*, a supreme ruler who governed multiple cities (or at least tried to), was elected from among the *ensi* and was responsible for public actions though eventually, perhaps as religious power was detached from rituals and shrines and reattached to representatives of the state, the *lugal* came to be considered a god. Perhaps instrumental to this transition was the intensely symbolic location of sacrality in the physical accoutrements of leadership, to the extent that a ruler could not exist separately from the signs of his authority. For example, "the scepter, the staff, and the nose-rope," which symbolized the ruler as a "faithful shepherd," were also considered to contain deities, as was the throne; meanwhile the flag and "the monument were the symbols of his power over the communities and the conquered territories where his monument was installed."[23] Sometimes thrones themselves received offerings, perhaps connected to the worship of deceased rulers. As for the dais in the temple, originally it was the place reserved for the statue of a god, but subsequently it became the place in the temple where the ruler sat, again illustrating a direct transference of authority.

Nonetheless, the deification of the ruler did not translate into despotic authority. On the contrary, the ruler was expected to earn respect and heed counsel.

> We know from the oldest royal inscriptions that Sumerian kings had to have remarkable force, huge energy, external appeal causing people's love, worship and trembling, as well as to be ruthless to their enemies and to pay their special attention to gods' and elders' advice.[24]

Early in this sequence, power was predominantly symbolic and religious, and Uruk was unrivaled as the holiest and most awe-inspiring site. This position would also have given it vital trade advantages in the regional network, allowing it to become the home of artisans and merchants who would have gradually surpassed the farmers in symbolic and spiritual wealth. At this time, before the appearance of organized warfare and supreme rulers, the most elaborate buildings were communal structures

---

23   Vladimir V. Emelianov, "The Ruler as Possessor of Power in Sumer," in *The Early State, Its Alternatives and Analogues*, 182, 184.

24   Ibid., 184.

rather than private palaces, and the sites of religious ritual (the ziggurats) were open-air structures, though their symbology was doubtlessly hierarchical and celestially oriented. With the greater concentration of spiritual power, a professionalizing priest class supported by religious offerings could monopolize the places of ritual and worship, changing the traditional belief systems to favor values of hierarchy and obedience.

Uruk's dominance excited the jealousy of elites in other nascent cities, leading to warfare. However, the increase in hostility only intensified the unity of this authoritarian regional system, creating the possibility for the elite of one city-state to dominate the others, exercising a power that was not only symbolic but also coercive. The day-to-day glue of the regional system, however, was still based in the commerce of spirituality and goods.

The priests of Nippur, for example, traditionally conferred the kingship for the whole of Sumer. Nippur was the home of the sacred shrine of Enlil, the second most important god; the city had no other claim to power. It was built, and rebuilt, on a site especially prone to flooding, and the settlement was maintained at great cost to the inhabitants despite repeated water damage. It was, in other words, not a pragmatic settlement located to profit off some economic advantage, but a religious settlement located at a site of spiritual importance, and this importance was recognized by all the other cities in the regional system.

The Tiwanaku state formed in the Andes around 300 CE. Like the Inca state that followed it, it was a fusion of Quechua and Aymara cultures that monopolized the rich trade between the products of the jungle valleys in Las Yungas (tropical fruits and staples, medicines, feathers) and those of the high plateau, the Altiplano (potatoes, cereals, salt, wool). People practiced agriculture in this region already starting around 5000 BCE, and going back at least to 1500 BCE there was a small farming settlement at the site that would later become capital. Archaeological evidence from this settlement shows neither social divisions nor religious monuments, though trade in ceramics, obsidian, gold, and silver was practiced. Starting around 100 CE, it is believed that the Tiwanaku site took on significance as a spiritual center.

It became the capital of the emerging state between 300 and 400 CE, and reached urban proportions around 600 CE. At its peak, the population of the capital city measured in the tens of thousands, and the three valleys that made up the center of the territory may have sustained a population in the hundreds of thousands or even surpassing a million.[25]

As in other regions, we see a relatively stable stateless period persisting for a long time after the development of agriculture and sedentary living, and a relatively rapid increase in hierarchy, stratification, and the centralization of power once an organized religious cult perfects the ability to shape the spiritual beliefs of the broader society.

Though at the empire's peak the population density was remarkably high, this is not at all reflective of the conditions pertaining to the pre-state period, when the population was so dispersed that would-be elites faced a major barrier to the concentration of power. The ceremonial centers created by religious cults, therefore, had an important seduction effect, bringing together populations, at least temporarily, in regions with dispersed settlements. Temporary, celebratory gatherings at ceremonial centers were useful for trade, creating a momentary super abundance that are probably better conceptualized as giant regional parties than as markets, but they were not useful for sustained economic activity until such time as a large number of people could be *captivated*, convinced to settle in a proto-urban location. Accordingly, from a statist viewpoint, the most important function of these periodic ceremonial gatherings was to erect an ephemeral but recurring school, a central point where the emergent priestly class could impart spiritual lessons, influencing the worldview of the rest of the society in a way that eventually favored state formation.

Trade between the highlands, the jungle, and the coast long predated the state and the religious cult. Since people practiced a gift economy, goods were more likely to be imbued with spiritual significance than with any kind of quantitative exchange value.

---

25   Wikipedia "Tiwanaku Empire," https://en.wikipedia.org/wiki/Tiwanaku_empire (accessed February 20, 2016).

The necessary evolution for state formation, then, was from spiritual commoning, in which everyone had access to sacred acts of creation, artistry, and gift-giving, to fixed spiritual values allowing for a centralized process of spiritual production. Some of the most important trade goods circulated in the network eventually dominated and intensified by the Tiwanaku state were ritual items, which, by the very nature of their being ritualized, possessed a fixed rather than a subjective spiritual value. By changing the value paradigm, the emerging priests could make themselves indispensable to trade by controlling the very rites by which goods were fixed with a value. The new spirituality, therefore, had to negate the subjective—what is useful, what is beautiful (to me)—and manufacture a social consensus on what was objectively valuable. Value, in its earliest iterations, is not the product of a free market, but of a professional conspiracy.

The Tiwanaku elite lived within a sacred compound—built with a moat to give it the appearance of a floating island—that commoners were allowed into, it is believed, only during special ceremonies. Cult knowledge, such as images from creation stories, was recorded in engravings exclusively located on the inside of the compound. Religious rites were complex, involving hallucinogens that had to be carefully administered, astronomical knowledge, and human sacrifice and ritual disemboweling. Sacred elites monopolized commerce and redistributed goods across the entire society. They expanded their empire by establishing trade missions and state cults in neighboring societies, gradually winning their subordination through peaceful means, though they were not above attacking and stealing the religious monuments of defiant neighbors. Stolen monuments were invariably placed in a submissive position within symbolic religious arrangements back at the capital.

Around 950 CE, possibly in response to a climatic change reducing agricultural productivity, a large part of the population abandoned the theocratic state. Its temples had fallen to ruins by the time the Inca state arose.

One of the most rapidly emerging early states appeared along the Nile River during the Early Dynastic period of ancient Egypt. The standard theories cite gradual population growth leading to

land shortages, warfare, and domination by the strongest chiefdom; or need for extensive irrigation to control flooding, but as
Dmitri Proussakov points out, settlement patterns were actually
irregular and population was low in Upper Egypt at the time
of politogenesis, and there is no evidence that a general irrigation system existed at that time (drainage, in fact, appears to be
the main infrastructural activity encouraged by the early state).
All the supposed preconditions for state formation are lacking: a
shortage of resources; an external military threat; or the influence
of other states.[26]

The Nile Valley was populated by numerous independent
chiefdoms that alternated between war and trade. Before the
reign of King Narmer, one of those chiefs, there was little to
suggest that any of them was on the point of erecting a state. The
chiefdom centered at This—the home of the pharaohs who would
eventually unify the Nile under one state—dominated Upper
Egypt, but even there their authority was more reciprocal or sta-
tus-driven than state-like. They did, however, excel in the use
of large boats to transport collective work crews, soldiers, cargo,
and the pharaoh himself in expeditions of a ritual, commercial,
or military nature.

Around 3100 BCE, possible flooding and a rise in sea level
seems to have sent a wave of ecological refugees out of the Nile
Delta and into to Upper Egypt, Canaan, and other neighboring lands. Something on the scale of 120,000 people, with all
their livestock arrived, in Upper Egypt, which was dominated
by the Thinite pharaohs. Symbolically defeated and subordinated
by King Narmer, they were "naturalized" and allowed to settle,
providing a basis for state power.

> Subjugation of such a multitude of people could not fail to
> result in unprecedented growth of [the] personal author-
> ity of Thinite rulers and to raise the military-economic
> potential of the "Thinite Kingdom". For instance, the

---

26   Dmitri B. Proussakov, "Early Dynastic Egypt: A Socio-
     Environmental/Anthropological Hypothesis of 'Unification,'"
     in *The Early State, Its Alternatives and Analogues*, 140.

'captives' might have been recruited to build Memphis, the future capital of Egypt, under Narmer's successor Horus Aha [..] Archaeological excavations reveal the Memphis region to be rather densely populated at the earliest Dynastic times.[27]

But in a powerful showing of reciprocity, the totem of the Delta people, the hawk, was elevated to become the chief deity of the emerging state; Horus replaced Seth, the traditional god of Upper Egypt, in preeminence.[28] Such reciprocity is a sure sign that state authority had not yet been established and that Narmer, at least at the beginning of his reign, was the head of a chiefdom and not a state.

The organization and administration of such a large population, dislocated at least in part from its traditional community structures, would have provided a unique opportunity for bureaucratic innovation, also liberating the king from his chiefly role as the head of a single kinship group, and the representative of a single localized deity. We can assume that the refugees were not transformed into a permanent subordinate caste, as the Aryans did with the conquered Dasas, since it was presumably the Delta people who returned to (re)build Memphis—now under the authority of the This pharaohs—during the reign of the very next ruler. This likelihood seems to confirm that the capture of the 120,000 was a primarily symbolic victory and not a full military humiliation that might have wreaked the psychological consequences necessary for creating a new underclass.

As the Egyptian polity grew and took on the features of a state, it did not spread as a cohesive territorial unit but as a network of discrete enclaves amidst weaker but independent chiefdoms. The capitals of the emerging Egyptian state, This and Memphis, were sites for the worship of deceased pharaohs, whereas the other enclaves, such as Hierakonpolis, Elkab, Koptos, Buto, and Sais, were each dedicated to a specific god or goddess. It was the River Nile that connected them all, allowing

---

27   Ibid., 145–46.
28   Ibid., 165.

a rudimentary state to govern dispersed settlements separated
by hundreds of kilometers and surrounded by neutral or hostile
chiefdoms.[29]

Boats and ritual activities on the river had long been
important to Egyptian tribal elites, and the use of large cargo
or troop boats powered by many rowers allowed "selective colonization of the Nile banks, sailing safely to occupied territories"
and "avoiding destructive overland battles." The pharaoh, representing Horus, sailed the Nile twice a year in an important
ceremonial procession, ensuring the administrative unity of the
state and also reenacting a creation myth in which the divine
ruler traveled the world with his possessions and "thus established the world order."[30] Boats were even buried next to kings
in their sacred tombs.

The Egyptian proto-state took advantage of its symbolic
monopoly of the river (or at least a privileged access to the river
that no chiefdom was powerful enough to obstruct) in order to
monopolize trade between the enclaves, which in addition to
displaying religious specialization also produced different material goods. By the time of Horus Den in the First Dynasty, the
state owned numerous granaries and other storage facilities that
conceded an advantage in trade and extra power when climatic
changes or Nile flooding provoked scarcity. Simultaneous to this
expansion, the number of administrative officials increased.

Commerce along the river in the form of ceremonial
gift-giving played an important role in the spiritual expansion
and political unification of the early Egyptian state. The This
kings made lavish gifts and built temples honoring local deities in
then-unconquered Middle Egypt or other autonomous stretches
of the river. Similar to the expansion strategy of the Inca state
and various Buddhist states of Southeast Asia, early Egypt did
not rely exclusively on military conquest but sought religious
alliances. In the temples, state gods were symbolically unified
with local deities, rendering a sign of respect to the unconquered
culture and also clearing the path for its integration. Granted,

---

29   Ibid., 147.
30   Ibid., 148, 151.

such gift-giving rituals are not typical of state authority, which is based on the command relationship; however, they do constitute a strategy for eventual incorporation. They also decrease hostilities that could interfere with the cohesiveness of the enclaves. Lesser chiefdoms that accepted the gifts were recognizing the Egyptian state as the uncontested power on the Nile. However, since the Thinite pharaohs had to give more valuable gifts than they received in order to preserve their supreme status, the semi-autonomous chiefs rose in status upon receipt of the gifts, especially relative to their own populations. In time, their accumulation of power allowed them to challenge the enclave state.[31] However, the symbolic power of the state was the motor of this crisis; though they were able to challenge state dominance, the other chiefdoms were also becoming more statelike. Pharaonic gift-giving was a cratoforming exercise that broke the power of the first state and laid the groundwork for the emergence of a larger and more unified state.

In the time of the early Second Dynasty, there was a political crisis that saw the fragmentation of the enclave-based state, with the result that the pharaohs, relocated in the larger city of Memphis, were cut off from their ancestral home at This. When the Egyptian state regained its force, it unified the whole of the Nile in one territorial body backed by the non-reciprocal force of military conquest, ending the enclave system and also the reliance on a spiritual, trade, and gift-giving network that followed the course of the river. Religious power remained central, as seen in the growth of the cult of the sun god Ra and the frenetic construction of pyramids to honor the divine pharaohs.

The Egyptian example is distinct from primary state formation in the Andes and Sumer. The position of a supreme ruler appeared earlier in the evolution of the Egyptian state than in these other examples. There may be elements of the royal court state model of politogenesis, with warfare between hierarchical chiefdoms enabling the emergence of a supreme ruler simultaneous to the establishment of spiritual trade networks; however, an anomaly among states, patriarchy in Egyptian society was

---

31   Ibid., 163.

remarkably light, with multiple women rulers. Massive monument building also followed rather than preceded state formation. It was not until the Third Dynasty that the first pyramids were built, though the Egyptian, Andean, and Sumerian pyramids make a poor comparison, since the pyramids of the former were not places of spectacular public worship but sites for the adoration and divinity-building of deceased pharaohs. It may be that the Nile itself provided the stage for the sort of spectacular ceremonies that Sumerian and Andean early states performed on their ziggurats and ceremonial platforms.

In any case, the models should be taken as rough patterns rather than strict typologies (the latter being a sort of production of knowledge in which classification and abstraction, with the advantage of allowing quantification, outweigh and obstruct observation and understanding). I think that this admittedly incomplete survey has shown that if our attention to detail is rigorous enough, we can describe as many pathways to state formation as there have been states in the history of the world. Overarching patterns, though, contradict a good deal of doctrine and help us to perceive the nature (and perhaps points of weakness) of the State.

But before we turn our attention to the lessons that might help us reclaim our freedom and our destiny from this leviathan that has dominated us for too long, I want to reach back a little further, to explore a few more questions that remain.

ON THE FERTILE PLAINS and river valleys north and west of
the Black Sea—the corridor through which agriculture entered
the European subcontinent—the stories of some of the first agricultural societies shed light on both the effects of agriculture on
society, and on the history of the State. The Cucuteni-Trypillian
culture existed from 4800 to 3000 BCE in the area that is now
western Ukraine, Moldova, and eastern Romania. They practiced
an agriculture based on the cultivation of wheat, rye, and peas.
Women carried out textile and pottery manufacturing, and men
hunted and herded, especially cattle. This culture built some of
the largest settlements in the world of that time, including cities
of up to fifteen thousand people. They invented the oldest known
proto-writing system in the world, manufactured and traded,
and lived in pit houses that gave way over time to above-ground
clay houses with thatched roofs.

Contrary to assumptions about the state being a more
advanced form of political organization, the Cucuteni-Trypillian
culture was stateless, egalitarian, peaceful, and non-patriarchal,
with a matrifocal spirituality. It ended with the arrival of the the
patriarchal and militaristic Indo-European Kurgan or Yamna culture, which was stateless but at least mildly hierarchical (for example, they buried their warrior-kings in special, lavish graves). How
this displacement played out is uncertain, and Marija Gimbutas's
hypothesis of a patriarchal Indo-European invasion is disputed.
There is evidence of coexistence between the two cultures. It is
known that they traded goods, and the Cucuteni-Trypillian inhabitants migrated west, abandoning settlements and creating new
ones, which is evidence of some kind of negative pressure coming from the east. Such a settlement disruption suggests a more

gradual process rather than invasion, slaughter, and conquest. However, the permanent settlements of the Yamna culture were in the Don basin at this time, far to the east. Radiocarbon dating suggests that there was almost no time window in which Yamna and Cucuteni-Trypillian settlements existed in adjacent territories. One possibility is that trade was carried out by intermediary populations who became increasingly hostile as a response to Yamna expansion, or that early waves of Yamna came to trade or make war but not to settle permanently.

Farther south, the Boian culture existed in similar conditions, but with different social organization and a different end. Existing between 4300 and 3500 BCE in what is now Romania and Bulgaria, the Boian culture practiced agriculture, lived in wattle and daub houses with wooden platform floors and thatched roofs, and made fine decorative pottery that was traded throughout the region. The culture descended from the Gumelniţa culture, which was famous for its anthropomorphic and zoomorphic art. Eventually, the Boians transitioned smoothly into several subsequent cultures of the region. Unlike the Cucuteni-Trypillian, starting around 4100 BCE they developed hierarchies within and between settlements, suggesting the development of a non-state elite that began to centralize political power in federations linking multiple villages and towns. Later in their development, these settlements grew to include defensive fortifications, suggesting an increase in warfare. The Boian culture may have intermingled with or been absorbed by arriving Indo-European populations, rather than having been destroyed or expelled.

And to the west, in the gentle valley where the Ljubljanice River snakes past wooded hills, a stateless people lived for millennia, until around 1000 BCE, in pile dwellings amidst the marshes and lakes, using stone and wooden tools until late in their existence. They sustained themselves with hunting, fishing, and primitive agriculture, traveling in dugout canoes. Though they might appear especially primitive in our eyes, they happen to be the inventors of the oldest known wooden wheel in the world. It seems that they were peaceful, non-patriarchal, and egalitarian. They may have been the ones to build the first fortified hilltop settlements in the valley, or this may have been the work of new arrivals; in any case their fortunes changed with the influx of various warlike Indo-European tribes.

The Illyrians were a grouping of hierarchical Indo-European tribes who established a kingdom in the Balkans and earned the hatred of their commerce-focused southern neighbors with constant piracy and warfare. They were eventually defeated and conquered by the Romans. After the arrival of various Celtic populations, the Taurisci, a militaristic Gallic federation, settled here following their defeat by the Romans at the battle of Telamon (225 BCE). They subsequently allied with the Romans but were defeated by invading Germanic tribes, the Cimbri and Teutons, in 112 BCE. The Romans extended their power to the eastern shore of the Adriatic and the region of the Ljubljanice River around 200 BCE, building a city in 50 BCE where Ljubljana now stands. It was the definitive arrival of state power, thousands of years after the advent of agriculture.

In the Pyrenees and on the Mediterranean coast of the Iberian Peninsula, where I now sit finishing this book, the indigenous inhabitants were Ibers and Vascones, a non-Indo-European people who are the ancestors of the present-day Basques, and who settled in the peninsula sometime around 4000 BCE. Celtic and Lusitanian (both Indo-European) tribes had arrived some time after 2000 BCE, but they moved on and settled primarily in the western half of the peninsula. The Ibers, the indigenous inhabitants most influenced by the Phoenicians and Greeks, lived in fortified hilltop settlements, raised crops, made bronze tools, herded animals, and oscillated between war and peace, engaging primarily in raiding rather than territorial conquest. Their society was organized in tribal confederations that could unite around war leaders but were relatively egalitarian. The Vascones lived in more mountainous regions. They practiced pastoralism, hunting, and gathering, and used even more decentralized, non-patriarchal, and horizontal forms of social organization. Starting around 1100 BCE, the Ibers began trading with Phoenician sailors, who established commercial colonies across the Mediterranean coast (in fact it was probably this commercial contact that began to distinguish the Ibers from the Vascones). In subsequent centuries, the Phoenicians were supplanted by the Greeks, who established even more trading colonies, including one where Barcelona now stands. Increasingly, the Ibers were integrated into a world economy, but they remained independent and stateless.

State power was finally imposed around 210 BCE, when first the Carthaginians under Hannibal, and then the Romans, defeated the Iberian and Celtic confederations in a series of wars and subjected them to a system of total colonization and forced production. Some, like the Lusitanian war leader Viriathus, proved indomitable; Rome put an end to the resistance of the tribal confederation he led by paying some of his own to assassinate him after luring him to peace talks. To their credit, they then executed the hired killers with the reasoning that "Rome doesn't pay traitors." Many war-captives were forced into slavery and made to work on the villas of the legionaries who had defeated them.

There is a common element in all of these stories. Agriculture could be adopted as an intensive practice or as a light complement to herding, hunting, and gathering. It made up a variable part of the repertoire of stable, non-patriarchal, egalitarian societies for thousands of years. Some such societies engaged in trade, others were relatively isolated; some were peaceful, others were warlike, although their bellicose practices were generally limited to raiding and not the conquest of territory. Hierarchical, non-state, patriarchal societies such as the Illyrians or Kurgans frequently disrupted or uprooted the non-hierarchical alternatives. Other times it was a fully formed state, such as the Roman Empire. In both cases, the conquerors used agricultural production as a sort of weapon and a way to sustain permanent military mobilization. Such a practice is not a consequence of agriculture but a specifically cultured way to understand and to organize agriculture reflecting a worldview and a strategy. What's more, at least a few hierarchical societies, such as the Bini and the Aryans, resulted when a nomadic society took over an agricultural society. The culture that reproduces an authoritarian and exploitive worldview and deploys militaristic and oppressive strategies will do so no matter what material conditions they are presented with.

We have seen enough examples, demonstrating myriad pathways of social evolution, to put to rest the progressivist assumption that agriculture and sedentary living inexorably lead to state formation. However, agriculture does seem to be a clear precondition for state formation. Sedentary hunter-gatherer societies (typically those with permanent villages near inexhaustible fishing spots) did not develop states, and the nomadic empires, though they did develop complex hierarchies incorporating huge populations, only founded states in the moment when they conquered preexisting agricultural polities. Is there anything in the invention of agricultural techniques that might shed a little light on state formation?

It is now known that agriculture was developed independently in at least eleven different regions of the globe, including multiple sites in Asia, Africa, and North and South America. The first area where it appeared was in the Near and Middle East. Recent research shows that agriculture was not a singular invention in the Fertile Crescent but that it was first developed across a broad region spanning what is now Syria, Palestine, Turkey, Iran, and points in between.[1] At multiple sites throughout this region, 11,500 years ago (9500 BCE) hunter-gatherers started sowing wild barley, wheat, and lentils. For thousands of years previously, they would have already been eating the seeds of these wild-growing grasses, but now they started taking extra steps to encourage their spread, collecting and sowing seeds rather than eating all of them, then storing seeds, and eventually taking the step of clearing land and planting directly, and also selecting seeds from the plants with the characteristics they preferred. Nothing about the beginning of this process is unique in hunter-gatherer practice, since such societies regularly influence their environments to make their food supply more abundant, the same way beavers, ants, and many other species do. Perhaps it becomes useful to dispense with the myth of pristine nature and distinguish between influenced and artificial environments.

For some reason, certain hunter-gatherers of the Fertile Crescent started expending the extra effort to store, to clear, and to plant, settling at sites that may first have been seasonal camps and later permanent villages. The critical point that signals the

---

1   Michael Balter, "Farming Was So Nice, It Was Invented at Least Twice," *Science* (July 4, 2013).

beginning of agriculture is domestication: the selection and guided evolution of a species, plant or animal, until a new species is created, corresponding to the characteristics desired by the cultivator and not to the species' relationship with its original ecosystem. The earliest domesticated plant species found in eastern Turkey, Syria, and Lebanon date to 10,500 years ago (8500 BCE).

Chogha Golan, in Iran, was continuously inhabited for 2,200 years starting 12,000 years ago (10,000 BCE). People began cultivating wild barley, wheat, and lentils more than 11,500 years ago (9500 BCE), with domesticated species appearing there 9,800 years ago (7800 BCE), a few hundred years later than in the western Fertile Crescent, though DNA testing confirms that domestication was an independent event at different places in the Fertile Crescent rather than a one-time invention that spread across the region.[2] At Chogha Golan they also kept wild goats in pens, a transition stage between the hunting of wild, free-range animals and the breeding of domestic species.

Because agriculture was developed simultaneously at so many sites across such a wide area, and in multiple regions across the globe, scientists—at least archaeologists, paleoecologists, archaeobotanists, and members of similar disciplines—insist that farming was "inevitable" once the Ice Age ended and conditions for a bountiful agriculture spread and improved.[3] On the one hand, we can accept the simple proposition that, given a large enough human population divided into a diverse enough range of separate societies (as unification and centralization tend to stifle innovation), anything that can be invented eventually will be invented. But there are certain cultural valuations that infiltrate discourses on inevitability that we would do well to question, not only because they normalize and naturalize occurrences that perhaps should spark our ethical disgust and condemnation, but also because they tend to erase a large part of the human panorama.

2   Simone Riehl, Mohsen Zeidi, and Nicholas J. Conard, "Emergence of Agriculture in the Foothills of the Zagros Mountains of Iran," *Science* 341 (July 5, 2013): 65–67.

3   Balter, "Farming Was So Nice, It Was Invented at Least Twice."

In this case, what about all the human societies that did not develop agriculture?

In fact, there is a huge body of evidence regarding the rejection of agriculture and a widespread aversion to laboring to achieve what nature can provide us freely. Many hunter-gatherer groups (and today, probably all of them) have demonstrated knowledge of agriculture, but choose not to partake. Probably most of the hunter-gatherer societies that have adopted agriculture and sedentary living in the last three hundred years—societies that covered a significant portion of the globe—were forced to do so by processes of colonialism, and some still resist deep in the Amazon or the Kalahari Desert.

Clastres discusses a number of societies that practiced agriculture and gave it up, such as the Lakota of the North American Great Plains, the indigenous inhabitants of the Chaco region in South America, and the Guayaqui in the Amazon. There are also numerous examples of societies that may have transitioned directly from hunting and gathering to nomadic pastoralism, such as the Sami of arctic Europe, the Khoikhoi of southern Africa, and maybe even the early Indo-Europeans.

Agriculture was not independently developed wherever it was ecologically feasible. In fact, it would be safer to say it was only developed in the places and during the climates where it was most favored and would be most abundant. This is no surprise, given that agriculture constituted a major decline in human well-being, with more work or poorer health.[4]

The earliest forms of proto-agriculture (the collecting, storing, and wild sowing of seeds) were not as labor-intensive as the later practice of clearing fields to plant domesticated species. The practitioners of proto-agriculture still sustained themselves on a diverse and healthy diet including hundreds of species of hunted, gathered, and cultivated food sources. At Chogha Golan, archaeologists found 116 different plant taxa and the remains of dozens of hunted animal species, from gazelles to boars to rodents to reptiles to birds to freshwater crustaceans. Wheat only constituted

4   Jared Diamond, "The Worst Mistake in the History of the Human Race," *Discover Magazine* (May 1987): 64–66.

20 percent of the plant remains found during the last centuries of the settlement, after a more than two-thousand-year-long trajectory towards agriculture.[5]

Once the hard work of domestication and tool innovation was accomplished, agriculture did not necessarily spread by adoption, but by population expansion. Most white Europeans are genetic descendants of farmers in the Fertile Crescent and the Levant.[6] Early farmers, buried eight thousand years ago in what is now Germany, are genetically most similar to the modern inhabitants of Turkey and Iraq. Certainly there are plenty of cases of societies voluntarily adopting agriculture, although we should also take into account that the spread of agriculture makes foraging in the same ecosystem untenable, as forests are cut down and animals over-hunted. But in many other cases, agriculture was spread as part of a cultural complex by a specific people, like the Sumerians, the Bantu, or the Han.

In other words, agriculture cannot be viewed as a mere technological shift, and certainly not as an improvement. It was in large part a cultural choice and many cultures were evidently disposed to avoiding it. What cultures, then, were disposed towards the development of agriculture? Is there anything within such a cultural make-up that might have favored the intensification of hierarchy in some of these societies, and not in others?

We know that while all hunter-gatherer societies are stateless and in material terms egalitarian, we also know that they cover a great range from mildly patriarchal and gerontocratic to resolutely anti-authoritarian. A society of the former type could potentially develop kinship and religious hierarchies once agriculture gave them the opportunities for denser populations, fixed territoriality, craft specialization, and inheritance.

---

5   Riehl, Zeidi, and Conard, "Emergence of Agriculture in the Foothills of the Zagros Mountains of Iran."

6   David *Derbyshire*, "Most Britons descended from male farmers who left Iraq and Syria 10,000 years ago," *Daily Mail*, January 20, 2010, http://www.dailymail.co.uk/sciencetech/ article-1244654/Study-finds-Britons-descended-farmers-left -Iraq-Syria-10-000-years-ago.html.

Examining studies on the earliest agriculture, a few things become apparent. For one, sedentary living preceded full-scale agriculture. At Chogha Golan, settlement began around 10,000 BCE, cultivation of wild cereals began around 9500 BCE, and the first domesticated crops appeared around 7800 BCE, roughly mirroring the timeline elsewhere in the Fertile Crescent. This is no paradox. Hunter-gatherer societies can be roughly divided into two modes, foragers and collectors. The latter, in response to ecological conditions, are not fully nomadic. Rather, in certain seasons, they settle in semi-permanent camps to take advantage of a temporary bounty (e.g. the salmon run or the ripening of an abundant fruit, nut, or grain) or to pass the winter, surviving off smoked meats, nuts and grains, or other foods stored up throughout the year. Collectors tend to specialize more in the gathering of especially abundant foods. Hunter-gatherers in the Fertile Crescent may have had semi-permanent settlements in the winter or in the summer months when the abundant wild cereals ripened, and they may well have returned to the same settlements year after year, eventually building permanent structures.

At these settlements, they would have noticed an increase in the growth of the very cereals they collected, as a result of transported seeds falling to the earth, seeds passing intact through the human digestive tract, and so on. Eventually, with just a little extra effort, they might begin to put aside a part of these seeds to sow later, making the natural supply even more abundant. But why take the labor-intensive next steps, when so many other collector societies did not? What else might have induced hunter-gatherers to take the step to permanent sedentary settlement?

We know that sacred sites played an important role in many early states and in the stateless agricultural societies that preceded them, some hierarchical, others horizontal. We also know that nomadic hunter-gatherers had sacred sites where they might go for visions or to perform certain rituals or make spiritual art, from rock carvings to more ephemeral kinds that have not survived the passage of time. Such sites were often in out-of-the-way places or along seasonal migration routes, and not connected to permanent settlement.

It turns out, though, that there is at least one example of hunter-gatherers erecting a permanent monumental site, and it just so happens to be in the Fertile Crescent, dating to a few hundred years before the appearance of proto-agricultural settlements.

The Göbleki Tepe site in the southeast of modern-day Turkey dates to around 11,600 years ago. There, hunter-gatherers made a monument consisting of rings of large stones, up to five meters high, arranged in concentric circles and engraved with animal motifs. The stones weighed between ten and twenty metric tons; placing them therefore required a large group of people and advanced techniques.

If hunter-gatherers in the region had permanent sites, what if these sites also had permanent residents, religious hermits supported by the offerings of visiting pilgrims and by their own activities, which came to include agriculture? It may be feasible that over-hunting in a region populated by many semi-sedentary bands of collectors forced the residents to either move away or take the step to more intensive forms of plant cultivation, yet the symbolic weight of such a decision and the role of spiritual and cultural criteria in its outcome should not be underestimated. The shift to agriculture could never have been a simple calculation of calories per unit of labor because it called into question the very worldview and relationship with nature of those who undertook it. Such a shift would have required a site of spiritual production.

Contrary to ideological mumbo-jumbo regarding "surplus" and "subsistence economies," hunter-gatherer societies are perfectly capable of supporting a large proportion of non-productive members, namely the old and the young. Supporting a specialized group of holy people would have been perfectly within their means. A minority of religious hermits living at monumental or sacred sites might not account for the greater part of proto-agricultural settlements. But given the widespread use of semi-permanent, seasonal dwellings by collectors across the world, I think that the greatest leap is not between pure hunting and gathering and a diversified cultivation of wild plants, but between the latter and the labor-intensive clearing of land to plant domesticated crops, together with permanent settlement.

Sedentary religious hermits not only would have aided in the process of innovation and domestication (living at a permanent site and without the distractions of society they would have been privileged observers to the natural processes that led to domestication),[7] they would also have provided an example for the holiness of sedentary living and the magic of co-opting natural processes, shaping the environment, tracing human aesthetics on the natural world (ever a fascination for a symbolic species), and giving birth to other species.

Over time, as sedentary settlements gave rise to trade networks and populations grew, the spiritual practice would have intensified. We can imagine shamans who were supported by offerings and gifts and who earned their status through charismatic performances, skill in healing, or ability in other artistic techniques, who lived at sites of spiritual significance that became the destination of pilgrimages and thus nodes of trade. As spiritual/material trade expanded, these holy people could take on disciples, eventually founding hierarchical religious orders that spread through the very trade networks that sustained them. Those orders that executed their functions more out of love for status than out of love for gift-giving, healing, and spiritual experiences would develop authoritarian values that would result in the expansion of internal hierarchies—initially just a pedagogical organization dividing masters, intermediates, and novices. Authoritarian orders within the network would unite, since their logic favored the accumulation of power over the unimpeded search for truth, meaning, and ecstasy. A clash between these different spiritualities may also be a point of origin for the first specifically anti-authoritarian, state-resisting cultural practices.

---

7   Additional research supports this hypothesis: it turns out that genetic analysis shows that the earliest samples of domesticated wheat originated from within thirty-two kilometers of Göbleki Tepe site (Manfred Heun, Ralf Schäfer-Pregl, Dieter Klawan, Renato Castagna, Monica Accerbi, Basilio Borghi, and Francesco Salamini "Site of Einkorn Wheat Domestication Identified by DNA Fingerprinting," *Science* 278 [November 14, 1997]: 1312–14.).

The development of agriculture was above all a spiritual development, and in every single instance in which this spiritual economy arose, it had the opportunity to promote a tolerance for hierarchy, the specialization of ritual, and the monopolization of occult knowledge, or to promote spiritual commoning and to make ecstatic, transformative experiences available to all. In the former case, the earliest predecessor to a politogen would be intimately connected to a cultural complex binding agricultural methods, spiritual values, and organizational principles. Authoritarian and anti-authoritarian versions of this cultural complex slowly spread across multiple continents.

In the thousands of years that followed, these cultures had the chance to blend, to reverse their directions, or to intensify. Once agriculture was generalized and became the practice, not of spiritual enclaves but of entire societies, hierarchy was probably forced to take several steps back. Next to a growing population that was no longer nomadic, and therefore less inclined to undertake pilgrimages, the preexisting spiritual centers probably faced a sharp decrease in their relative importance. It would take a long time for spiritual hierarchies to either reemerge in each agricultural settlement, or for the earlier spiritual centers to reestablish themselves as regional capitals, once the growth of population and crafts broke the immobility and self-sufficiency of the agricultural settlements and allowed spiritual/material trade to flourish again.

XIII.
From Clastres to Cairo to Kobane:
Learning from States

THROUGH THE COURSE OF this book, we have looked at several models of secondary and primary state formation. Primary state formation, rare in world history, is a process by which a society with no knowledge of existing states forms a state through autochthonous processes. Secondary state formation, much more common, is when a society develops a state influenced or aided by an already existing state. We might refine the latter category by detaching from it a third one, tertiary state formation, which requires direct intervention and administration by a fully formed state, in order to restore state power to previously statist populations in which state authority had been weakened or destroyed, or to impose its authority on a population that had previously resisted full integration under a state.

Tertiary:
the **progressive state**
the **colony state**
the **neo-colonial state**
the **revolutionary state**
the **settler state**

Secondary:
the **imitative state**
the **rebel state**
the **reluctant client state**
the **conquest state**
the **projectual state**
the **true believers' state**

Primary:
the **royal court state**
the **holy father state**
the **raider state**
the **sacred commerce state**

These models are not intended to be strict typologies nor any kind of pseudo-objective classification of different "species" of state. Most historical instances of politogenesis will likely include characteristics from more than one model. Taken individually, the models provide a simplified version that allows the dynamics of a specific case of state formation to be conceptually appreciated. Taken together, they trace broad patterns with two important theoretical results. The first is to communicate unmistakably that state formation is a multilineal process and not a teleological, progressive evolution. The second is to outline the broad patterns that have characterized very different histories of state formation throughout world history; the range of these patterns completely refutes classical statist doctrine, both Hobbesian and Lockean variants, as well as Marxist and primitivist doctrine about state formation, and it seriously problematizes environmental determinist theories of state formation. The evidence presented confirms the theoretical suggestions regarding state formation made by anarchist thinkers like Bakunin and Kropotkin, as well as the more systematic theoretical framework offered by Clastres. Though significant modifications are necessary in light of a larger body of research, their fundamental arguments stand: the State is a motor of economic exploitation, and an institutional development that allows the enslavement of society.

The purpose of this book, however, is not to simply make a theoretical contribution, a proffering of data on the altar of science, and move on. My interest in studying the state flows directly from my lived experiences as a state subject, which I could politely characterize as unfavorable, unhealthy, involuntary, and antagonistic. These experiences leave me and many others with an unambiguous desire to destroy the State, and this book is one among many initiatives intended to sharpen the struggle against all domination. Information alone accomplishes nothing. Learning is only worthwhile if it helps us to fight, to live healthy, to live free.

Pierre Clastres offers us one story of a society that was in the process of bucking social hierarchy when European colonization interrupted their way of life. Among the Tupi-Guarani, in the lands today occupied by the states of Paraguay and Brazil, were the largest and densest of the stateless Amazonian societies. Many villages included thousands of inhabitants, and their chiefs were steadily concentrating more power. Within this context, a seemingly endless supply of prophets arose, urging people to listen to the gods, warning against "the Evil of One," and organizing periodic mass pilgrimages to the sea, which, if the people had sufficiently purged themselves through fasting and observance of righteous conducts, would open up for them, delivering them from the Bad Earth. Clastres argues that this religious movement, which began before the arrival of the Portuguese and traces of which survive to this day, is a movement against the unification, centralization, and stratification accompanying the growth of political power, a movement that seeks to abandon what were the first outlines of an emerging state.[1]

We know that attempts to abandon states or evade state power are universal; they have probably affected every state in the history of the world. But we have fewer opportunities to see, or at least to imagine, the mass abandonment of a hierarchical political structure that does not yet have coercive authority, as an effective measure of state prevention. What we do have are numerous archaeological "mysteries," states and proto-states that collapsed without any clear environmental or external political cause. As a rule, scientists refuse to consider the possibility of popular rebellion. From an ironically anthropological perspective, it would be fair to describe scientists as among the most important priests of the state, who, like the priests of nearly all other states, also accomplish objectively useful outcomes in the fields of architecture, astronomy, mathematics, medicine, and so forth, but the unifying principle of their activity is its integration within a worldview and an institutional operationality that favors

---

1   Clastres, *Society Against the State*, 206–207.

state power. The exceptions to this rule are valuable indeed, just as heretical prophets using the same charismatic performances and some of the same methods as state priests, were valuable to numerous anti-authoritarian rebellions.

If a mass abandonment like those incited by the Guarani prophets were to succeed (e.g., if they had somewhere to go other than into the sea), the results, recorded archaeologically, would probably be identical to the mysterious collapse of so many civilizations: the loss of writing, the abandonment of cities, the dispersal of population.

The difficulties and consequences of state formation are not relegated to prehistory. All states are constantly trying to augment their power, all states are closer to the brink of collapse than they would like to let on. The last decade has been extremely useful for those interested in understanding states, thanks to the spread of popular revolts against every model of state currently in existence.

When the Arab Spring came to Cairo, hundreds of thousands of people organized a horizontal resistance in order to occupy Tahrir Square, defend themselves from the police and paramilitaries, communicate their ideas worldwide, quickly innovate solutions to problems of first aid and healthcare, defend against dangers ranging from tear-gas to sexual assault, sidestep the government's internet blockades, overcome religious and ethnic divisions, and feed and otherwise sustain their movement. The crisis in government they provoked forced the military dictatorship to allow elections.

When a rightwing religious party began capitalizing on the movement, trying to turn a widespread opposition to authority into an opposition to secular as opposed to religious authority, the military launched a coup and took control of the government again. In any case, it was clear that the rightwing party was in the process of establishing its own dictatorship, albeit through democratic means, similar to the democratic dictatorship ruling in Turkey under the authoritarian Erdogan.

The particular state model in force clearly has a huge impact on our day-to-day life. The kinds of oppression we face, and even the likelihood we have of getting imprisoned or killed, will differ depending on whether our government is a two-party police state democracy like the United States, a multi-party police state democracy like Turkey, a social welfare democracy like Sweden or Germany, a military dictatorship like Egypt, and so on. However, we mustn't lose sight of the fact that the similarities between these forms of government far outweigh the differences. In Egypt, the transition between democracy and dictatorship occurred overnight, going both ways. It was not a thousand-year process of evolution but a simple switch in the control strategy of the ruling elite. The vast majority of governmental and economic institutions continued unchanged. And in all of the governments mentioned above, from the military dictatorship to the social welfare democracy, people are locked up in cages, immigrants and other outsiders are occasionally or routinely killed, nature is ravaged, people are not allowed free access to the land, and people who do not submit themselves to economic exploitation are subject to forms of exclusion that range from marginalization and bureaucratic controls to starvation.

In a historical perspective, a sort of anthropological long view, the pretensions of certain states to be different, to be anything other than structural complexes for the accumulation of power, are absurd. At the fundamental level, all states are the same. Thus, the Arab Spring and the many movements it spawned or influenced, from the Rojava Revolution to the plaza occupation movements, became contestations of state authority. Within each of these movements, there appeared a dynamic tension between those currents that wished to use the movement to renew state authority in a different form, and those who wished to abolish such authority completely.

The nonviolent, pro-democracy Color Revolutions forced out ruling parties in Serbia, Ukraine, Lebanon, and other countries. But popular resentment surged anew within a year or two of the new government taking power, fueled by the unbroken continuity of exploitation and disempowerment that sparked the initial rebellions. The message could not be clearer that more elections or another form of government do not address our fundamental powerlessness and the many inequalities that arise from this. The problem is not corruption or lack of democracy or a particular political party, but the very fact we are governed.

Even in the countries of North America and Western Europe
where capitalism was successful, according to its own metrics, at
producing prosperity, misery reigned. Well before the financial
bubble had people talking about crisis, the proliferation of mental
health problems, loneliness, and unhappiness—or diseases like
obesity and cancer—were out of control. And in each of these
lands of opportunity were sizable minorities who slept on the
streets, lacked access to healthcare, were controlled by the humil-
iating social service and welfare bureaucracies, or were locked
up in mental hospitals, prisons, juvenile centers, and immigrant
detention facilities. And any social movement that tried to question these failings outside of a reformist framework were aggressively marginalized by the media and the police.

The Occupy and plaza occupation movements that broke
out in Spain, Greece, the United States, and other countries
turned into battlefields between those who wanted to pressure
the government for reform and those who wanted to spread the
practice of popular self-organization. The latter were repressed
by the State, particularly with heavy anti-terrorism operations
in the United States and Spain, whereas the former proved to be
their own worst enemy, ruining their hopes for change exactly at
the point that they got what they wanted. In Greece, a populist,
grassroots political party—Syriza—rode the wave of social movements into power and proceeded to institute the most insulting,
devastating austerity measures in history, even after losing a popular referendum against the measures. In Spain, the Podemos
party arose from the plaza occupation movement and quickly
converted into another bureaucratic political party engaged in
all the same power plays and either unable to or uninterested in
stopping the austerity measures that bankers, technocrats, and
centrist politicians were demanding. Every generation can tell
the same stories of betrayal, and every political party that at one
point claimed to be progressive or revolutionary hides the same
sordid history. No party has ever stood in the way of capitalism,
yet people keep on voting.

Given state responsibility for colonization, nationalism, and
the subjection of minority ethnicities, in the twenty-first century there are still hundreds of movements for national liberation

and struggles against occupation. In the previous century, most of these movements aimed to create independent states, unconsciously emulating Western values in order to disprove racist stereotypes or consciously seeking power in Western terms. However, many of these movements have since rejected the goal of state formation, realizing that states are incompatible with freedom. In the dungeons of the democratic United States, revolutionaries locked up for fighting for black liberation—like Russell "Maroon" Shoatz, Lorenzo Komboa Ervin, Kuwasi Balagoon, and Ashanti Alston—developed anti-state positions. Mapuche communities fighting for the recovery of their land, usurped by forestry and mining corporations with the backing of the Chilean and Argentinian governments, have broken with the leftist movements working to install socialist governments— since not even the socialists have wanted to put a decisive end to colonialism—and now reject the State as a Western imposition and an irremediable tool for domination.

One of the most well-known examples of this pattern comes from Kurdistan. For decades, the Kurds have been fighting against the occupation of their lands by Turkey, Syria, Iraq, and Iran. In the eighties and nineties, they followed the well established Marxist-Leninist model of national liberation through the creation of an independent state. Through experience and reflection, however, they came to the conclusion that socialist governments are incapable of breaking with capitalism and all the misery and exploitation it produces, and that states can never be a tool for emancipation because they will inevitably centralize the dominant culture and repress minority cultures. In Rojava and Bakur—the parts of Kurdistan occupied by the governments of Syria and Turkey—the people are currently fighting off the brutal and genocidal imposition of state authority (primarily by Turkey and the Islamic State) and engaging in a dedicated experiment with freedom, building confederal structures of communitarian organization from the ground up.

They are not doing this in a typically anarchist way, because they have not made a complete rupture with preexisting governmental and capitalist institutions, but neither are they trying to change these institutions from within—as so many naïve reformists have done—so much as trying to supplant them with autonomous organizations. The Rojava experiment involves a confederal structure united by an anti-authoritarian ethos. One of the most lively debates of the decade concerns whether they can emancipate themselves with such a structure. So many revolutionary movements have condemned themselves to new kinds of authoritarianism in the past, that skepticism is healthy and inevitable.

A critical position asserts that the structure being used in Kurdistan is pyramidal, and will therefore result in the central-ization of power and the formation of a new state. Even some proponents of the model admit it to be pyramidal. In fact, every confederation is a pyramid, uniting local organizations into a sin-gle entity through multiple levels of coordination. The Haude-nosaunee—the League of the Six Nations—successfully resisted state formation and promoted harmony and reciprocity using such a model for centuries. With the Six Nations, however, the pyramid was inverted, and most of the power was in the local groups. There were also multiple, complementary forms of power that prevented centralization—such as spiritual power and social power, or power in the household and power in times of war—and a deeply rooted autonomy by which delegates could not impose decisions on other community members, and the large-scale coordinating bodies (the "higher" levels of organization in a Western logic) could not impose decisions on the communities. Because of the principle of voluntary association, leaders could at any time be abandoned by their followers.

What allows a pyramid to be inverted or upright? Experi-ence and continued struggle will give the clearest answers, but our study can suggest a number of factors. Is there a strong, anti-authoritarian ethos in the society in question, or is power worshiped? Are leaders mistrusted or adored? Is leadership frag-mented and complementary, divided among the fields of spiritu-ality, coordination, sustenance, healing, history, artistry, warfare, conflict resolution, and so forth—allowing everyone to exercise some kind of non-coercive leadership—or is the principle of authority unified, allowing government by a single ruler or ruling body? Is the economy based on local self-sufficiency and shared access to the commons, or on an industrial organization that requires massification and large-scale coordination? A healthy anarchist idealism would suggest pushing for the former against the latter in each of these tensions, or avoiding confederal structures and delegation altogether; however, the struggle in Kurdistan may throw light on how much wiggle room a society has to strike a balance on these diverse organizational questions without creating a new state. And there is also the strategic question of whether, given an armed uprising, we can supplant existing institutions or whether we need to rupture with them unequivocally. Lenin already proved that states do not wither away if we are using them as instruments for change; the Kurds may show whether or not certain state institutions may be left intact while we build grassroots structures.

Like capitalist exploitation and the oppression of dominated ethnicities, climate change is another state effect that governments are incapable of solving. The process of colonization that extended the private property regime across the globe and allowed for intercontinental deforestation was organized by states. The infrastructure of automotive transportation, industrial agriculture, and electricity generation, which are responsible for the majority of greenhouse gas emissions, are built and regulated by states (though they are often privatized once governments have forced people to pay for them). The industries responsible for destroying the planet depend on government regulation, police protection, and financing, and form part of an economic complex that is integrally connected to government and that is best viewed as part of the state apparatus, given that all states have conducted their business in both public and private spheres. Through a series of global summits, the State has also attempted to present itself as our savior against the ravages of climate change, but in practice, it is completely inefficient, even unable to moderate ecological disaster where it negatively affects its own interests. For decades, governments have been organizationally defunct, even unable to implement their own measly accords, which by the admissions of their own scientists are inadequate to prevent the crisis. By continuing to trust states as the potential solvers of climate change and mass extinction rather than spreading information and tools designed to enable grassroots direct action (most of which would be illegal), climate scientists are complicit with catastrophe.

We need to stop thinking of the State as a potential vehicle for emancipation. It has never been anything other than a tool for the accumulation of power, and accumulating power is harmful for individuals, for communities, and for the entire planet. A critical appreciation of the effects of state-forming currents within social movements today, an unflinching look at the records of the most powerful states now and in the past, an analysis of the ability of states to respond to critical problems like environmental destruction, genocide, alienation, and exploitation, and an understanding of the history of the State, make it impossible to trust any claim that in the long-run the State can work for the common good. And since states will use any conflict or opportunity to enhance their powers, relying on the State for short-term benefits ensures the proliferation of the problems we seek to overcome. Examples of this pitfall abound, such as the way the reformist sector of the workers' movement achieved the welfare states that bureaucratized and dismantled the movement, blunting their momentum with hand-outs that broke the self-organization and tenacity of the workers, and enabled the eventual imposition of austerity measures that an alienated population with a middle-class ideology was unable to resist. Seeking reform within the State is like taking out loans to keep the creditor at bay. The State is incompatible with our freedom and well-being.

Continuing to cover up the lines of antagonism that run between us and the institutions of authority can only perpetuate the problem. There is no social contract and there never has been. Our submission to state authority is wholly involuntary because it is the only choice we are given. The states that rule today are the same ones that enslaved our ancestors at sword- or gunpoint. The form that slavery has taken and the mechanism for achieving it has changed drastically, but it is no less effective. In many ways we are worse off today because liberated zones free of state authority are ever more removed or ever more fleeting.

Perhaps the last time that a whole society in the West attempted to organize itself in a horizontal, solidaristic fashion free of State authority, the major institutions—military, Church, landowners, business owners associations, and representative government—drowned their aspirations in blood in an intensifying series of crackdowns that culminated in the Spanish Civil War and subsequent fascist dictatorship, killing half a million people while the neighboring governments watched in silence or lent their support. And every decade in the last century, if not every year, an indigenous people have attempted to reassert their sovereignty, to cast off the State and live according to their traditional forms, only to be evicted, imprisoned, or murdered, adding yet another episode to the largely unwritten chronicle of genocide and colonialism that has accompanied the State since its inception. The most recent peoples to be targeted include the Kanôc, Yanomami, Aché, Karen, Maya, Chakma, Mbuti, and Standing Rock Sioux; and the locations of the atrocities range from Pine Ridge, in the United States, to West Papua.

Open debate is always necessary for the development of our ideas and practices, but in the present context, anyone who claims that states are not antithetical to our freedom cannot be taken seriously. If it really were a question of free debate, of the exchange of ideas, of what was best or what was necessary, why have they massacred us every time we have put stateless forms of social organization into practice? This is one atrocity that all forms of government are guilty of, whether democratic, fascist, or socialist. Given that the debate is in fact not free, the apologists of state mythology in effect become hacks who are simply preaching the official truths they are paid to proclaim, or worse, naïve puppets who repeat for free what they have heard from the professionals.

Honestly expressing the nature of our relationship with the State is the first step to solving the ills that this relationship reproduces. New elections or new government programs cannot even begin to address our lack of freedom. States must be made to answer for their usurpation of our right to organize our own lives, as well as for their unbroken history of genocide, enslavement, tyranny, exploitation, spying, indoctrination, abuse, alienation, warfare, and the despoliation of nature.

Fortunately, we can learn a great deal from the State's historic evolution. Entering into dialogue with the State is always an error. Societies that sought peaceful, neighborly relations with an encroaching state can be commended for their benevolence but the lesson has by now become clear: there can be no peaceful coexistence with the State. Those who wish to protect or recover their freedom can disparage state representatives, insult them, mock them, ignore them, or silence them, but conversing with them is to mistake them for reasonable human beings rather than the organic masks that an insatiable machine wears in order to extend its power.

We can also learn that states require obedience. Disobedience to the State is therefore an important practice among those who value freedom. The popular heroes that might exemplify an anti-authoritarian ethos are the bandits, the fugitives, the prisoners, the rebels, and the rioters, especially the Robin Hoods and Harriet Tubmans who subvert established hierarchies rather than the mafiosos and Nathaniel Bacons who emulate them. Practices that foster disobedience include refusal to pay taxes, to participate in elections, to collaborate with police investigations, or to perform military service; a further step would be willfully breaking every law that one can get away with, provided the delinquency hurts rulers and owners and obstructs the infrastructures of control and economic accumulation without hurting common people.

In order to rule, states must also organize society to favor legibility—observation, organization, and control from above. Nowadays, rejecting legibility largely means rejecting or abstaining from the private communications technologies that states increasingly use to monitor their subjects; recovering the practices of face-to-face communication rather than mediating all our relationships through Facebook, Google, Twitter, and cell phones; using cash instead of credit cards and even better, developing black market or currency-free economies.

A study of history shows that state authority has a religious aspect: the adoration of leaders and the worship of power itself. People in rebellion must cultivate the contrary, viewing not only politicians but all power-holders and the professionals of para-state institutions (the media, the universities) as torturers, murderers, exploiters, liars, parasites, bullies, snitches, mercenaries, or at best, desperate and unethical opportunists.

We need to learn how to trust again in our own histories and our own capacities for problem solving. An anti-authoritarian history arises from an affinity with the egalitarian "Dark Ages" and not the Golden Ages of opulence above and misery below; with the barbarians and savages and not with the civilizations and empires. It arises from a sympathy with the outlaws and the slaves rather than with the rulers and the generals; with the Indians and not with the cowboys, with the witches and the heretics, and not with the Inquisitors or the reformers. Every historical gaze posits a center; if we truly value freedom over hubris, ours must be rooted among the underclasses who have born the weight of grandeur, and among the marginalized who have ever fled the State's expanding borders.

Progressive historians will admit the atrocities the State has inflicted, but ignore the possible solutions. The progressive historian bemoans the genocide of indigenous societies, while pretending such societies have already disappeared, and while erecting essentialist, impassable barriers between those who were colonized by state authority before 1492 and those who were colonized after. Yet whether a society succumbed to the Babylonians, to the Romans, to the conquistadors, or to the US Army, colonialism is the shared inheritance of every human being on this planet.

State pretensions to absolute power within a territory, we should remember, are fictive; they are only true to the extent that inhabitants of that territory believe in them. And even now, everywhere in the world, there are people who live in conflict with and sometimes in open negation of state authority. We have not disappeared. We are still fighting.

A reformist historiography that acknowledges the undeniable truth of state atrocities must prevent radical (which is to say, realistic) solutions by instilling victimization. And while it is true that states have done horrible things to us and continue to do horrible things, proportional to how rebellious or how marginalized we are, it is equally true that we have always fought back. We are not victims; many a time the powerful have been afraid of us, and with good reason. Writing of an anti-authoritarian society in Southeast Asia, James C. Scott emphasizes "one 'tradition' to which most Lisu proudly point: namely, the tradition of murdering headmen who become too autocratic."[2] The anarchists of Europe and the Americas, through a practice of revenge for the massacres of thousands of common people demanding freedom, dignity, or mere survival, laid low dozens of monarchs, generals, presidents, and governors. And peoples like the Lakota, the Cheyenne, and the Mapuche have put more than a few genocidal butchers into early graves, ending the atrocities of Custer, Oñez de Loyola, and others. No matter what continent we are from, those who choose to align ourselves with an anti-authoritarian history can be proud: we are the ones who have killed kings.

The reason why states so violently interrupt us every time we try to organize society on the basis of mutual aid and solidarity, or to recover pre-colonial traditions of reciprocity and respect for the earth, is because these horizontal, decentralized methods work. Many a healthy, egalitarian society structured itself in such a way in the past, and the degraded communities of today can choose to do so again, adapting to changing circumstances and to modern needs, because self-organization is an innate human ability. In fact, only by seizing power over our own lives—taking responsibility for ourselves, engaging with our community, and refusing to rule or be ruled—can we intelligently and fairly solve the problems of poverty, alienation, warfare, and the destruction of the planet.

Many anti-authoritarian societies in the past were limited in their resistance by a healthy, libertarian rejection of perpetual warfare. For example, Geronimo, an important war leader of the Apache, often went into combat with just a handful of supporters, because most of his compatriots refused to participate in one war after another. They preferred to seek peaceful solutions with their encroaching neighbors. In hindsight, we can appreciate that peaceful coexistence with a state is impossible, even if we also admire the anti-state practices of the Apache. Avoiding the logic of militarization is key to preventing authoritarianism or politogenesis in our present-day struggles. But we would do ourselves a favor by recognizing that the very existence

---

2   Scott, *The Art of Not Being Governed*, 276.

of the State constitutes an unending war against the planet and all its inhabitants.

The necessity to reject the State transcends ideology. The questions of how we are to free ourselves and what we will do with our freedom remain open, and there exist hundreds of cultural and historical traditions that suggest possible answers, as well as an infinity of utopian possibilities that remain to be explored.

We have the chance, however, to secure one point of common ground that might allow a thousand different worlds to flourish side by side. Just as we refuse to be ruled, we refuse to rule over anyone else. The State is an idea that has been given one chance after another for thousands of years, and the result has always been disastrous. Let us raise our voices against ignorance and complicity until the refusal of domination becomes the common sentiment of all humankind: never again!

Bibliography

Abu-Lughod, Janet. *Before European Hegemony: The World System A.D. 1250–1350*. New York: Oxford University Press, 1989.

Ahern, Emily. *Chinese Ritual and Politics*. Cambridge: Cambridge University Press, 1981.

Algarra Bascón, David. *El Comú Català*. Barcelona: Potlatch Ediciones, 2015.

Anonymous. "Fire Extinguishers and Fire Starters: Anarchist Interventions in the #SpanishRevolution." *CrimethInc.* June 2011. http://www.crimethinc.com/texts/recentfeatures/barc.php.

Anonymous. "From 15M to Podemos: The Regeneration of Spanish Democracy and the Maligned Promise of Chaos." *CrimethInc.* March 3, 2016. http://crimethinc.com/texts/r/podemos/.

Arrighi, Giovanni. *The Long 20th Century: Money, Power, and the Origins of our Times*. New York: Verso, 2010.

Bakunin, Mikhail. "Rousseau's Theory of the State." 1873.

———. *Statism and Anarchy*. 1873.

Balter, Michael. "Farming Was So Nice, It Was Invented at Least Twice." *Science*, July 4, 2013. http://www.sciencemag.org/news/2013/07/farming-was-so-nice-it-was-invented-least-twice.

Barclay, Harold. *People Without Government: An Anthropology of Anarchy*. London: Kahn and Averill, 1996.

Baum, Richard. "Ritual and Rationality: Religious Roots of the Bureaucratic State in Ancient China." In *The Early State, Its Alternatives and Analogues*, edited by Leonid E. Grinin, Robert L. Carneiro, Dmitri M. Bondarenko, Nikolay N. Kradin, and Andrey V. Korotayev, 41–67. Volgograd, Russia: Uchitel Publishing House, 2004.

Beliaev, Dmitri D., and Andrey V. Korotayev. *Civilizational*

Models of Politogenesis. Saarbrücken, Germany: LAP Publishing, 2011.

Berent, Moshe. "Greece: The Stateless *Polis* (11th to 4th Centuries B.C.)." In *The Early State, Its Alternatives and Analogues*, 364–87.

Berezkin, Yuri E. "Alternative Models of Middle Range Society. 'Individualistic' Asia vs. 'Collectivistic' America?" In *The Early State, Its Alternatives and Analogues*, 61–71.

Boehm, Christopher. "Egalitarian Behavior and Reverse Dominance Hierarchy." *Current Anthropology* 34, No. 3 (June 1993).

Bondarenko, Dmitri M. "From Local Communities to Megacommunity: Biniland in the 1st Millennium B.C. to the 19th Century A.D." In *The Early State, Its Alternatives and Analogues*, 325–63.

———."Kinship, Territoriality and the Early State Lower Limit." In *Social Evolution and History: Thirty Years of Early State Research*, edited by Henri J.M. Claessen, Renée Hagesteijn, and Pieter van de Velde, 19–53. Moscow: Uchitel Publishing House, 2008.

Bondarenko, Dmitri M. and Andrey V. Korotavey, eds. *Civilizational Models of Politogenesis.* Moscow: Institute for African Studies of the Russian Academy of Sciences, 2000.

Bondarenko, Dmitri M., Leonid E. Grinin, and Andrevy V. Korotayev. "Alternatives of Social Evolution." In *The Early State, Its Alternatives and Analogues*, 3–27.

Boxer, Charles R. *The Dutch Seaborne Empire: 1600–1800.* London: Hutchinson, 1965.

Braudel, Fernand. *The Perspective of the World.* New York: Harper & Row, 1984.

Burton, Antoinette. *The Trouble with Empire: Challenges to Modern British Imperialism.* Oxford: Oxford University Press, 2015.

Carneiro, R.L. "A Theory of the Origin of the State." *Science* 169 (1970): 733–38.

Chabal, Patrick, Gary Feinman, and Peter Skalník. "Beyond States and Empires: Chiefdoms and Informal Politics."

In *The Early State, Its Alternatives and Analogues*, 46–60.

Chemaly, Soraya. "What witches have to do with women's health." *Salon.com*. October 31, 2013. https://www.salon.com/2013/10/31/what_witches_have_to_do_with_womens_health/.

Claessen, Henri J.M., Renée Hagesteijn, and Pieter van de Velde, eds., *Social Evolution and History: Thirty Years of Early State Research 7*, No. 1. Moscow: Uchitel Publishing House, 2008.

Clastres, Pierre. *Society Against the State: Essays in Political Anthropology*. 1974. Translated by Robert Hurley and Abe Stein. New York: Zone Books, 1989. (My citations are from a Spanish language edition, translated by Paco Madrid. Buenos Aires: Editorial Tierra del Sur, 2011).

Coquery-Vidrovitch, Catherine. "Research on an African Mode of Production." In *Perspectives on the African Past*, edited by M.A. Klein and G.W. Johnson. New York: Little, Brown and Company, 1972.

Davis, Wade. *The Serpent and the Rainbow: A Harvard Scientist's Astonishing Journey into the Secret Societies of Haitian Voodoo, Zombies, and Magic*. New York: Simon & Schuster, 1985.

Derbyshire, David. "Most Britons descended from male farmers who left Iraq and Syria 10,000 years ago." *Daily Mail*. Jan. 20, 2010. http://www.dailymail.co.uk/sciencetech/article-1244654/Study-finds-Britons-descended-farmers-left-Iraq-Syria-10-000-years-ago.html.

Diamond, Jared. *Guns, Germs, and Steel: The Fates of Human Societies*. New York: W.W. Norton, 1997.

———. "The Worst Mistake in the History of the Human Race." *Discover Magazine* (May 1987): 64–66.

Donald, Moira, and Linda Hurcombe, eds. *Representations of Gender from Prehistory to Present*. New York: St. Martin's Press, 2000.

Dozhdev, Dmitri V. "Rome," in *Civilizational Models of Politogenesis*, 255–86.

Durrenberger, E. Paul. "Lisu: Political Form, Ideology, and Economic Action." In *Highlanders of Thailand*, edited by

John McKinnon and Wanat Bhruksasri, 215–26. Kuala
Lumpur: Oxford University Press South East Asia, 1987.

Ealham, Chris. *Anarchism and the City: Revolution and Counter-
Revolution in Barcelona, 1898–1937*. Oakland: AK Press,
2010.

Earle, Timothy K. "Hawaiian Islands (AD 800–1824)." In
Civilizational Models of Politogenesis, 73–86.

Ehrenreich, Barbara and Deirdre English. *Witches, Midwives,
and Nurses: A History of Women Healers*. New York: The
Feminist Press, 1993.

Emelianov, Vladimir V. "The Ruler as Possessor of Power in
Sumer." In *The Early State, Its Alternatives and Analogues*,
181–95.

Engels, Frederich. *The Origin of the Family, Private Property,
and the State*. 1884.

Evans, Arthur. *Witchcraft and the Gay Counterculture: A Radical
View of Western Civilization and Some of the People It Has
Tried to Destroy*. Boston: Fag Rag Books, 1978.

Fanon, Frantz. *The Wretched of the Earth*. New York: Grove
Press, 1961.

Federici, Silvia. *Caliban and the Witch: Women, the Body and
Primitive Accumulation*. New York: Autonomedia, 2004.

Finkelstein, Israel, and Neil Asher Silberman. *The Bible
Unearthed: Archaeology's New Vision of Ancient Israel
and the Origin of Its Sacred Texts*. New York: Simon &
Schuster, 2001.

Fried, Morton H. *The Evolution of Political Society*, New York:
Random House, 1967.

Gelderblom, Oscar, and Joost Jonker. "Completing a financial
revolution: The finance of the Dutch East India trade and
the rise of the Amsterdam capital market, 1595–1612."
Journal of Economic History 64, No. 3 (2004): 641–72.

Gelderloos, Peter. *Anarchy Works*. Berkeley: Ardent Press, 2010.

———. *How Nonviolence Protects the State*. Harrisonburg,
Virginia: Signalfire Press, 2005.

Gimbutas, Marija. *The Civilization of the Goddess: The World of
Old Europe*. San Francisco: Harper, 1991.

Gorrion, Alex. "Anarchy in World Systems: A review

of Giovanni Arrighi's *The Long 20th Century*." *The Anvil Review*. Published December 18, 2013. http://theanvilreview.org/print/anarchy-in-world-systems/.

———. "Science." *The Anvil Review*. Published May 29, 2015. http://theanvilreview.org/print/science/

———. "You don't really care for music, do ya?" *The Anvil Review*. Published July 21, 2011. http://theanvilreview.org/print/you-dont-really-care-for-music-do-ya/.

Graeber, David. *Fragments of an Anarchist Anthropology*. Cambridge: Prickly Paradigm Press, 2004.

Grinin, Leonid E. "Early State and Democracy." In *The Early State, Its Alternatives and Analogues*, 419–63.

———. "The Early State and Its Analogues: A Comparative Analysis." In *The Early State, Its Alternatives and Analogues*, 88–136.

Grinin, Leonid E., Robert L. Carneiro, Dmitri M. Bondarenko, Nikolay N. Kradin, and Andrey V. Korotayev, eds. *The Early State, Its Alternatives and Analogues*. Volgograd, Russia: Uchitel Publishing House, 2004.

Guisepi, R.A., ed. "Africa and the Africans in the Age of the Atlantic Slave Trade." *History World International*. history-world.org. Accessed January 7, 2016.

Gumplowicz, Ludwig. *The Outlines of Sociology*. 1899. Reprint, Kitchener: Batoche Books, Ltd., 1999.

Heun, Manfred, Ralf Schäfer-Pregl, Dieter Klawan, Renato Castagna, Monica Accerbi, Basilio Borghi, and Francesco Salamini. "Site of Einkorn Wheat Domestication Identified by DNA Fingerprinting." *Science* 278 (1997): 1312–14.

Hill, Gord. "Never Idle: Gord Hill on Indigenous Resistance in Canada." *The Portland Radicle*, March 18, 2013. https://portlandradicle.wordpress.com/never-idle-gord-hill-on-indigenous-resistance-in-canada/.

Hoogbergen, Wim S.M. *The Boni Maroon Wars in Suriname*. Leiden: E.J. Brill, 1990.

Hsu, F.L.K. *Americans and Chinese: Passage to Differences*. Honolulu: The University Press of Hawaii, 1981.

Oppenheimer, Franz. *The State*. 1908. Available online, oll.

libertyfund.org/titles/1662.

Irwin, L. "Cherokee Healing: Myth, Dreams, and Medicine." *American Indian Quarterly* 16, No. 2 (1992), 237–57.

James, C.L.R. *The Black Jacobins.* New York: Random House, 1963.

Kaczynski, Ted. "Letter to a Turkish Anarchist." ca. 2003. *the anarchistlibrary.org,* June 9, 2009. http://theanarchistlibrary.org/library/ted-kaczynski-letter-to-a-turkish-anarchist.

Katsiaficas, George. *The Imagination of the New Left: A Global Analysis of 1968.* Boston: South End Press, 1987.

Khan, Tariq. "'Come O Lions! Let Us Cause a Mutiny': Anarchism and the Subaltern." *Institute for Anarchist Studies,* April 2, 2015. https://anarchiststudies.org/2015/04/02/come-o-lions-let-us-cause-a-mutiny-anarchism-and-the-subaltern-by-tariq-khan/.

Kradin, Nikolay N. "Early State Theory and the Evolution of Pastoral Nomads." In *Social Evolution and History,* 107–30.

Kuta Yahaya, Mohammed. "The Nupe People of Nigeria." *Studies of Tribes and Tribals* 1, No. 2 (2003): 95–110.

Korotayev, Andrey V. "The Chiefdom: Precursor of the Tribe? (Some Trends of Political Evolution in North-East Yemeni Highlands)." In *The Early State, Its Alternatives and Analogues,* 300–24.

Kropotkin, Pyotr. *The Great French Revolution.* 1909. Translation, London: Heinemann, 1927.

———. *Mutual Aid: A Factor of Evolution.* London: Heinemann, 1902.

Le Goff, Jacques. *Time, Work, and Culture in the Middle Ages.* Translated by Arthur Goldhammer. Chicago: The University of Chicago Press, 1980. (Note that the articles edited in the collection were originally published between 1963 and 1976.)

Levack, Brian P. *The Witch-Hunt in Early Modern Europe.* New York: Pearson Education, 2006.

Linebaugh, Peter, and Marcus Rediker. *The Many-Headed Hydra: Sailors, Slaves, Commoners, and the Hidden History of the Revolutionary Atlantic.* Boston: Beacon Press, 2000.

Lozny, Ludomir R. "The Transition to Statehood in Central Europe." In *The Early State, Its Alternatives and Analogues*, 278–87.

L'vova, Eleonora. "The Formation and Development of States in the Congo Basin." In *The Early State, Its Alternatives and Analogues*, 288–97.

Maalouf, Amin. *The Crusades Through Arab Eyes*. Translated by John Rothschild. New York: Schocken Books, 1984.

Maeckelbergh, Marianne. *The Will of the Many: How the Alterglobalisation Movement is Changing the Face of Democracy*. London: Pluto Press, 2009.

Marcus, J. and K.V. Flannery. *Zapotec Civilization: How Urban Society Evolved in Mexico's Oaxaca Valley*, London: Thames and Hudson, 1996.

Marín, David. "Terra de Bruixes." *El Punt Avui*, January 2, 2016. http://www.elpuntavui.cat/societat/article/-/929459-terra-de-bruixes.html. (Article about the as-yet-unpublished research by Pau Castell on witch-hunts in the Pyrenees.)

McWorter, John. *Our Magnificent Bastard Tongue: The Untold History of English*. New York: Gotham, 2009.

Moore, R.I. *The War on Heresy: Faith and Power in Medieval Europe*. London: Profile Books, 2012.

Moskvitch, Katia. "Migrants from the Near East 'brought farming to Europe.'" BBC, November 10, 2010. http://www.bbc.co.uk/news/science-environment-11729813.

Native Heritage Project, "Tuscarora Populations." *Native Heritage Project*, June 24, 2012. nativeheritageproject.com/2012/06/24/tuscarora-populations/. Accessed January 13, 2016.

Paillal, José Millalén. "La Sociedad Mapuche Prehispánica: Kimün, Arqueología y Etnohistoria." In *¡…Escucha, winka…! Cuatro ensayos de Historia Nacional Mapuche y un epílogo sobre el future*, edited by Pablo Marimán, Sergio Caniuqueo, José Millalén, and Rodrigo Levil. Santiago de Chile: LOM Ediciones, 2006.

Perlman, Fredy. *Against His-story, Against Leviathan!* Detroit: Black and Red, 1983.

PG, "A Critical Review of Anarchism and the City," *The Anvil Review*. May 24, 2012. http://theanvilreview.org/print/criticalreviewanarchismcity/.

Pognon, Edmond. *La vie quotidienne en l'an mille*. Paris: Hachette litterature, 1981.

Proussakov, Dmitri B. "Early Dynastic Egypt: A Socio-Environmental/Anthropological Hypothesis of 'Unification.'" In *The Early State, Its Alternatives and Analogues*, 139–80.

Purkiss, Diane. *The Witch in History: Early Modern and Twentieth-Century Representations*. Abingdon: Routledge, 1996.

Ramnath, Maia. *Decolonizing Anarchism: An Antiauthoritarian History of India's Liberation Struggle*. Oakland: AK Press, 2011.

Riehl, Simone, Mohsen Zeidi, and Nicholas J. Conard. "Emergence of Agriculture in the Foothills of the Zagros Mountains of Iran." *Science* 341 (July 2013): 65–67.

Rijkeboer, Henk. "History of the Dutch East India Company—The Asian Part." *European Heritage*, 2011. http://european-heritage.org/netherlands/alkmaar/history-dutch-east-india-company-asian-part Accessed January 12, 2016.

Ronan, C.A. and Needham, J. *The Shorter Science and Civilization in China*. Vol. 1. Cambridge: Cambridge University Press, 1978.

Schmidt, Klaus. "Göbekli Tepe, Southeastern Turkey: A Preliminary Report on the 1995–1999 Excavations." *Paléorient* 26, No. 1 (2000): 45–54.

Scott, James C. *The Art of Not Being Governed: An Anarchist History of Upland Southeast Asia*, New Haven: Yale University Press, 2009.

Seneca Nation of Indians website, https://sni.org, January 13, 2016.

Serjeant, R.B. "South Arabia." In *Gazetteer of Historical North-West Yemen in the Islamic Period to 1650*, edited by C. van Nieuwenhuijza, IX–XII. Hildesheim etc.: Georg Olms, 1977.

Severino, John. "The Other Gods Were Crying: Stories of Rebellion in the Bolivian Highlands." *theanarchistlibrary*.

org, 2010. https://theanarchistlibrary.org/library/john
-severino-the-other-gods-were-crying.

———. "With Land, Without the State: Anarchy in Wallmapu."
theanarchistlibrary.org, 2010. https://theanarchistlibrary
.org/library/john-severino-with-land-without-the-state
-anarchy-in-wallmapu.

Shoatz, Russell "Maroon." "The Dragon and the Hydra: A
Historical Study of Organizational Methods." Published
from prison, decentralized edition and distribution, ca.
2010.

Spencer, Charles S., and Elsa M. Redmond. "Conquest
Warfare, Strategies of Resistance, and the Rise of the
Zapotec Early State." In *The Early State, Its Alternatives
and Analogues*, 220–61.

———. "Multilevel Selection and Political Evolution in the
Valley of Oaxaca, 500–100 B.C." *Journal of Anthropological
Archaeology* 20 (2001): 195–229.

Stafford, Saralee, and Neal Shirley. *Dixie Be Damned: 300 Years
of Insurrection in the American South*. Oakland: AK Press,
2015.

Tacitus. 98. *The Agricola and the Germania*. Translated by H.
Mattingly. Baltimore: Penguin Books, 1948.

Thapar, Romila. *A History of India*, Vol. I. New York: Penguin
Books, 1966.

Thompson, E.P. *Whigs and Hunters: The Origin of the Black Act*.
New York: Pantheon, 1975.

Turnbull, Colin M. *The Forest People*. New York: Simon &
Schuster, 1961.

Tymowski, Michal. "State and Tribe in the History of Medieval
Europe and Black Africa—A Comparative Approach."
In *Social Evolution and History*, 171–96.

Van Allen, Judith. "Sitting On a Man." *Canadian Journal of
African Studies* II (1972): 211–19.

Vorobyov, Denis V. "The Iroquois." In *Civilizational Models of
Politogenesis*, 157–174.

Weber, Max. *The Religion of China: Confucianism and Taoism*.
New York: The Free Press, 1951.

———. *The Theory of Social and Economic Organization*. New

York: The Free Press, 1947.

Werner, K.F. *Structures politiques du monde franc (VI – XII siècles)*. London: Ashgate-Variorum, 1979.

Wikipedia. "Ashanti Empire." Accessed January 7, 2016. https://en.wikipedia.org/wiki/Ashanti_Empire.

———. "Cherokee." Accessed July 20, 2015. http://en.m.wikipedia.org/wiki/Cherokee.

———. "Cucuteni-Trypillian Culture." Accessed February 20, 2016. https://en.wikipedia.org/wiki/Cucuteni-Trypillian_culture.

———. "Dahomey." Accessed January 7, 2016. https://en.wikipedia.org/wiki/Dahomey.

———. "Dutch East India Company." Accessed January 5, 2015. https://en.wikipedia.org/wiki/Dutch_East_India_Company.

———. "Erlitou Culture." Accessed February 20, 2016. https://en.wikipedia.org/wiki/Erlitou_culture.

———. "Kingdom of Israel." Accessed January 8, 2016. https://en.wikipedia.org/wiki/Kingdom_of_Israel_%28united_monarchy%29.

———. "Kingdom of Judah." Accessed January 8, 2016. https://en.wikipedia.org/wiki/Kingdom_of_Judah.

———. "Late Bronze Age collapse." Accessed January 14, 2016. https://en.wikipedia.org/wiki/Late_Bronze_Age_collapse.

———. "Longshan Culture." Accessed February 20, 2016. https://en.wikipedia.org/wiki/Longshan_culture.

———. "Nupe people." Accessed January 7, 2016. https://en.wikipedia.org/wiki/Nupe_people.

———. "Oyo Empire." Accessed January 7, 2016. https://en.wikipedia.org/wiki/Oyo_Empire.

———. "Shang Dynasty." Accessed February 20, 2016. https://en.wikipedia.org/wiki/Shang_dynasty.

———. "Tarumanagara." Accessed February 20, 2016. https://en.wikipedia.org/wiki/Tarumanagara.

———. "Tiwanaku Empire." Accessed February 20, 2016. https://en.wikipedia.org/wiki/Tiwanaku_empire.

Wright, H.T. "Recent Research on the Origin of the State."

Annual Review of Anthropology 6 (1977): 379–97.

Wright, Robert. *The Evolution of God.* New York: Back Bay Books, 2009.

Yi, Jianping. "Non-Autocracy in Pre-Qin China." In *Social Evolution and History,* 222–44.

Zerzan, John. *Future Primitive and Other Essays.* New York: Autonomedia, 1994.

Zlodey, Lev, and Jason Radegas. *Here at the Center of the World in Revolt.* Anonymous edition, ca. 2011.

Index

"Passim" (literally "scattered") indicates intermittent discussion of a topic over a cluster of pages.

A

abandonment and flight. *See* flight and abandonment
Abbasid Caliphate, 65
accumulation, 67, 81, 126, 132, 137–41 passim, 149–57 passim. *See also* power accumulation; status accumulation
Afghanistan, 66
Africa, 29, 56, 59–60, 140–41, 118, 201–2, 207, 227. *See also* Benin; Congo states; Egypt; Egypt, ancient; Mali, ancient
African Americans, 102, 103, 239
Against His-story, Against Leviathan (Perlman), 12–13
The Agricola and the Germania (Tacitus), 40n4, 46–49 passim, 97–98, 193
agriculture, 43, 49, 80, 139; Americas, 114, 141, 213, 215; ancient Greece, 131; Aryans, 177, 178; Central Europe, 153; Cretans, 149, 150; development of, 221–32 passim; Hawaiian Islands, 173; hierarchy and, 156; Indus Valley, 143; Java, 145; resistance to,

227; stateless peoples, 99, 100, 105–6; tribute systems, 57; West Africa, 117–21 passim; Zapotec, 188–92 passim. *See also* granaries
Amazonia, 186–87, 227, 235
American Civil War, 103
Americas, 82–83, 140, 141, 187–91, 218; agriculture, 114, 141, 213, 215; British colonialism, 31, 33–34, 115, 116. *See also* Amazonia; Andes; Native Americans; United States
Anabaptists and Anabaptism, 62, 71
anarchists in Spanish Civil War, 54
anarchist theory, 138, 154, 158
ancestor cults and ancestor worship, 120, 122, 164–66 passim, 178, 198, 201
ancient Egypt. *See* Egypt, ancient
ancient Greece. *See* Greece, ancient
ancient India. *See* Aryans
ancient Mali. *See* Mali, ancient
ancient Mexico. *See* Mexico, ancient
ancient Rome. *See* Roman Empire
Anderson, Benedict, 45
Andes, 82–83, 141, 196, 205, 208,

division of labor, 49, 88, 97, 221
generosity, 156–57, 161
Genghis Khan, 118
genocide, 22, 30, 32, 34, 115, 144,
   245
The Germania (Tacitus). See *The
   Agricola and the Germania*
   (Tacitus)
Germanic peoples, 22, 32, 37–51
   passim, 55, 62, 78, 97, 168;
   gender relations, 89; Illyrians
   and, 223; slavery, 30
Germany, 32, 42, 45, 228
Geronimo, 246
gerontocracy. See elders, rule by
gift economy, 138–39, 214
gifts, obligatory. See tribute
gifts, ritual, 116, 120, 150, 207,
   215, 218–19
Gimbutas, Marija, 221
gleaning, 104, 228
global warming. See climate
   change
Göbleki Tepe, 230
goddesses, 47, 180, 206, 217
Gorrion, Alex, 94
Goths, 40n4, 44–45
Graeber, David, 50
granaries, 106, 114, 218
Granny Nanny, 35
Great Britain, 41, 86; anti-terrorism wars, 186; Black Act, 104;
   Dutch relations, 144; Hadrian's
   Wall, 106, 107. *See also* British
   colonialism; England
Great Dismal Swamp, 102
Greece, 40, 129, 238
Greece, ancient, 50, 55, 157,

196, 223–24. *See also* Athens,
   ancient; Spartans
Grinin, Leonid E.: *The Early State,
   Its Alternatives and Analogues*,
   2–3n1
Guarani, 8n9, 235, 236
guerrilla warfare, 23, 24, 31, 32,
   34, 35

H

Hadrian's Wall, 106, 107
Haiti, 34, 35–36
Hammurabi's Code, 180, 211
Hannibal, 40, 224
Haudenosaunee, 112–16 passim,
   240
Hawaiian Islands, 173–76
herders and herding, 116, 131,
   149, 221, 223, 224
heretics and heresy, 71, 72, 80,
   81, 86–89 passim, 102. *See also*
   witch hunts
high-prestige crafts, 141, 149, 189
Hill, Gord, 113
Hindus and Hinduism, 67, 70,
   145–47 passim, 180, 182
holy father states, 165, 167–68,
   178, 185, 234
homosexuality, 55
human sacrifice, 215
Huns, 116
hunter-gatherers, 6–7, 11, 12,
   195n, 223–30 passim; belief
   systems, 194, 195; Bini, 118;
   Indus Valley, 143; religion,
   193–95 passim; San, 22; South
   Asia, 182
hunting, 78, 100; African

216, 217

religion, 42–43, 67–74 passim,
244; China, 197–99, 207;
Hawaiian Islands, 174; symbolic power, 193–220 passim; syn-
cretism, 44, 101–2; South Asia,
180, 182; West Africa, 119, 121,
124, 205. *See also* ancestor cults
and ancestor worship; atheism; Hindus and Hinduism;
intermediaries, religious/spir-
itual; salvation religions; state
religions

religious hermits, 230–31

religious purification, 72

reluctant client states, 25–26, 233

rent, 47, 93, 104

resistance, 75, 85–89 passim,
102–4 passim, 112, 129,
182–88 passim, 227; Arab
Spring, 236; Buddhist, 71; to
Christianization, 118; to colonization, 102, 113; guerrilla/
armed, 23–24, 32, 113; Haiti,
34–36 passim; Iberian, 40; Java,
147; maroon communities, 34–
35; Native American, 31, 32,
102, 113, 159, 240, 246; South
Asia, 182–83; spirituality and,
195, 231; to state authority/
power, 3, 32, 100, 111, 160, 207;
to state formation, 2, 16, 21–22,
32, 72, 98, 204; Zomia, 99, 100;
zones of, 103–4, 130–31. *See
also* flight and abandonment

revolution and revolutions, 236,
237; aftershocks, 91; models,
131

Rickahoken, 33–34

rights, 1, 11, 156, 157, 161, 175,
211; ancient Greece, 132; of
commoners, 92; of dependent
class, 30, 211; Rome, 53

ritual gifts. *See* gifts, ritual

Rojava, 237, 239, 240

Roman Catholic Church. *See*
Catholic Church

Roman Empire, 22, 30, 38–72
passim, 82, 99, 116, 118, 224;
architecture and, 196; Aryans
compared, 178; Catholic
Church and, 61; cities, 223;
collapse, 40, 46, 78, 89, 91, 101;
democracy and, 157; Hadrian's
Wall, 106, 107; Illyrians and,
223; law, 94; numerology, 199;
patriarchy, 89; religion and spirituality, 199–200; slave trade, 52

Romania, 221, 222

royal court states, 163–64, 165,
185, 234

royalty, expatriate. *See* expatriate
rulers

rotation of authority, 126

runaways, 35, 116, 131, 174. *See
also* flight and abandonment

Rus people, 38, 44

S

sachems, 113–14, 115

sacred commerce states, 185, 210,
234

sacred sites, 206, 229, 230

sacrifice, 180, 199, 200, 207. *See
also* human sacrifice

sagrera model, 101

West Africa. *See* Benin; Congo;
Mali
West African slave trade. *See* slave
trade: West Africa
Westphalia Settlement. *See*
Settlement of Westphalia
wheat domestication, 231n7
Whigs and Hunters (Thompson),
86
Wielkopolska, 38, 39
*Witchcraft and the Gay
Counterculture* (Evans), 55, 86
Witches, Midwives, and Nurses
(Ehrenreich and English), 88
witch hunts, 72, 86–87
women gods. *See* goddesses
women-men relations. *See* gender
relations
women priests, 149, 150
women's hunting. *See* hunting: by
women
women's status, 54, 179. *See also*
gender relations; matriarchy
work. *See* labor
workers' movement, 14, 19, 242
written language. *See* language:
written

Y
Yamna culture, 221, 222, 224
Yemen, 63–64, 75

Z
Zapotec state, 141, 187–91
ziggurats, 196, 197, 210, 211, 213,
220
Zinn, Howard, 13
Zomia, 39, 97–109

AK Press is small, in terms of staff and resources, but we also manage to be one of the world's most productive anarchist publishing houses. We publish close to twenty books every year, and distribute thousands of other titles published by like-minded independent presses and projects from around the globe. We're entirely worker-run and democratically managed. We operate without a corporate structure—no boss, no managers, no bullshit.

The Friends of AK program is a way you can directly contribute to the continued existence of AK Press, and ensure that we're able to keep publishing books like this one! Friends pay $25 a month directly into our publishing account ($30 for Canada, $35 for international), and receive a copy of every book AK Press publishes for the duration of their membership! Friends also receive a discount on anything they order from our website or buy at a table: 50% on AK titles, and 20% on everything else. We have a Friends of AK ebook program as well: $15 a month gets you an electronic copy of every book we publish for the duration of your membership. You can even sponsor a very discounted membership for someone in prison.

Email friendsofak@akpress.org for more info, or visit the Friends of
    AK Press website: https://www.akpress.org/friends.html

There are always great book projects in the works—so sign up now to
    become a Friend of AK Press, and let the presses roll!